FESTIVALS & CELEBRATIONS

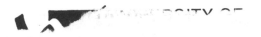

Rowland Purton

FESTIVALS & CELEBRATIONS

Basil Blackwell · Publisher

Reprinted in 1982, 1987, 1990

First published in paperback 1989

British Library Cataloguing in Publication Data
Purton, Rowland W.
  Festivals and celebrations.
  1. Festivals
  I. Title
  394.2   GT3930

ISBN 0–631–90413–1 Pbk

Phototypeset in VIP Palatino by
Preface Ltd, Salisbury.
Printed in Great Britain by
T.J. Press (Padstow) Ltd.
Padstow, Cornwall.

Contents

Acknowledgements   vii

Introduction   ix

Festivals and celebrations   1

Religions and Festivals   5

    Many gods . . . or one?   6

    Humanism   10

    Shinto   11

    Hinduism   12

    Buddhism   14

    Taoism   16

    Confucianism   17

    Judaism   18

    Christianity   20

    Islam   26

    Bahá'í Faith   29

    Sikhism   30

    Jainism   32

    Zoroastrianism   33

    Communism   34

Festival themes   35

    A new start   36

    Calling for help   42

    Early spring   48

    Maytime   52

    Summer   58

    Harvest   62

    Autumn celebrations   68

    Light and fire   72

    Christmastide   78

New Year (Religion) 84

Celebration and worship 90

Holy Books 102

Triumph over evil 106

Pilgrimage 110

Fasting and penance 114

Special remembrance 120

Patron saints 126

Wakes and fairs 130

Pageantry and processions 132

Flowers 138

Water and the sea 142

Music, dancing and culture 148

Festivals of sport 152

Work and business 154

Beginnings 156

Ceremonial 160

National festivals 168

Gatherings and assemblies 170

Family festivals 172

Birth and naming 176

Initiation 178

Marriage 184

Death and burial 186

Anniversaries 188

Pronunciation guide 194

Calendar of festivals 196

Index 203

Acknowledgements

The author wishes to express his thanks to those who have given permission to reproduce copyright material.

Extracts from the *Authorised King James Version of the Bible* and the *Book of Common Prayer* of 1662, which are Crown Copyright, are reproduced by permission.

The quotations on pp. 36, 98, 116, 117 and 144 are from the *Good News Bible*— Old Testament: Copyright © American Bible Society 1976; New Testament: Copyright © American Bible Society 1966, 1971, 1976.

The verse by Anthony G. Petti (p. 99) is reprinted from *The New Catholic Hymnal* by permission of the publishers, Faber Music Ltd.

The prayer on page 62 from *The Illustrated Prayers Blessings and Hymns* translated by Abraham Burstein is by permission of Ktav Publishing House Inc., New York.

A prayer (p. 172) from *Prayers at Breakfast* by Beryl Bye is by permission of The Lutterworth Press.

The prayer on page 83 is from the *Methodist Service Book*, published by the Methodist Publishing House 1975 and the verse on page 154 is from *Hymns and Songs*, published by the Methodist Publishing House 1969.

Sections 9:26 and 11:36 from *The Bhagavad Gita* trans. Juan Mascaro (Penguin Classics, 1962) pp. 82, 93, Copyright © Juan Mascaro, 1962, are reprinted by permission of Penguin Books Ltd. (pp. 106, 190).

Extracts (pp. 85, 103) from *Children's Siddur for Sabbaths and Festivals* are reproduced by permission of United Synagogue, London.

Reference has been made to many publications. Should any copyright have been unwittingly infringed, the author extends his sincere apologies. Any omission will, if notified, be gladly corrected in future editions.

The author also wishes to express his gratitude to many who have kindly supplied information on their respective religions but especially Mr Clive Lawton and Mr Mervyn Leviton (Jewish), Mr A. S. Chhatwal (Sikh), Mr Cyrus P. Mehta (Zoroastrian) and Mr G. W. Buddhadasa (Buddhist); to his staff colleagues, Cyril Sherbourne, Alauddin Ahmad, Md Shafique Rahman and Surindar Sethi; and to his wife Sylvia, whose practical help and encouragement has been invaluable.

Introduction

Festivals play an important role in the life of any school, both in assembly and in Religious Education schemes. They are also important to the community at large, for they give an opportunity to share one another's joys. In the urban environment containing people of various cultures and faiths they can provide a meeting point and perhaps the ground for better understanding and a greater degree of tolerance.

But how much do we know about the festivals of others? For that matter, how great is our knowledge of the Christian festivals and traditionally British celebrations? We cannot assume as great a knowledge as once existed. This book has been written in response to numerous requests for some information about the festivals of people of all faiths as well as those which are secular or folk celebrations.

It is anticipated that the book will be of particular value in assembly and, for that reason, a short prayer has been included with each. It is of necessity short. For longer prayers and for additional information on some themes, attention is drawn to the author's previous books DAY BY DAY and ASSEMBLIES. Prayers from various faiths have been included. Where no indication of source is given, prayers have been written for this book.

This is, however, more than a book for assembly. The information will prove invaluable as background material for Religious Education in general and in the staff reference library

It will soon be apparent that the festivals have not been set out in chronological order or according to individual religions. It was felt that it would be more helpful to arrange them thematically so that kindred festivals from different faiths and many parts of the world would give opportunity for comparison. There is a considerable degree of cross referencing within the text and a comprehensive index.

An important feature is the Calendar of Festivals (p. 197), which gives as much information as possible about the dates of festivals so that they can be incorporated to the greatest advantage in assemblies and schemes of work.

In giving dates throughout the book, the letters BC and AD have been discarded in favour of the letters currently used in books that refer to different religions—BCE for Before the Common Era and CE for Common Era (sometimes interpreted as Christian Era).

It is not always easy to give an accurate rendering of some of the foreign words that are translated into English. Hebrew words, for example, will be spelt in many different ways. Ch and H are both used to indicate a gutteral H. In general the Ch has been used here (e.g. Chanukkah rather than Hanukkah). In the Arabic the H is a throaty one and normally sounded. Translations from the Hebrew and some Indian dialects may variously transpose B and V (e.g. Hebrew month of Ab or Av and Indian *Varanasi* = *Benares*). Often the Indian S is pronounced Sh (Sri = *Sh*ri). So one could go on. A brief guide to pronunciation of those names and words marked* throughout the book is given on page 195.

The scope of the book has been made as wide as possible so that it includes not only major festivals but some of the interesting customs, traditions and celebrations that are observed. By including such things, however briefly, it is hoped that interest may be engendered and encouragement given to delve more deeply into a fascinating subject. There is much more to many of the celebrations than can be included in a book of this size and information on many of them is comparatively easy to obtain.

Finally, it is sincerely hoped that this will not be regarded as a book of ready-made assemblies to be taken as they stand but rather as a source book of information upon which a great deal of interesting work can be built.

RP.

Festivals and Celebrations

Feeling very pleased with yourself? Good news received? A chance of a life-time? A piece of good fortune? You feel on top of the world and want to share your joy with others, so you invite your family and friends to a special celebration, a sumptuous meal, some music and dancing, perhaps some other entertainment. People have a chance to forget everyday things, to let their hair down and have a whale of a time! It is an enjoyable occasion for all—a celebration, a festival. Festivals are fun! And as we consider the many kinds of festival and celebration we realise how much enjoyment they bring to those who share in them.

A glance in the dictionary will serve as a reminder that a festival is a feast day, a celebration, a time for merry-making. It is related to the word feast, which is not only a sumptuous meal but a joyful religious anniversary, a recollection of the Spanish fiesta, which is a very happy occasion, and the fête, which, again, has its entertainments and relaxed happy-go-lucky atmosphere. Nor does one have far to look to see the relationship with the fair—from the Latin feria (sing) and feriae (holiday). And holidays were 'holy days' on which people refrained from working because they were days set apart for religious observance.

When we say festivals are fun, we must remember that this goes for most religious festivals too, for so often these are a combination of fun and frivolity with solemnity and dedication. Fasting is usually preceded and succeeded by feasting. Religion, after all, has connotations with the whole of life, with the mundane as well as the spectacular, with the daily task as well as the inexplicable mystery. Man celebrates his blessings and seeks yet more. Festivals so often provide the opportunity of expressing his hopes as well as his thankfulness—and in company with others.

Festivals are public occasions when people share their feelings with a much wider company, when the deeply religious may share a happy occasion with the adherent and even with the non-believer. There is something special about a festival, be it religious or secular, which breaks down barriers of aloofness and of intolerance. Our festivals today can help to bring far greater understandings if we make the fullest use of them.

For many people, the festivals serve as a seasonal calendar. The festivals of all the religions are annual reminders of the familiar yet important stories that need to be remembered.

Festivals give an ordered structure to the year and, in the past, even the minor festivals of saints' days served as a calendar for everyday life.

Many of the world's festivals are centred around local places of worship or on sites which become temporary holy places for thanksgiving and petition. For others, one has to travel to a holy place that has especial significance. The Hindu may travel to Varanasi* to bathe in the sacred Ganges, whilst the Jew and the Christian may visit the Holy Land. Some make a kind of pilgrimage to a shrine or a holy island such as Iona or Lindisfarne, where there are historic religious associations or perhaps the relics of a saint—though these are of lesser importance than the relics in the Buddhist stupa or temple and the pilgrimage at a different level from the Muslim pilgrimage to his holiest of shrines, the Ka'ba at Mecca.

At such holy places there is a certain aura of reverence as one remembers those holy people who had a vision of God and were enabled to enlighten others. For this reason, too, there is often a deep sense of awe amid the rejoicings at festivals as one recalls the reasons for their institution.

Each festival has its particular customs and traditions, many of which go back to the ancient times of darkness, fear and superstition but which have become intertwined with later beliefs. This is very true of the great Christian festivals of Easter and Christmas. The eggs associated with the former are very ancient symbols, whilst Christmas is a strange mixture of the pagan tree, the Yule fire, the excesses of Saturnalia and the story of God incarnate, born in a stable.

Symbolism is very important in festivals and celebrations. The enactment of life and death in ancient dances can still be seen in the symbolic death of winter or of evil, played by the Fool in the Morris or sword dance. Fertility has always been a central theme, as it is in many places to this day, with the symbolism of images or dance and the central pole or tree.

Neither is the clothing worn on festive occasions just a matter of chance or choice. The masks worn in some ancient or primal religions, the complete covering of the body and the blackened faces, were often intended to conceal the identity of the person so that spectators saw not the man but that which he represented. At a different level, the vestments worn by the clergyman or religious leader are intended, when put on, to transform the wearer from time in the everyday world to 'holy' time. The vestments themselves are covered in symbols, each of which has its special significance.

Symbols abound, not surprisingly perhaps, for these, in a way, have been the visual and aural aids of generations—the means by which man has been taught or reminded of the great facts of life and religion. The cross is a constant reminder to the Christian of the fundamental teaching of his faith; the Jewish Menorah* speaks of the relationship between God and His people. The wheel is significant as probably the most ancient of symbols. To the Buddhist it is the symbol of succession but it also symbolises the rays of the sun, prominent in so many ancient religions. The swastika, used by Hindu and Jain is a broken wheel, whilst the cross no doubt originated as the spokes of a wheel or rays of the sun. The statues of the Hindu or the Buddhist and the icons of the Orthodox Church are similarly the means by which people are helped in their religious life and observance.

But religion is a part of the whole of life and such things must overflow into the everyday sphere. Nowhere is this more obvious than with the symbolic Five Ks of the Sikhs. Such symbolism is evident at the festivals of all the great religions, where it is prominent in parades and processions as well as in the holy places.

Festivals are feasts; and food features highly in the celebrations. Here again symbolism serves as a reminder of deeper things. At his Sabbath feast the Jew has the two challot*, a reminder of God's providence in the wilderness. Most Christian festivals involve the celebration of Mass, the Eucharist or Holy Communion with the bread and wine symbolic of the body and blood of Jesus Christ.

The Sikh, at every service in his temple or gurdwara*, shares food as a reminder of the equality of all men before God. At many festivals and celebrations, both religious and secular, the kind of food eaten is also bound up with tradition, as is also the way in which it is prepared. Matzos for Passover, for example, may be exactly the same as those eaten throughout the year but they must be made under strict religious supervision.

Rituals of many kinds form a part of celebrations, especially those involving worship. The ritual lighting of candles and fires is often associated with the coming of light into the world and purification of that which has been tarnished. Water for cleansing is an integral part of most of the major religions.

There are certain prescribed rituals such as the positions and postures adopted in the prostration of the Muslim or the meditation of the Buddhist. The Jew puts on his tallith* and tefillin* for prayer: the high churchman may cross himself or genuflect before the altar. The Hindu dancers, portraying the stories of the gods, observe strict rules regarding dress. The Red Indians taking part in the Sun Dance have a complicated ritual which must be observed to the minutest detail.

It is natural that one should want to do things 'properly' when presenting them to God, whether they be prescribed or whether they come naturally from a sincere desire to offer one's best. Festivals and celebrations have this element of procedure and tradition built into them alongside all the enjoyment and periforal trimmings.

Yes. Festivals *are* fun! They are even more enjoyable when we are able to understand more of the background that has made them what they are. It is hoped that this book will serve just a little to whet the appetite for a deeper study of those many observances which mean so much to so many people and help to bring brightness and enjoyment to everyday life.

Religions and Festivals

Many of the festivals which are celebrated in countries all over the world have their roots in the religion of the people. Some, in fact, go back far into the realms of mythology, legend, superstition and fear. It is natural that people would wish to celebrate those things which mean a lot to them and for many people in all ages this has been their religion, their God or gods and their remembrance of special people or events.

It is helpful to know a little about all religions as a background to the festivals and a brief summary is given in this first part of the book. With each religion is a note of the main festivals to be found later in the book. This introduction must of necessity be limited and it is strongly recommended that a few reference books should be available. A few that would be very useful are:

The Concise Oxford Dictionary of the Christian Church, E. A. Livingstone (Ed.) Oxford, 1977

A Dictionary of Non-Christian Religions, Geoffrey Parrinder, Hulton Educational, 1971

Words in World Religions, P. D. Bishop, SCM Press, 1979

World Religions: A Handbook for Teachers, W. Owen Cole (Ed.), Commission for Racial Equality and Shap Working Party, 1972 (Reprinted 1978)

Religions of the World, John Ferguson, Lutterworth, 1978

What men believe, F. G. Herod, Methuen, 1968

Many gods . . . or one?

It is very easy to try to over-simplify the development of religion and to suggest some progression from fear and bewilderment, superstition and magic, to a religion in which belief in a God or gods eliminates such things. Most people who have studied religions recognise that there is no progression, that faith seldom completely banishes fear of the unknown and that superstition and magic are often interwoven with religion.

Scientific knowledge explains many of the mysteries of the past, yet people still cling to ancient customs. And, in the underdeveloped parts of the world, there are many who still adhere to the old tribal or primal religions.

Perhaps the simplest of these can be summed up in the Polynesian word *mana*. It was a belief in a force or forces that cannot be recognised or understood. Any person or object which behaved in an unusual or an inexplicable way might contain *mana* and should therefore be treated with respect. Things which could harm were well left alone and became 'taboo'. People who might be able to control such forces were in great demand and so there arose the witch-doctor, the medicine man and the shaman, practices of black magic, white magic and voodoo.

Another thought was that the earth, rivers, trees, stones, and other objects contained spirits which could be helpful or harmful. We call this *animism*. Objects thought to contain a helpful spirit are sometimes worn on the person or fixed at the doorway as a kind of talisman or amulet. Spirits with powers of life and death, fertility and good harvest must be humoured or appeased with gifts or sacrifices, dance, worship or self-inflicted pain. These practices form a part of many of today's festivals and celebrations.

Such spirits feature prominently in the beliefs of many of the primitive peoples of the world. For others the spirits grew in importance until they became gods to be worshipped and served. A fine example of this is seen in the Shinto religion of Japan (p. 11) with its thousands of *Kami* (Gods). The belief in and worship of many gods is called *polytheism*.

In most polytheistic religions there are gods who control the earth, the weather and the forces of nature, but there is usually one great creator god who planned and made all things, including the other gods. Usually referred to as 'He' or 'Father', God is not necessarily regarded as male, but He is certainly a god of many names. To the African He may be Amma, Mawu,

Ngewu, Nyambe, Mulungu or Olodumare; to the Maori He is Io and to the aborigine of Australia Baiami. Amongst ancient people, the Hittite Kumarbi was 'Father of the Gods', the Sumerian Anu was 'King of the Gods' and the Phoenician El was the 'Creator of Creation'.

For some peoples the supreme power is not so much a person as a force or a spirit. The Eskimos look to Sila, a watching controlling power: the Hindus believe in the Brahman as the great soul of the universe.

In most religions there is an ultimate aim in life—to be with or be united with the great creator in a place where all is bright and fair—a 'heavenly' place. The idea of heaven depends upon the earthly circumstances. The Eskimo, accustomed to long winter nights, looks for a place where it is eternal sunshine: the American Indian dreams of the 'Happy Hunting Ground'.

But to reach that sublime place one has to pass through death and death is something that has played a very important role in man's thinking and in his religious life. Indeed long ago, and in many parts of the world today, the spirits of the dead are to be feared or, at least paid great respect. What happens to the spirit of the departed? Where is it? Can it come back to haunt or harm?

No doubt it was thinking such as this that lay behind many of the customs that emerged, such as praying for departed souls or offering them gifts. It certainly gave rise to the regard in which one's ancestors have been held in some parts of the world (pp. 120–2). With some peoples is the thought that the spirits of the ancestors could help the living. Zulus will make offerings of food and drink to such spirits or Amadlozi, believing that the ancestral spirits will help them.

Many funeral rites and practices were designed to make the passage to 'the next world' as easy as possible and to provide the wherewithal to reach the desired haven—but all ultimately depended upon the quality of the life that had been lived.

The beginnings of religious thought are lost in the mists of time. They belong to that period of prehistory when man was trying to explain the mysteries that surrounded him yet had no means of recording his conclusions save that of passing them on by word of mouth. It was in that early period, aptly known to the Australian aborigine as *The Dreaming*, that myth and legend had their origin and the multitude of gods, most of them gods of creation or of nature, began to appear.

To primitive people in most parts of the world the greatest wonder was the vastness of the sky and the power of the sun. Inevitably the greatest and most powerful god was the one who personified the sun or who ruled the sky. To the ancient Egyptians he was *Re*, to the Aztecs *Huitzilopochtli*, to the Maoris *Rangi*. Usually male, there were a few exceptions, one being *Amaterasu*, the Sun-Goddess of Japan. If the sun-god were male it was natural for many that the moon was personified as a goddess.

The earth, too, had its mysteries. What was the secret of life? How did things grow? Why did they grow better in some years than in others? Naturally fertility was a female attribute and so there was an earth-mother or fertility goddess. Numerous images have been found, in many parts of the world, depicting such a deity. Often referred to as Venuses, they take many forms but obviously female. So *Anu* was the mother-goddess of the ancient Celts, *Ala* of the Ibo of Nigeria, *Gunabibi* of the Australian aborigines and *Astarte* of the Phoenicians. Among the many goddesses of agriculture were *Chicomecoatl* (Aztec), *Demeter* (Greek) and *Ceres* (Italian). The Maoris had a god of agriculture, *Rongo.*

Alongside these were many other deities, usually of lesser importance, gods or goddesses of the sea, rain, weather, war, love and peace, some of whom were good and others mischievous or rebellious, if not decidedly evil.

Such was the explanation by some people of the opposites of this world—good and evil, light and darkness, summer and winter, matters which feature time and time again in the festivals which are celebrated in many parts of the world. If the creator god was good, there must obviously be an evil god or force, a trickster or an adversary responsible for all the evil in the world. If the creator gave life, someone must cause death. Even the seasonal changes were a result of a never-ending battle between two deities one of whom began to win in spring, reigned throughout the summer and was overcome in autumn.

Naturally the gods suited the people who served them. It was a case of making god in one's own image. The warlike Norsemen had warlike gods, looking very much like themselves but much larger and the Norsemen's aim was to reach Valhalla, the dwelling place of all dead warriors.

In each of the polytheistic communities would be told the

myths, legends and tales of the gods, their strivings, their loves, their hates, their contributions to the world of man and their relationships one with the other. There are obvious parallels between the deities of Greece and Rome but it is interesting to look back further and see the parallels with other religions too. The Greek father-god *Zeus* ('sky' or 'brightness') is related to the ancient Sanskrit *Dyaus* and the Teutonic *Tyw*.

Polytheism was a very convenient system for some but not for others. How could there be so many? they reasoned. People such as Abraham (p. 18) and Zarathustra (p. 33) believed there was only one true god—known to the Israelites as *YaHVeH*, to the Zoroastrians as *Ahura Mazda* or *Ohrmazd*, to Muslims as *Allah* and to Christians as *God*.

Hinduism is, on the face of it, polytheism but that would be an over simplification, for the offering of praise to one of the gods is regarded as an offering to the supreme spirit of the universe. This is sometimes called *henotheism*.

Today people's beliefs vary as much as ever they have done. Those who believe in a God or gods wish to make offerings or live lives that are worthy in every possible way. So the great religious festivals and celebrations, often a mixture of past and present, of folklore, tradition and belief, sometimes reach spectacular proportions as the people enter heart and soul into their celebration.

Humanism

There are people who believe in many gods and there are those who believe in only one but there are also people who have no belief whatever in a god or any spiritual power. A person who disbelieves the existence of God is called an *atheist*. There are others who hold that we know nothing of things which are outside the material phenomena and there is therefore no reason to believe in a god or supernatural powers. Such a person is an *agnostic*.

Throughout the years, in ancient civilisations as well as modern, there have been those who, rejecting a god or religion, have maintained that the salvation of mankind rests with man himself. Such people are *humanists*. They are people who are 'humane' in outlook, who are normally very concerned for the well-being of the poor and oppressed, not for any religious reason but because it was, and is, man's world.

The French philosopher Auguste Comte argued that man was the centre of the universe and all his problems could be solved by sociology and science, which would replace religion. It was man who should be worshipped.

The poet A. C. Swinburne (1837–1909) ends his *Hymn of Man*:

> 'Glory to Man in the highest!
> For Man is the master of things.'

Humanism is to be found in many countries today in humanist associations devoted to reform but not through religion. They have rejected belief in God because this requires faith which betrays reason. In fact they aver that not only is religion unnecessary but it has sometimes stood as a barrier to social reform. It is a matter upon which the humanist and the religious will inevitably disagree. Religious people will point to many reforms which have resulted from the dedication of people to their religious beliefs.

If we believe in a life after death and in a great power in the universe necessary to man, we are religious: if we reason that these things are illogical and that man himself has the answers to his problems, we are humanist.

Shinto

Origin: The ancient religion of Japan.

Founder: None.

Symbol: Though not officially a symbol of Shintoism, the *Torii* is sometimes used. This is the archway through which the visitor to a shrine passes from the everyday world into the presence of a god.

Writings: The *Kojiki* ('Records of ancient matters') is the oldest Japanese book and the nearest to being a sacred scripture. Next in importance, the *Nihongi*, records ancient mythology with stories of creation, gods and men.

Long ago the Japanese believed in many kinds of god, nature spirit or objects of worship, possibly as many as eight million of them. They were known as *Kami* and the religion which arose from the worship of these was Kami-no-Michi ('The Way of the Gods'). Chinese Buddhists called this, in Chinese, *Shen-Tao*, westernised as *Shinto*.

Supreme among the gods was the sun-goddess, Amaterasu-omi-kami, whose son, Prince Ninigi, married Kono-hana-sakuya-hime, goddess of the mountain Fuji-yama. From their descendents, the kings of Japan were thought to have come. It is easy to see how *Jinja* (shrine) Shinto became known also as *Kokka* (state) Shinto. A collection of Japanese government regulations, produced in 967 CE, the *Engi-Shiki*, gives details of Shinto ritual as well as listing 3,000 gods worshipped in 2,000 temples.

During the last century or so, a number of 'New Religions' have emerged. They are known as *Kyoha* or *Shuha* ('Sect') Shinto.

The Jinja, or shrine, contains an object sacred to a god, and halls for worship, prayers, making offerings, ceremonial dances (p. 46) and festivals (*matsuri* pp. 101, 173). Priests make daily offerings (*Nikku*) of green twigs and recite prayers. At the entrance is a *Shimenawa*, a rope with hanging pieces of folded paper, cloth or metal—a symbol of the god's presence and of sanctity.

A smaller Shimenawa hangs above the *Kami-dana* ('God-shelf'), the shelf or altar in the home where daily worship is offered.

Hinduism

Origin: India, c.13th Century BCE

Founder: None. Hinduism developed from the ancient Vedic traditions of the Aryan people who settled around the River Indus (of which 'Hindu' is a form).

Symbol: The OM or AUM (p. 13), which is a part of all Hindu prayers.

Sacred books: The *Vedas* ('knowledge') consist of four collections of hymns, of which the *Rigveda** (Royal knowledge) is best known. *The Brahmanas** are rules for offerings, sacrifice and ceremony. Later writings, the *Upanishads** (an invitation to learn), are philosophical and mystical. There are also two great epics: the *Ramayana** which tells the story of Rama and Sita; and a tale of war, the *Mahabharata**, which incorporates the *Bhagavad Gita** (Song of the Lord), the revelation of the Lord Krishna.

Hinduism is a religion but it is also a way of life, interpreted freely by millions of people in the Indian sub-continent and elsewhere.

The Vedic literature had tales of many gods, the gods of the sky who ruled, gods of battle, gods of nature, gods who created and those who destroyed—gods to whom sacrifices had to be made. So there grew out of this the Brahmins, who were the priests, and the caste system, which was to dominate Indian life for many centuries. The Brahmins were responsible for writing the Brahmanas.

From the Upanishads came a belief in the Brahman, a great spirit or soul that existed beyond this world and could never be approached directly. All living things have an *atman** (soul), which is part of the Brahman. This soul will eventually join the Brahman but this cannot be achieved in a single life span. Hindus therefore believe in reincarnation.

Of the hundreds of gods, the one who came to be regarded as the most important was Brahma*, the creator (not to be confused with the Brahman). He also had two other personalities, Siva*, the destroyer, and Vishnu, the preserver and god of love. Vishnu may also appear in other forms, e.g. as Rama* or Krishna.

Although Hindus worship any of the gods, they believe that, in so doing, their offerings are made to the Brahman. To assist in their worship they often use a *yantra* (instrument for controlling). This may be a statue or a pattern known as a *mandala**,

(a) AUM

(b) Shri Yantra

the most famous, the Shri Yantra, being a design of triangles and lotus flowers. They also use *mantras*, which are words to recite. The most commonly used is the Gayatri Mantra from the Vedas: 'We meditate on the excellent glory of the radiant sun (or *the creator*); may he inspire our minds.'

This, and any other prayer, is preceded by the AUM and a pause. This, too, is a mantra. The A represents the state of wakefulness, the U of dreaming and the M of dreamless sleep. The silence which follows is a symbol of the ultimate reality—the unspeakable, the Brahman. In uttering the AUM, the worshipper tries to be in tune with the Brahman.

Hindus worship alone or with their families but there is collective worship at festivals. Each temple has at least one week-long festival in honour of the god to whom it is dedicated and these are happy occasions with much festivity, processions and bathing in the temple pool or river.

Main festivals:

Diwali* (p. 87), Holi (p. 49), Sarasvati* Puja (p. 149),
Dashara and Durga* Puja (p. 106),
Raksha Bandhan* (p. 173),
Janam Ashtami* (p. 190), Ram Navmi* (p. 190),
Shiva Ratri (p. 47), Ratha Yatra (p. 113),
Ganesh* Chaturthi* (p. 101).

The birthdays of great Hindus, Sri Ramakrishna (19th Century 'saint') and Swami Vivekananda (reformer) are also celebrated (p. 191).

Buddhism

Origin: India, 6th Century BCE.

Founder: Gautama* *(family name)* Sid-dhartha*, also called Sakyamuni* ('sage of the Sakyas'), who, after his enligh-tenment, became known as the Buddha*.

Symbol: The eight-spoked wheel, sym-bolic of the Eightfold Path. The lotus flower is another symbol.

Sacred writings. There is no single book and some Buddhists use more than others. The canonical writings of Therevada* Buddhists are the *Tripitaka* (*Tipitaka*), the 'Three Baskets', con-sisting of rules for monks and teachings. Of the other books the *Lotus Scripture* and *The Way of Virtue* are important, many Buddhists learning the latter by heart.

Buddhism, one of the world's largest religions, began after Gautama, the son of a north Indian ruler, was brought face to face with suffering and began looking for answers. Beneath a tree, now called the Bo-tree or 'Tree of Enlightenment', he found these answers and so became a Buddha (an 'enlightened one'). He then expounded his ideas at Varanasi (Benares) (p. 105).

He spoke of *Four Noble Truths*:

*Dukkha**: Suffering is a part of life.

*Samudaya**: Suffering is caused by *tanha* (desire, selfishness).

*Nirodha**: Suffering will end if selfishness is destroyed.

*Magga**: The way to destroy suffering is the Eightfold Path.

The Eightfold Path consists of

Right understanding: to see life as it is.

Right thought: a pure mind free from lust, ill-will, cruelty.

Right speech: avoiding lying, harsh words, gossip.

Right action: no killing, stealing, adultery, drunkenness etc.; positive action—love, charity, generosity, honesty etc.

Right vocation: an occupation which harms no-one.

Right effort: prevent new evils and expel old ones: seek new good and maintain existing good.

Right mindfulness: concentrate to become aware of truth about body, mind, feelings and thoughts.

Right concentration: meditation to understand the imperma-nence of things.

By following this path, one would reach *Nirvana**, a state of bliss.

Buddhists do not believe in a creator god; neither do they worship gods. They seek enlightenment and improvement through their following of the Eightfold Path or with the help of the monks. Monks have played a very important role in Buddhism since the first Buddhist Council met after the death of Gautama and laid down the main principles of monastic discipline.

About a century later, a second council met at which a division of opinion led to the development of Buddhism along two different paths. In the north of India and neighbouring lands they wanted a broad way by which all men might seek salvation. They called themselves *Mahayana** ('Great Vehicle'). Those in the south preferred to leave more in the hands of the monks and became known as *Hinayana** ('Little Vehicle'), though they are more frequently known as *Therevada** ('Way of the Elders').

Buddhism gradually died out in India but by that time, by missionary zeal, it had spread far and wide. Therevada Buddhism is now widespread in Sri Lanka, Burma and South-East Asia. Mahayana Buddhism developed in Tibet and spread to China, Korea and Japan. In China it became mixed up with Taoism (p. 16). In Japan it took the name of *Zen* (from the Chinese *Ch'an*). Zen Buddhism emphasizes meditation as a means of reaching 'englightenment' and has spread in recent years to Western lands.

Buddhists may have shrines in their homes with a small image called a *Buddharupa*[1]. They may visit a pagoda or stupa (p. 112) or a temple where there is a relic or image of the Buddha. Some Buddhists seek the help of the *Sangha** (monks) or *Bodhisattvas** (saints). Many will sit cross legged, perhaps before an image of the Buddha, meditating. Others may use a mantra or mandala (p. 13).

Main festivals:

   Mahayana: Bodhi Day; Parinirvana (p. 189).
   Therevada: Vesakha Puja* (Wesak*) (p. 189);
   Dhamma Vijaya (Poson) and Dhammacakka* Day (p. 105);
   Temple festivals, e.g. Esala Perahera* at Kandy (p. 101).
   (Perahera = Procession)

Taoism

Origin: China, probably 6th Century BCE

Founder: Traditionally Lao-Tzu (or Lao-Tse) but he is now considered a mythical person. Taoist concepts may have been collated in the 4th century from earlier writings.

Symbol: The *T'ai-chi T'u* or Yang-yin symbol (illustrated) is not exclusive to Taoism.

Writings: The classic of Taoism is *Tao-Te-Ching* (the 'Book of the Way' or The Way-Power Book). *Tao Tsang*, the Taoist canon includes some 1,120 books.

Taoism may be described as the Way of Heaven which the way of man should follow. The Way is not a personal God, as is accepted in other major religions, but an attempt to express in simple terms the ultimate in the universe.

The Supreme Ultimate is symbolically portrayed in the *T'ai-chi T'u*, a device which is commonly seen in China on buildings, furnishings and elsewhere. It consists of two separate, yet interlocking, shapes known as the Yang and the Yin. The Yang (literally 'the bright side'), the male half of the symbol, represents light, warmth, heavenly powers and all that is positive. The Yin (the dark side) stands for darkness, coldness, earthly powers, negative attitudes and femininity. The Yang is thought to dominate the world in summer and the Yin in winter. They are, however, interdependent and all life springs from the two working in harmony.

Behind Taoist teaching lies the belief that the Supreme Ultimate Way is indescribable and beyond comprehension. It is man's responsibility to be still and contemplative so that the Tao can overflow and envelop him.

In many ways Taoism has declined or has been discouraged but its influence on Chinese history and way of life has been very considerable.

Festivals

For Chinese festivals see page 17.

Confucianism

Origin: China, 6th Century BCE.

Founder: Confucius is the Latin form of the Chinese K'ung Fu'tzu ('Master K'ung'), who lived about 551–479 BCE and is regarded as the greatest and wisest of Chinese teachers.

Books: Five books have been attributed to Confucius but his main teachings are summed up in *The Analects*, a collection of ideas collated about 70 years after his death.

Confucianism has been described by some as the traditional religion of China, whilst others regard it not as a religion so much as a way of life. Although there is an indication of a belief in *T'ien*, the Chinese heaven and True God, it is fundamentally humanistic, consisting of treatises on ethical and political matters.

Confucius was a self-educated man, who was held in great respect by many students, possibly some 3000, to whom he taught many aspects of morals and duties both in home and society. There are rules for ceremonial occasions and ritual concerning the remembrance of ancestors (p. 120). He was given such titles as 'Teacher of Ten Thousand Generations' and 'Grand Perfection'.

Confucianism declined and was discredited once China had become Communist, but the new regime continued to recognise the heritage of centuries and respect by many for the one who, long ago, taught the fundamental principle of not doing to others those things that you would not wish others to do to you.

Main Chinese festivals

Chinese New Year (p. 40) and Lantern Festival (p. 48);
Dragon Boat Festival (p. 147); Moon cake Festival (p. 67);
Festival of Maidens (p. 184);
Birthday of Confucius (Chinese Confucian) (p. 191);
Yue Lan (Hungry Ghosts) (p. 121);
All Souls' Day (Chinese Buddhist) (p. 124);
Ch'ing Ming (p. 120); Chung Yeung (p. 122);
Time of sending winter clothes to ancestors (p. 121).

Judaism

Origin: Palestine, 20th Century BCE.

Founder: Abraham.

Symbol: *The Shield (Star) of David* and the *Menorah** (seven-branched candlestick).

Sacred Writings: The *Torah* ('Law') (p. 103) which, with the Prophets, Psalms and other writings, forms the Jewish Bible. The *Talmud*, supplements the Bible and consists of the *Mishnah* (six orders of Laws) and *Gemara* (comments of the Rabbis).

In the early pages of the book of Genesis we read how God called Abraham to go where God would send him, with the promise, '. . . I will bless thee and make thy name great . . . and in thee shall all the families of the earth be blessed.' Abraham's descendents settled in Egypt, where they were enslaved, delivered by God through Moses and led to the promised land. On Mount Sinai, Moses was given the Ten Commandments and many other laws.

Jews believe in one God, known as JHVH (*Yahweh*)—'The Lord'. He is the creator of heaven and earth, the Lord of nature and the Lord of history, who controls the empires of the world and the affairs of man. He is holy, awesome and righteous, yet compassionate, filled with mercy and loving kindness. He is a living God and a personal God. He demands the obedience of his people and promises his presence and help to those who remain faithful.

The Jewish faith, or creed, is summed up in the *Thirteen Principles*, tabulated by *Maimonides** (12th C.) and used in daily prayer to this day: Faith in God as Creator; God is a Unity; He has no Form; He is the First and the Last; it is right to pray to Him alone; all the words of the prophets are true; Moses was the chief of the prophets; the whole law is the same that was given to Moses; this law will not be changed and there will never be any other; the Creator knows every deed and thought of men; He rewards those who keep his commandments and punishes others; the Messiah will come; there will be a resurrection of the dead.

The words of the *Shema** (*Deuteronomy 6, verses 4–9, 11 and 13–21*) are a constant reminder of God.

Part of the Shema* is written on a scroll inside a *mezuzah**, which is nailed to the door posts of the home and is also inside the *tefillin** (phylactery), which a Jew wears when praying on weekdays. The tassels on the *tallith** (prayer shawl) are also a

(a) Star or Shield of David

(b) Menorah

reminder of God's commandments.

Home life is very important and family meals, especially that on the eve of the Sabbath (p. 90), are happy occasions. Here, and in the synagogue, God is constantly remembered daily but especially at the great festivals listed below.

Jews who observe strictly all the Jewish laws, customs and rituals are known as *Orthodox Jews*. Services and prayers in their synagogues are in Hebrew. Those who have modified some of the beliefs and customs and pray in the vernacular are *Reformed* or *Liberal Jews*. They live mainly in Britain and America. *Conservative Jews* fall between the two. *Chassidic Jews* are very pious Jews, who dress distinctively in black, and are found mainly in eastern Europe.

Jews are very tolerant of the beliefs of others. They do not try to convert others but they are determined, despite persecution, to remain true to their own beliefs, as they have done through the centuries.

Main Festivals

Rosh Hashanah* (*New Year*) (p. 85); Yom Kippur (p. 117);
Sukkoth* (p. 63); Simchath Torah* (p. 103);
Chanukkah* (p. 73); Purim (p. 107);
Tu b'Shevat* (*New Year for trees*) (p. 158);
Pesach* (*Passover*) (p. 108); Shavuoth* (*Pentecost*) (p. 62);
Tisha b'Av* (Fast of 9th Av) (p. 116);
Shabbat* (*Sabbath*) (p. 90); Rosh Chodesh* (*New Moon*)
(p. 37).

Christianity

Origin: Palestine, 1st Century CE
Founder: Jesus Christ

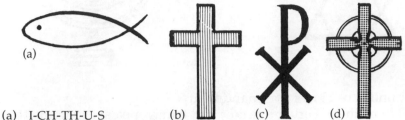

(a) I-CH-TH-U-S
(b) Latin cross
(c) Chi-Rho Monogram
(d) Celtic cross

Symbol: The earliest symbol of the Christian Church was the fish (a), adopted because the letters of the Greek word for fish, *i-ch-th-u-s*, are also the initial letters of the Greek words for Jesus Christ, God's Son, Saviour. Generally accepted as the symbol of Christianity is the cross, which may take one of many forms. The Latin cross (b) has a longer upright than arms, whereas the Greek cross has four equal arms. The Chi-Rho monogram (c) is a combination of the Greek letters with which Christ begins. The Celtic cross (d) incorporates a circle. Sometimes called a 'resurrection cross', the circle symbolises everlasting life.

Sacred Book: The *Bible* ('The Book'), divided into two parts—the Old Testament, which is the Jewish Bible, and the New Testament, which tells of the life of Jesus Christ and the growth of the Church. It contains the teachings of Jesus and others. The *Apocrypha* consists of Jewish sacred writings not included in the canon of the Bible.

Christianity has its roots in Judaism. Jesus Christ was born into the home of a Jewish carpenter and was brought up to have a good understanding of the scriptures (*St. Luke 2; 46—7*). When asked what was the greatest commandment, he naturally quoted the Shema:

> *'Love the Lord your God with all your heart,*
> *with all your soul and with all your mind.'*

St. Paul, the great teacher of the early Church, was also steeped in Judaism, having been brought up a strict Pharisee.

The Jews had long awaited a Messiah, one who would come to save his people. Christians believe that Jesus Christ was the Messiah, able to save people and bring them back into a true relationship with God because of His unique position as 'Son of God' and yet a man living a normal life on earth.

'Son of God' is interpreted in various ways but the accepted teaching of the Church is that Jesus Christ was God incarnate—God in human form, as part of the Trinity (p. 98), God the Father, God the Son and God the Holy Spirit.

We know little of the early life of Jesus. At the age of 30 He was baptised (*St. Mark 1; 10–11*) and began calling on people to repent and believe the Good News. He had many followers, from whom He chose twelve 'apostles' to be His close friends. He aroused the anger of religious leaders who had Him arrested, tried and crucified. After His death (Good Friday) He was placed in a tomb but rose from the dead on the third day (Easter Sunday). After appearances to His friends He ascended into heaven.

Christian beliefs are summed up in The Apostles' Creed: *'I believe in God the Father Almighty, Maker of heaven and earth: and in Jesus Christ His only Son our Lord, Who was conceived by the Holy Ghost, Born of the Virgin Mary, Suffered under Pontius Pilate, Was crucified, dead and buried. He descended into hell; the third day He rose again from the dead; He ascended into heaven, and sitteth on the right hand of God the Father Almighty. From thence He shall come to judge the quick and the dead. I believe in the Holy Ghost, The Holy Catholic Church, The Communion of Saints, The Forgiveness of sins, The Resurrection of the body, And the Life everlasting. Amen.'*

Not surprisingly, the main Christian festival is Easter, though this no longer has the popular appeal outside the Church that Christmas enjoys. The Christian year begins with Advent (p. 84) and includes festivals of Christmas (pp. 81–2), Epiphany (p. 83), Candlemas (p. 73), Lent (p. 115), Easter (pp. 94–5 & 109, Ascension (p. 96) and Whitsun (p. 97).

There are other festivals and celebrations which are kept mainly by certain communions in the church. They include The Immaculate Conception (p. 99), The Annunciation (p. 99), Corpus Christi (p. 93), Trinity Sunday (p. 98), and All Saints' Day (p. 125).

The Christian Church is sometimes referred to as the 'Body of Christ'. Just as a body has many parts or members, so the Church has many parts or denominations, all of which may be called Christian. The reasons why they exist are many and various. Differences of opinion regarding doctrine or organization led to break-away movements. People also like to worship in differing ways, as is evident from forms of service and the celebration of certain festivals.

The Church began in Jerusalem and spread to other cities, such as Antioch where the name 'Christian' was first used, thence to Rome, the heart of the Empire. The head of the Church became Bishop of Rome, the title held to this day by the Pope, the head of the *Roman Catholic Church*. Catholic means 'all-embracing' and, without the word Roman, may be used, as in The Apostles' Creed (p. 21), to mean the whole body of Christians worldwide.

In the 4th Century CE, Constantine built a new eastern capital at Constantinople, which became an important church centre. Councils at nearby Nicea examined the basic teachings and beliefs of the church. But differences of opinion arose between east and west. In 1054 CE the *Orthodox Church* broke its ties with Rome. Today it has subdivisions such as the Russian and Greek churches but they are all part of the one Orthodox Church.

During the 16th Century, certain religious thinkers questioned some beliefs and practices of the Roman Catholic Church. They protested against these and so their followers became known as *Protestants*. From the teachings of Luther in Germany and Hus in Bohemia, came the *Lutheran* and *Moravian* Churches. From Calvin came the *Calvinist* and *Presbyterian* churches, including the *Church of Scotland*.

In England the major break from Roman Catholicism came with the declaration, in 1534, by Henry VIII, that the *Church of England*, or Anglican Church, was no longer subject to the Pope.

In succeeding years, many did not wish to worship in the style of the Anglican Church. We call them *Nonconformists*. Because they broke away from the established Church, they are sometimes called *Separatists*.

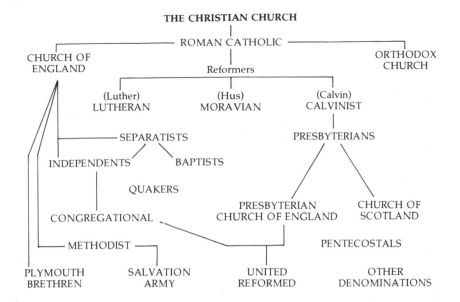

THE CHRISTIAN CHURCH

ROMAN CATHOLIC

CHURCH OF ENGLAND

ORTHODOX CHURCH

Reformers

(Luther) LUTHERAN

(Hus) MORAVIAN

(Calvin) CALVINIST

SEPARATISTS

PRESBYTERIANS

INDEPENDENTS   BAPTISTS

QUAKERS

PRESBYTERIAN CHURCH OF ENGLAND

CHURCH OF SCOTLAND

CONGREGATIONAL

METHODIST

PENTECOSTALS

PLYMOUTH BRETHREN

SALVATION ARMY

UNITED REFORMED

OTHER DENOMINATIONS

Nonconformists included *Independents, Congregationalists, Baptists* and *Quakers* (Society of Friends).

During the 18th Century, the message and enthusiasm of an Anglican clergyman, John Wesley, were not acceptable to the Church. Wesley's followers separated to become *Methodists*. It was a Methodist minister, many years later, who founded the *Salvation Army*. Another group to separate from the Anglicans in 1827 was the *Plymouth Brethren*. Many today also like the lively services of the *Pentecostals* (*Elim* and *Church of God*) and their seeking after the power of the Holy Spirit.

So the Church divided into many denominations all accepting the fundamental teachings of the Christian Church but with differing interpretations, emphases and practices. Recently there have been many moves to unite the Churches. Some have, in fact, come together. In 1972, Congregationalists and Presbyterians joined to become the *United Reformed Church*.

Ecumenical movements and closer co-operation are welcomed and many churches unite each year for special services and meetings in the week 18th–25th January, the Week of Prayer for Christian Unity.

There are many churches or sects which had foundations in Christianity but which have rejected some of the fundamental beliefs of the Church or have additional beliefs which the mainstream of Christianity would find unacceptable.

Unitarians

Unitarians do not accept the doctrine of the Trinity or the deity of Christ. Their foundation goes back to Faustus Socinius, born in Sienna in the 16th Century. John Biddle first preached Unitariansm in England in the 1640s.

Seventh Day Adventists

A Christian denomination which looks in anticipation to the return of Christ in person. They are fundamentalist, accepting the Bible literally in every respect. They hold their Sabbath on Saturday, the Seventh Day, as decreed in the Old Testament. The movement was started by F. William Miller and formally organised in 1863.

Christadelphians ('Christ's Brethren')

A movement founded in 1848 by John Thomas. It is an adventist movement, looking for Christ to return to set up His Kingdom on earth. It has no clergy. Baptism is by total immersion. The Bible is inspired and infallible. Christadelphians reject the Church, the doctrine of the Trinity and the belief that Christ is the incarnate Son of God.

Jehovah's Witnesses

An exclusive group believing that salvation is for them alone. They are Unitarian, denying that Christ was the Son of God and rejecting ideas of the incarnation or of atonement. Their founder, Charles Taze Russell, in America, formed discussion groups and, in 1874, the Watch Tower Bible and Tract Society. Their second leader, Joseph Rutherford named his followers 'Jehovah's Witnesses' in 1931. Witnesses meet in a Kingdom Hall, where worship is 'functional' rather than formal. Once a year they observe 'Memorial' (Holy Communion). Their doctrines are Bible based but they are guided strictly by the Watch Tower publications.

Mormons

The Mormon Church is the name commonly given to *The Church of Jesus Christ of Latter-day Saints*, one of the fastest-growing religions of the present time. Its founder, Joseph Smith, claimed that an angel, Moroni, directed him to a place where two inscribed golden plates would be found. From these plates he produced the *Book of Mormon*. Mormons later migrated to Utah and established a headquarters at Salt Lake City. Mormon missionaries are active today in many parts of the world. This is an adventist movement which accepts the Book of Mormon as more accurate than the Bible, which is considered to contain errors.

Christian Scientists

The movement was founded by Mary Baker Eddy (1821–1910) and much of its teaching is based on her book *Science and Health with Key to the Scriptures*, in addition to the Bible. 'Divine Mind' is used as a synonym for God. Man, who is in the image and likeness of God, is seen as the manifestation of the 'Divine Mind'. Christian Scientists believe that prayer is the sole means by which physical and moral deficiencies in mankind can be solved. Despite its name, the movement denies most Christian teachings.

Rastafarianism

This religion, which began in the depressed areas of Jamaica in the 1930s, is now found in many places where there are West Indian communities. In those days of oppression the Rastas looked upon Haile Selassie, then the only black ruler in Africa, as a Black Messiah. Since his death, he is still so regarded. Recent black power protagonists have helped increase the popularity of Rastafarianism.

The Rasta religion is based mainly upon the Old Testament and on the Book of Revelation: it is expressed partly through reggae music and heightened by smoking marijuana. The characteristic appearance of a Rastafarian is his long hair braided in 'dreadlocks'.

Other new religions

Other new religions are springing up, particularly in the developing countries, many being Christian or Bible based but with deviations from traditional Christianity.

Islam

Origin: Arabia, 7th Century CE

Founder: Muhammad

Symbol: The star and crescent moon, much used in Islamic lands, is not strictly a religious symbol. For Muslims, beautifully written words (calligraphy) about Allah* (God) are holy and none more so than His name.

Sacred books: The Qur'an* ('a reading'), also referred to as 'The Book', is regarded as the Word of God, eternal, uncreated, written in heaven and revealed to Muhammad. It has 114 *suras* (sections), which contain 6,200 *ayyats** (verses). Another holy book, the *Hadith*, a collection of the sayings of Muhammad, is of lesser importance.

In Arabia, in the 7th Century CE, religion and religious practices varied from tribe to tribe. Many gods and goddesses were worshipped, the best known ones around Mecca being the goddesses Lat, Uzza and Manat. It was against this background that Muhammad was born about 571 CE. Muhammad thought a lot about God, the one God, whom he called Allah. At the age of about 40 he had a vision of the angel Gabriel carrying a piece of silk on which was the word, 'Recite'. When he protested his inability to do so, he was instructed still to recite (*Qur'an 96, 1–5*). So he told others and they wrote it down.

This was the first of many revelations. The words were written on scraps of leather, parchment, board and bone. Traditionally they were gathered by the first Caliph, Abu Bakr, to form the Qur'an.

Muhammad proclaimed a belief in a God who is almighty and all knowing, a God with absolute power. *Islam* is submission and obedience to this God, Allah, and a person who has so submitted is a *Muslim*. Man should be a slave (*'abd*) of Allah.

Allah is described in 99 'beautiful names', some of them from the Qur'an and some traditional. A Muslim rosary has 99 beads. A Muslim will describe Allah in beautiful words but is forbidden to attempt to draw a picture of Allah. The worship of Allah is more than a religious duty: it is a part of life.

Muslims believe in one God, His Angels, His Books, His Prophets, the Day of Judgement, good and evil, and life after death. Muhammad declared that Islam was built on five pillars and every Muslim is expected to observe these.

1. *Shahada**: The confession of faith: 'There is no god but God (*Allah*) and Muhammad is the Apostle of God.'
2. *Salat**: Prayer: to be offered at five set times daily, with congregational prayer on Friday.
3. *Zakat**: The giving of alms to the needy.
4. *Saum**: Fasting during the month of Ramadan* (p. 118).
5. *Hajj**: The pilgrimage to Mecca to pray for forgiveness on Mount Arafat and visit the Ka'ba.

There is an additional duty of *Jihad* (striving for *Islam*), which is the use of force if necessary to extend the influence of Islam. There are also strict rules, based on the Qur'an, concerning such things as food, dress and relationships.

The sacred shrine of Islam is the Ka'ba ('cube') at Mecca. In the wall of the building is a Black Stone and nearby a holy well, Zamzam. The whole is now in the courtyard of a great mosque.

A mosque, or *masjid** ('place of prostration') is where Muslims gather for prayer. There are no seats but carpet or prayer mats are on the floor. A *mihrab** (recess) indicates the *qiblah*, the direction of Mecca, always faced at prayer time. An *imam** will lead prayers and may preach from the *minbar* (pulpit). A lectern holds a copy of the Qur'an. There are no images or pictures but art shapes, designs and texts in Arabic script.

On 16th July, 622 CE, Muhammad, to save his life, fled to Yathrib (now Medina). It is from this date that the Muslim calendar begins (p. 86). It is a lunar calendar of twelve months. This means that each year the festivals are held about 10–12 days earlier than in the previous year.

Main Festivals

Day of Hijrah* (1st day of Islamic Year) (p. 86).
Eid ul-Fitr* (p. 175); Eid ul-Adha* (p. 111).
Ramadan* and 10th Muharram* (p. 118).
Lailat ul-Qadr* (p. 102); Lailat ul-Bara'h (p. 203);
Muhammad's Birthday (p. 193); Lailat ul-Isra (p. 193).

Sunna or Sunni ('Custom')

This orthodox mainstream of Islam includes some 80% or more of all Muslims today. It follows the traditional ways of Muhammad and the expositions of orthodox teachers. Sunnis are normally peaceful and tolerant and, although divided into four schools of laws (Hanafi, Shafi'i, Maliki and Hanbali) each recognises the others. Sunnis accept the first three Caliphs of Baghdad, Abu Bakr, 'Umar and 'Uthman*, as 'rightly guided'—the cause of the early 7th Century CE rift in Islam.

Shi'a* or Shi'ites ('Party' or 'Followers')

The major break-away movement. The Shi'a do not accept the first three caliphs but recognise the fourth, 'Ali, as the first. To the Shahada (p. 27) they add 'Ali is the friend of Allah'. Some-times called the 'Twelvers', they believe in twelve Imams, the last of whom, Muhammad al-Mahdi, went into hiding. They anticipate, one day, the reappearance of 'The Mahdi*'. Less than one fifth of world Muslims, they live mainly in Iran, Iraq, Pakistan, India, the Yemen and East Africa.

Isma'ilis*

A division of the Shi'a, they are also known as the 'Seveners', because they accept only seven Imams and look for the return of the seventh, Muhammad ibn Isma'il.

Kharijis* or Kharijites

This oldest sect of Islam, which withdrew support from 'Ali, remained very orthodox. Sole survivors today are the Ibadis, mostly in Oman, East and North Africa.

Wahhabis*

Founded by 'Abd al-Wahhab (1703–87). Puritanical and opposed to reform. Dominate Arabia.

Sufism

A very important movement dating back to the 8th Century. Sufis* (suf—a woollen cloak) were mystics who practised meditation and believed in a more personal God. Regarded as heretical but now accepted.

Bahá'í Faith

Origin: Persia, 19th Century CE
Founder: Bahá'u'lláh*, who based this faith on the teachings of *the Báb*. ('The Gate').
Sacred book: The *Kitab Akdas* ('Most Holy Book').

The Bahá'í* faith owes its origin to Sayyid A. G. Muhammad, born in Shiraz, Persia in 1819. He adopted the title of 'the Báb', a term given by Isma'ili Muslims to spiritual teachers. In 1844, he declared his divine mission. Charged with sedition against the Shah, he was martyred by firing squad in the barrack square at Tabriz* at noon on 9th July, 1850. More than 20,000 of his followers were also executed but the new ideas could not be suppressed.

The Bahá'í calendar, introduced by the Báb, dates from Naw-Ruz (p. 89) of the year of the Báb's declaration. It is a calendar of 19 months, each having 19 days. The days 26th February to 1st March are Ayyam-i-Ha (between calendar). Festival dates do not vary from year to year.

The most important festival is Ridvan (p. 193), a twelve day festival celebrating the period in 1863 when Bahá'u'lláh declared his mission. Bahá'u'lláh ('Splendour of God') was the title adopted by Mirza Husain 'Ali. He set up his headquarters at Akka (Palestine), where he died in 1892. Bahji, near Akka, is the holiest shrine for Bahá'ís and is the qiblah to which they turn during worship. Centre of the Bahá'í faith today is a golden domed building at Haifa, which contains symbols from various religions

Bahá'ís claim that theirs is the universal religion, teaching the unity of God, the truth of his prophets and a continuous revelation. They recognise nine great religious teachers of the world and consider no religion to be superior to the others. They believe in progress after death but not in reincarnation. All men should love one another and seek after peace.

Main festivals

Naw-Ruz* (p. 89); Ridvan* (p. 193);
Various anniversaries concerning the life of the Báb and Bahá'u'lláh (p. 193).

Sikhism

Origin: Punjab*, India, 16th Century CE

Founder: Guru Nanak* (1469–1538 CE)

Symbol: The *Khanda**—a two edged sword of true knowledge to defeat ignorance and superstition, a circle (*chakra**) to remind of one God who has no beginning or end, and two cutting swords (*kirpans**) to defend the truth.

Sacred book: The Guru Granth* Sahib—Guru because it is a teacher, Granth means 'Book' and Sahib to indicate that it is alive. It is sometimes referred to as the *Adi Granth** (First Word) to distinguish it from Dasam Granth, the book of the tenth Guru.

'There is One God. His name is Eternal Truth. He is the maker of all things and He lives in all things. He is without fear and without enmity. His image is timeless. He is not born: neither does He die to be born again. By the grace of the Guru He is made known to men.'

This *Mul Mantra**, translated from the Punjabi, is the basic teaching of the Sikhs, given by Guru Nanak. The founder of the religion. He had lived amongst Hindus and Muslims but was satisfied by neither. Sikhism draws on both these religions and upon Nanak's own insight. The one God, in whom he believed, Nanak called *Nam** (The Name) or sometimes the *Sat Guru* (True Guru).

There were ten Gurus, all of whom the Sikhs regard as perfect men, through spiritual union with whom they believe they can find salvation. Each Guru chose his own successor. The tenth Guru, Gobind* Singh chose no man. The great teachings of the Gurus had been recorded in the Guru Granth Sahib, which would thereafter be the only teacher.

It was Guru Gobind Singh who was responsible for forming the Sikhs into a religious community that was easily recognisable. It was at the festival of Baisakhi*, in 1699 CE, that he formed that *Khalsa** (p. 88), the brotherhood into which Sikhs are initiated (p. 180) and promise to obey the rules, to work for the community and give part of their income for religious or social work.

Members of the Khalsa promise to wear certain articles, usually known as the Five Ks. *Kesh*, the uncut hair and beard, is a symbol of devotion to God. It is usually covered by a turban, as worn by the Guru. The *Kanga**, the comb which keeps the hair in place, is an indication of cleanliness. The *Kara**, a bracelet on the right wrist, symbolises the unity of the Sikhs. The *Kirpan**, a short sword, is a reminder to defend the truth and the weak. The *Kaccha**, shorts, gave greater freedom than the cumbersome Indian clothing. In Western society the Five Ks have sometimes to be adapted.

The Sikh place of worship is the *gurdwara**. There is no special day for attending. Prominent in the gurdwara is Guru Granth Sahib. Before worship it is placed ceremoniously on its stand on the *takhat** (dais), covered with a richly decorated cloth. The whole is underneath a canopy. The Book is prominent in all Sikh services and ceremonies. It is read from beginning to end prior to all religious and personal festivals (p. 104).

In the gurdwara, after the Opening of the Book, there are hymns, music and prayers, including the *Anand**, a great prayer of thanksgiving. There are no clergy or priests because Sikhs believe that all men are equal. They sit cross-legged on a carpet as a sign of equality before God. At the conclusion of the service they all eat the *karah prasad** (a mixture of wheat flour, butter and sugar),—for anyone wishing to be a disciple must share as a symbol of equality. After this they may share a meal (*langar*) in an adjoining room. Anyone of any faith is welcome to partake of this meal. Sikhs regard all men as their brothers.

This equality is demonstrated at the Sikh Golden Temple at Amritsar (p. 88). This has four sides, doors and gates, so that people of any caste or religion can enter from any side. Steps lead down into the Temple: everyone, however humble, must go still lower to meet with God.

Main festivals:

Baisakhi* (p. 88); Diwali* (p. 87); Hola (p. 53);
Birthday of Guru Nanak* (1st Guru) (p. 192);
Martyrdom of Guru Arjan Dev (5th Guru) (p. 192);
Martyrdom of Guru Tegh Bahadur (9th Guru) (p. 192);
Birthday of Guru Gobind* Singh (10th Guru) (p. 192);
Anniversary of Guru Granth Sahib (pp. 104, 192).

Jainism

Origin: India c.8th Century BCE

Founder: Now believed to be Parsva*, born in Varanasi* about 850 BCE. Took form under Mahavira* (once regarded as founder) in 5th C. BCE

Symbol: The Swastika (Sanskrit *Svastika* —'well-being').

Sacred books: The *Agama* ('manual' or 'code') consists of 45 texts approved by a Jain Council in 5th or 6th century CE. There are eleven *Angas* (branches) but each sect also has other sacred books.

Jainism sprang out of Hinduism and has developed into a separate religion which is a mixture of Hinduism and Buddhism. The name Jain comes from the root word *ji* (to conquer)—the conquering of the body and the material world.

Jains believe that there are countless souls in the universe needing to be freed so that they can reach Nirvana*, a state of bliss or peace. To reach this state, they are born higher or lower according to their deeds (*karma**). Since every living creature has a soul, Jains believe in non-violence (*ahimsa**); they will avoid harming any living creature and will never take life. Strict Jains sweep insects from the footpath and wear a cloth mask. They refuse to go to war or engage in occupations such as butchery or hunting.

The four principles of Jainism are right knowledge, right faith, right conduct and austerity. The five vows (*vratas*) of Jain monks are non-violence, a regard for all living creatures, truthfulness, not stealing and not coveting.

Jains have a set hour for morning worship but it is individual worship. Their temples contain images of the 24 conquerers (*jinas*—saints) to whom offerings are made. These jinas are regarded more highly than any god. The chief centres of Jainism are in Gujarat and Mysore.

Main festivals:

Mahavir Jayanti* (p. 192)
Paryushan* (p. 119)

Zoroastrianism

Origin: Persia, 6th Century BCE

Founder: Zarathustra (Greek-Zoroaster)

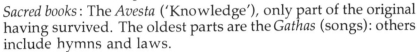

Symbol: Fire, often accompanied by the Avestan words Humata-Hukhta-Hvarshta or modern Pahalavi words Manasni-Gavasni-Kunusni ('Good Thoughts-Good Words-Good Deeds'). See also *Fravashi** (p. 122).

Sacred books: The *Avesta* ('Knowledge'), only part of the original having survived. The oldest parts are the *Gathas* (songs): others include hymns and laws.

'There is one God only, Ahura Mazda*, the Lord of Light, the wise Lord, the Holy One.'

Zarathustra, a courageous, far-seeing priest, taught this about *Ahura Mazda*, the one God who engaged in battle with *Ahriman** the Prince of Darkness. Zoroastrians recognise two forces or spirits—*Spenta Mainyu* (Holy or Good Spirit) and *Angra Mainyu** (Evil Spirit). The whole of life and of creation is a battleground and man must choose whether he will join forces with the Light.

Zoroastrians are enjoined to 'contemplate the beams of fire with a most pious mind'. They are not fire worshippers but regard the fire as symbolic. There are many analogies that can be drawn between fire and God, as Lord of Light, between the characteristics of fire and the nature of our world.

So a Zoroastrian worships in a Fire Temple, in which a sacred fire is kept burning by priests, using gifts of wood that have been brought by the worshippers at *Boi** and *Matchi** ceremonies. In the temple there are no statues or images. People of other beliefs are forbidden to enter.

When Persia was conquered by Muslims in the 8th Century CE, many Zoroastrians migrated to India, where they became known as *Parsis* (Persians).

Main festivals:

Jamshedi Naoroze*, Shahenshai* & Kadmi New Year (p. 89); Khordad Sal* (p. 191); Zarthostno Diso* (p. 191); Farvardin (p. 122); Farvardegan* Days (p. 122).

Communism

Origin: Germany, 19th Century CE
Founder: Karl Marx

Symbol: The Red Star is often used as a symbol of Communism.

Writings: Das Kapital, written by Marx and based on his Communist Manifesto, is the basic text-book of Communism.

It may rightly be argued that Communism is not so much a religion as an ideology, yet insofar as its members are dedicated to the furtherance of Communist principles, it becomes something of a 'religion' in the wider sense.

Karl Marx, a German Jew, rejected Judaism and became atheist. In Brussels he met Friedrich Engels and, in 1848, they issued their Communist Manifesto. It called upon the workers of the world to unite for they had nothing to lose in the battle against a capitalist society. It was only right that everyone should be able to share the benefits of work. The end-product would be a classless society with complete equality and justice. The guiding principle would be: 'From each according to his ability, to each according to his need'.

It was not until 1917 that the first step toward a Communist state was taken. In Russia the Tsar was overthrown and a totalitarian regime instituted. The revolution was bitter and the means ruthless. All opponents were put down and 'rival' organisation, such as the Christian Church, repressed. Communism spread by force through eastern Europe and into China. Other emerging nations adopted Communism as a basis for government.

In some ways Communism has had remarkable success; in others it has failed. It has certainly not succeeded in providing all man's needs nor satisfying his spiritual longings. The Church, repressed for more than half a century in Russia, remains a stronghold of faith. In the 1980s we are seeing the re-emergence of old customs, traditions and celebrations in both Russia and China.

In a rapidly changing world, Communism is recognising that people need their religion too.

Festival themes

Festivals and celebrations have been grouped by theme rather than by religion or country so that it is possible to gain a wider concept, appreciating some of the similarities and the differences, particularly of people from differing backgrounds in a multi-cultural community.

We begin with those themes which are mainly seasonal, albeit many of them having a strong religious connotation. These are followed by religious celebrations, festivities and practices. There are themes on everyday things and on ceremonial occasions as well as festivals of a personal nature.

Whilst it may often be beneficial to take a theme as a whole, there will obviously be times when one subject will need to be extracted for use on its own. Each one is therefore complete in itself with a concluding prayer, but there is also much cross referencing to provide additional information or background material.

A new start (1)

How did you begin today? Did you awaken bright and cheerful, glad to be alive? Did you feel like singing, 'Glad that I live am I, that the sky is blue'? And, if so, did you thank God for a new day? We have many kinds of celebration in life and many things for which to be thankful. A new day is the one that occurs most frequently and it is, perhaps, for this reason that it is often forgotten.

Yet all over the world, people of many faiths celebrate the new day with a prayer of thanks and an act of worship of their God.

Each morning, as he steps out of bed, a Hindu offers a special prayer as his foot touches God's earth. Then, after washing, he worships in the worship room of his home or outdoors beside a river. Each morning, Jains, whose worship is similar to that of Hindus, recite sacred texts as they get up and say prayers, using prayer beads. Each morning a Sikh rises, bathes and then recites from memory the great prayer of remembrance the *Japji**. Each morning Japanese people worship in front of the *Kami-dana* (God-shelf) in their homes.

In Muslim lands, the faithful are called to prayer at daybreak and reminded that 'prayer is better than sleep'. In Christian monasteries, monks have always risen early to worship and *matins* (morning prayers) are offered in churches. Jewish people remember, as they awake, to thank God for safekeeping and later offer their morning prayers in the home or synagogue.

If you are awake at dawn you may hear the 'dawn chorus' as the birds seemingly join in thankfulness for a new day. It is a lesson we might learn and remember.

An ancient Jewish prayer of praise (from Psalm 92)
How good it is to give thanks to you, O Lord, to sing in your honour, O Most High God, to proclaim your constant love every morning and your faithfulness every night. Because of what you have done, I sing for joy.

A new start (2)

Every so often you glance at the night sky and perhaps notice, quite by chance, that there is a new moon—a very thin crescent. You may remember an old superstition that you should turn over your money when you first see the new moon: or you may take no further notice.

Yet, in many parts of the world, people will have been looking for that new moon because it marks the beginning of a new month and, in some instances, the beginning of a very important festival.

Nowadays we have printed calendars and we know well in advance when events are likely to take place. We know how many days we must wait for Christmas or birthdays. Long ago, before most people could read or write, they found that the moon was very helpful. Each new moon came about $29\frac{1}{2}$ days after the previous one and the shape told them how 'old' the month was. This period is a lunar month. People in many lands still use a lunar calendar today.

But 12 lunar months do not make a full year of 365 (or 366) days. Muslims take no notice of this. Each year their festivals come about eleven days earlier. People of other faiths have found ways of adjusting their calendars so that festivals come at the right season (p. 197).

Long ago, Jewish people used to have a festival to celebrate the New Moon. It was called *Rosh Chodesh* and, at one time, it was more important than the Sabbath. Today it is not regarded as a great festival but it is still remembered. In some places a special blessing is spoken on *Rosh Chodesh*, the beginning of a new month, to be announced in the synagogue on the preceding Sabbath, known as the 'Sabbath of Blessing', when a special blessing or benediction is given.

Blessed art Thou, O Lord our God, King of the universe, who, in Thy wisdom, hast given us days and nights, times and seasons; teach us anew to dedicate each day, each month, each year to the glory of our God.

A new start (3)

It is good sometimes to be able to make a fresh start, to put the past behind us and look to a better future. New Year provides such an opportunity and many people use this occasion to resolve to do better than in the past.

We are familiar with the New Year symbol of an old man carrying a scythe, representing the dying old year, with a very young lad holding an hour glass with great hopes for the new life ahead. Some Red Indians symbolically extinguish their old fires and scatter the ashes before lighting new ones and seeking the blessing of their gods.

The lighting of New Year fires is a very old custom, dating back to pre-Christian times. Such celebrations continue to this day at Allendale, Northumberland, where barrels of burning tar are carried in procession to light a fire at midnight. At Comrie, Tayside, torches are carried in a Flambeaux Procession to the town square, where there is merrymaking and dancing.

These are but two of the many parties and festivities held in Scotland and the North of England to celebrate Hogmanay, as New Year's Eve is called. For many, these celebrations are greater than those at Christmas.

Eyes are on the clock as the midnight hour approaches. Then, perhaps, there will come a knock at the door and the family will hope it is a tall, dark stranger carrying a piece of coal for the fire, in exchange for which he is offered food and a drink. This, it is believed, will ensure prosperity.

Elsewhere bells are rung, ships' syrens sound, people dance at balls and in public places, sing *Auld Lang Syne* and greet each other with a kiss.

Yet others quietly celebrate the New Year at a watchnight service in a place of worship, where they dedicate themselves—and the coming year—to God.

Guide and bless us, O God, so that our future lives may prove a blessing to others and our days be filled with happiness, contentment and peace.

A new start (4)

NEW YEAR FESTIVALS

The Romans had a God, Janus, who was especially remembered at New Year. He had two faces, one looking backward to the year that was ending and one facing the future. Perhaps we do this too. If so, we know that there are things in the past that we regret and wish we had not said or done. Some people spend days in sorrow or fasting before the New Year begins (see also p. 119).

So New Year can be time for a 'clean sweep' to remove anything evil. In some places it is literally a clean sweep. In Japan, for example, there is a 'Beginning of Things' holiday on 13th December, when homes are thoroughly cleaned out and decorated. There are the ceremonial cleansings of temples and shrines, too, and at the Joya no kane ceremonies on the eve of New Year, 108 peals of bells are rung at all Hindu and Shinto shrines to mark the removal of evil.

For the Japanese, Ganjitsu (New Year) is the most important of all holidays and lasts for six days. it is a family festival comparable to Christmas in many Western lands. It is a time of family reunions and homecomings. Those unable to return home may be sent a piece of soil containing their family-god or *Uji-gami*.

There are many special foods and decorations, most of which have a symbolic meaning. There are those which represent good fortune, long life, good health, happiness and all the blessings that one would wish for oneself and for others.

The second day of the festival is the time for processions, when businessmen decorate vehicles and exhibit goods. There are often displays and exhibitions at the end of the holiday. Then it is back to work—with a desire to make the best of a new start.

We confess, O God, that we have sometimes been hurtful and thoughtless in our words and deeds. Forgive us for these things and help us in the coming days to be the best we can.

A new start (5)

CHINESE NEW YEAR (YUAN TAN)

'*Kungshi fa ts'ai!*'— A happy and prosperous New Year—a traditional greeting in many lands but given in these words by millions of Chinese people as they celebrate their most important festival It comes a little later than in some lands, for the Chinese New Year begins on the first day of the first month of their lunar calendar, which falls between mid-January and mid-February.

In fact, preparations begin a week earlier with the cleaning of homes, for tradition says that the kitchen god reports on the home before the festival begins. These gods are welcomed back on the eve of the New Year with firecrackers and incense.

The festival, which may last 15 days (usually less in Chinese communities in Western lands), is a great family occasion. Students return home; friends and relatives are visited; and ancestors are never forgotten. It is a time for new beginnings. New clothes are worn; debts are paid; and quarrels or bad relationships are forgotten.

In the home there are parties for which special foods are prepared, often including Jiaozi— white flour dumplings, some containing hidden coins. Children are also given 'lucky money' in red envelopes and coins are shaken from a 'money tree', to bring good fortune. Presents are exchanged and the house filled with plum and peach blossom, chrysanthemums, daffodils, fruits, sweets and lanterns.

And what excitement in the streets! Flags, banners and lanterns decorate the streets, where there are colourful processions, music, dancing and monster dragons—and none more so than in each tenth year, the Year of the Dragon (1976, 1986, etc.).

The colourful, yet deeply religious, festivities end with the Lantern Festival (p. 48) on the 15th day.

Grant unto us, O God, true happiness and prosperity and help us to use all our blessings to bring joy to others.

A new start (6)

Spring Equinox

For people who are used to celebrating New Year according to the Gregorian Calendar on 1st January, it may seem strange to think of a new year beginning at any other time. New year for some people begins as late as the autumn. One of the old Indian calendars began as late in the year as October. For some people, New Year is tied closely to religion and this has determined when their New Year would begin (pp. 85–6).

Many years ago, people in Iran were faced with the difficulties of working out a calendar. In ancient times there had been no continuous calendar. Records consisted of events in the reign of a particular king. Eventually it was decided that the calendar should be based on the seasons of the year (*fasal*). It is known as the Fasli Calendar (p. 198). It seemed that the best time for it to start was 21st March, the day we call the Spring Equinox, when day and night are of equal length. This is the day generally regarded as the end of winter and the beginning of spring—the time of new birth in the world. What better time to celebrate New Year than on 'Nature's birthday'?

In Japan, too, there is a festival at this time called Setsubun ('Change of Season'). People celebrate the festival in their homes and in temples as well as in the streets. It is the custom to scatter roast beans in the home as a symbol of driving away evil spirits. Beans are thrown in the streets, too, at imaginary devils! It is all good fun, yet a reminder to make a new start with anything evil banished into the background.

There are many people who reflect on the past at the end of the year, to try to make amends for anything that was wrong and resolve to make the next year better.

O Thou who art ever the same, grant us so to pass through the coming year with faithful hearts, that we may be able in all things to please Thy loving eyes; through Jesus Christ our Lord.

Mozarabic Liturgy

Calling for help (1)

Each year, on 17th January, the villagers of Carhampton, in Somerset, go to one of the orchards, as people have done for hundreds of years, and make a circle around one of the largest apple trees which will bear the fruit used in making cider. They decorate the branches of the tree with toast that has been soaked in cider; and they pour cider over the tree. Guns are fired into the branches and a song is sung to the tree, urging it to have a good crop of apples.

This old ceremony, known as Wassailing the Apple Trees, is intended to do two things—to scare away with the guns any evil spirits and to make an offering to the spirits of the tree itself. This may seem a strange belief but, from the earliest times, people have believed that there are spirits in the tree that are good and able to help them. Many believed, too, that the spirits in the trees would help them to have children or would give them good harvests.

As far back as people have any knowledge, man has had the greatest respect for trees. The earliest story in the Bible tells of the trees in the Garden of Eden, the tree of life and the tree of knowledge of good and evil. Groves of trees led to many a place of worship and maybe groups of trees formed the first 'temples'.

And people sought the help of the spirits that lived in the trees. A single tree was often a symbol of life and was the centre of many fertility rites. When people long ago set up the Maypole (p. 53) it was for this reason. And the dances performed around it were not the carefully rehearsed ones seen today: they were vigorous dances designed to arouse the spirits in the tree. Red Indians, likewise, set up a cottonwood tree at the centre of their summer festivals (p. 60).

In these, and many other ways, at many kinds of festival, people throughout the world have sought the help of spirits or gods to obtain for themselves the most important things in life.

Lord God, giver of all good gifts, grant us such things as You know that we need.

Calling for help (2)

Plough Sunday/Monday

Early in the year, farmers are busy in their fields preparing the ground for the sowing of crops. Bright coloured tractors chug across the field pulling ploughs which can turn several furrows at a time. How different from the days when all ploughing was done with simple hand ploughs—hard work which had to be done as soon as Christmas festivities were over.

But before the work on the land began, there used to be a special festival when people would ask God's blessing on their work. The day was Plough Monday and it fell on the first Monday after the Feast of Epiphany (January 6th). A plough was decorated with ribbons and then pulled through the village by farm labourers, who were accompanied by two characters, Bessie and the Clown. The proceedings varied from place to place but usually the party would stop, performing a short play, which told of the battle between good and evil, or doing some kind of noisy dance. It was great fun and villagers enjoyed watching them.

The playing and dancing was part of a ritual that went back long before Christian times. The dancing and the noise was intended to drive out evil spirits so that the land would produce a good harvest. Some prayers and gifts might be offered to the ancient gods and spirits. Christian teachers persuaded people to ask the blessing of God instead. So, for hundreds of years, Plough Monday was a time when this was done.

Times have changed but the ceremony of blessing the plough is still held as farm workers gather round on Plough Monday. Elsewhere, in cathedrals and churches, special services are held on Plough Sunday to ask God's blessing on those who work the land.

O God, bless the work of our hands and grant us the satisfaction of seeing good results from our labours.

Calling for help (3)

Each year, at Abbots Bromley, Staffordshire, a dance is held, which is the only one of its kind in Europe. The Horn Dance begins outside the church, then tours the countryside to bring good luck to the farmers and fertility to the crops. The dancers have jerkins over green shirts, patterned breeches and large berets. Six dancers carry reindeer horns, three of which are painted black and three white. There is also a Hobby-horse, a Fool, Maid Marian and a young Bowman. The bowman twangs his strings and the Hobby-horse snaps his jaws in time with the musicians. During the dance, there is a mock battle between those with the black horns and those with the white.

No one is quite sure how the dance originated but, like Morris dancing and other folk dances,it was probably symbolic of the battle between good and evil, life and death, winter and spring.

The characters accompanying the dancers are found in many other old folk dances (pp. 43, 55). The Fool, who carried a bladder on a stick, was the leader, who also 'died' symbolically in the dance. Maid Marian was a man dressed as a woman, representing both sexes and therefore connected with fertility. This man-woman was sometimes called the Betsy, Betty or Moll.

Many of the dances were concerned with the death of winter and birth of spring. Long, long ago, the process of death and resurrection was acted out in mummers' plays. Of many of these only the dances remain, some interesting ones being the sword dances, found mostly in the north of England. At the end of the dance, the swords are often locked together in a star formation. The ancient symbolism of all these dances belongs to a bygone age but the dancing enhances many a present day festival.

Almighty God, Lord of all worlds, Judge of all men, Giver and Taker of all life; hear our humble prayer: In life grant us prosperity and in death raise us up to a new life with You.

Calling for help (4)

One of the oldest forms of seeking help from the gods is the ritual dance drama, so often associated with festivals and, in particular, with seasonal festivals when help was sought for the growing crops, for rain (p. 145) and for the sunshine to make them ripen.

Such dance drama was often of the imitative kind, in which the dance movements represented historical events, the underlying hope being that something similar would happen again. Some imitated the action of whatever was required. So the hunter might mime the killing of an animal or the rain dancers the falling rain and growing crops.

At some festivals there were other kinds of dance, in which performers hoped to communicate with the gods without words, perhaps to entertain the gods (cf. p. 120), thus pleasing them, or to arouse or excite them (p. 42), encouraging them to respond. Sometimes they hoped, in some special way, to receive power. The old custom of dancing round an altar (representing the presence of a god) was to enable his power to jump from the altar to the encircling dancers.

Dance drama still forms an integral part of the festival worship at Shinto shrines. The old Jewish ceremonial dancing during Temple sacrifices and harvest festivals has its counterpart in modern Israel. Dance rituals, opposed by the Christian Church as superstition, continued to find a place at major festivals, some being performed before the altar. Dance still has a part in some worship today.

In another form, dance drama appeared as the Mummers' play, performed in every part of Britain year after year. No doubt originally associated with the winter and spring festivals, it became linked with the Christian festivals of Christmas and Easter. There were no written words and so there were many variations of the play, all of them being an enactment of the triumph of good over evil, the death of the old year and the new birth.

Almighty God, grant that whatever we offer to You—be it our voices, our music, our dancing, our talents or ourselves—our offering may be the very best we can make it.

Calling for help (5)

Witch-doctor and Medicine-man

There are often times when people who have problems seek the help of others who may be able to help them. They may go to a priest or other religious person and ask that a prayer may be said for them.

All over the world, for centuries, people have sought help from those who were believed to have special powers or means of communicating with gods or spirits. Sometimes they did so with rituals or on great ceremonial occasions, when they would dance, sing or go into a trance or state of ecstacy.

People who do this may be known as *shamans*. The original shamans were religious leaders in Siberia. The name is now given to many kinds of priest, magician, sorcerer or medicine man. The shaman may go into a trance, in which he is believed to visit other worlds, where he seeks the spirits who could help.

The Eskimos' *angakok* sang magic songs, which sent him into a trance in which he might travel as far away as the sun, the moon or the depths of the ocean. Sometimes he organised song or drum contests at which he would consult the spirits. In Islam we find religious beggars or teachers called dervishes. Some, the whirling dervishes, go into wild ecstacies as they dance.

Many shamans are consulted in time of illness. The Red Indian shamans were men with some knowledge of bone-setting and herbal medicines. Cures were normally accompanied by song and dance movements. The Zulu *isangoma* is a man who has special contact with ancestors as well as a knowledge of medicine. Medicine men in many lands are sometimes called witch-doctors, a reminder that there is little distinction between shamans and witches. A witch is a man or woman who is believed to have unusual powers through contact with the devil or some other supernatural power. Groups, or covens, of witches have their sabbaths and celebrations.

Thank You, O God, for people who can help us because of their knowledge of You. Help us to come to know You for ourselves.

SHIVA RATRI   *Lord of the Dance*

Dancing plays a very important part in many festivals and celebrations, whether they be religious or otherwise. People have learned to express their feelings in their dancing, just as they may in words.

There are many forms of dance throughout the world. Some of the most expressive is that performed by Indian dancers, who regard dancing as the most beautiful of the arts. Every movement of the body, head, neck, shoulders, stomach, back, legs, lips and so on, has a particular meaning, so that whole stories can be told in mime.

This is a form of dance drama that has been used for centuries to tell the stories and legends of the Hindu gods and so help people to understand their religion. Such dancing is popular at Diwali* and other festivals but may be especially remembered at Shiva Ratri, the Festival of the Dance of Shiva*, who, according to tradition, was the god who taught people to dance—though the dancing probably started in ancient times as a form of nature worship.

Shiva is one of the three most important Hindu gods, the others being Brahma and Vishnu. He is referred to as the first dancer, the 'King of dancers', or as Nataraja*, 'Lord of the Dance'. He is usually pictured dancing a frantic Tandava, his world-shattering dance, within a ring of fire, representing the life process of the universe, in which Shiva acts as both creator and destroyer. He has four hands—two to hold the balance between creation and destruction and two to offer people salvation and protection. He dances on the back of a demon—ignorance, which must be destroyed if souls are to be enlightened.

There are many Hindus who worship Shiva and call upon him to help them and give protection.

A prayer from the Rig-Veda
We praise you with our thoughts, O God. We praise you even as the sun praises you in the morning: may we find joy in being your servants. Keep us under your protection. Forgive our sins and give us your love.

Early spring (1)

Most people feel like celebrating when they see the first signs of spring. The snowdrops pushing their way through the hard ground and the first bright, golden crocuses give the message that winter is passing and brighter days are ahead. The days are slowly lengthening and the sun becomes that bit warmer. The world seems to be coming back to life.

Long ago, the people of China began celebrating the new birth of the world on the first full moon of the year with a Lantern Festival (*Teng Chieh*). It came at the end of the Chinese New Year celebrations and was the day on which public offices reopened. The lanterns represented the increasing light and warmth after the chill and darkness of winter. Lanterns in traditional styles were displayed on market stalls and in shops. Brightly coloured lanterns, made from silk, paper, glass, imitation pearls and straw had scenes from legends painted on them. Some villagers set up tent-shaped strings of lanterns fixed to a central pole. Lanterns were carried in procession and fireworks of all kinds let off.

Changes in government have meant a curtailing of Chinese festivals, which are not celebrated as they once were, but some survive in China and amongst Chinese communities abroad. One that has done so is the spring festival of *Ch'ing Ming*, the Festival of Pure Brightness, which comes about a month after the Lantern Festival. It is a time for family reunions (p. 174) and is the first occasion in the year for visiting and tidying the family graves. Gifts are offered to the ancestors (p. 120).

The Japanese have a festival called *Setsubun*, which marks the last day of winter and the beginning of spring (p. 41); and the Hindus celebrate Holi (p. 49), a bright festival. Spring is a happy season of the year, celebrated world-wide with festivals of many kinds to herald new birth in the world.

(*Some schools like to hold their own spring festivals, decorating the school with spring flowers.*)

Almighty God, in the awakening world, grant that we may see the light of Your truth and feel the warmth of Your love giving us new life with You.

Early Spring (2)

Hindu and Sikh Spring Festivals

One of the most carefree times of the year for people living in the North West or Central parts of India is the festival of Holi, a name which is associated with happy singing, much as people might sing 'Hallelujah!'

Holi comes at the time of the full moon towards the end of February or in March, which is about the time of the spring harvest. Fires play an important part in the festival and are lit in the homes. Community fires are lit by the priests. People remember a legendary character named Holika, who was burned. So images of Holika are made and burned on the fires.

The length of the festival varies from place to place. It may be five days, but certainly three. During this time there is a carnival type atmosphere of gaiety, singing, street dancing and processions. Bright clothes are worn. People also recall stories of Lord Krishna's games with the milkmaids and how cowherds and milkmaids smeared or sprayed each other with red powder. So, today, part of the fun is to spray others with coloured water or powder and to play pranks on one's neighbours.

Of course there are always people whose pranks can be hurtful and not funny for those on whom they are played. It is no joke to be covered in grease or mud instead of powder! This is nothing new. Long ago, Guru Gobind* Singh was concerned at such things and he called the Sikhs to a great gathering at Anandpur at the time of the festival. There were mock battles and competitions of horsemanship. Since then, the Sikhs have kept the festival of *Hola* (or *Hola-Mohalla*), a kind of fair which lasts for two or three days. The emphasis is on physical pursuits, but there is aslo plenty of fun and good humour.

Thanks be to You, O God, for all the blessings that are ours to enjoy. Thank You for good food, for our families and for friendship. Thank You for festivities and frolics, for sports and skills. As we enjoy ourselves, make us always aware of the needs and the feelings of others so that we can all be happy together.

Early spring (3)

Pancake Day

The period of forty days before Easter is known as Lent—at one time kept very strictly as a period of fasting and solemnity. It is not surprising that the few days before Lent began were ones when people let their hair down and engaged in all sorts of fun and merrymaking.

These days are known as Shrovetide. The name comes from the Roman Catholic practice of confessing sins and being forgiven, when a person is said to be shriven or shrove.

Amongst the many restrictions that applied in Lent were some concerning food. Fat, butter and eggs were forbidden, so people had a real feast to eat those that remained on the day before Lent, Shrove Tuesday. This became known in Europe as *Mardi Gras*—Fat Tuesday—when people not only feasted but enjoyed colourful noisy carnivals (p. 137).

The other way of using up the fat and eggs, and that with which people are familiar today, was to fry them up and make pancakes. So Shrove Tuesday also became Pancake Day.

There is a story told that, many years ago, in 1445, a housewife in Olney, Buckinghamshire was so busy making her pancakes that she did not notice how time was passing. When she heard the church bell, she rushed to church still wearing her apron and carrying her frying pan.

Nowadays there is always a pancake race at Olney on Pancake Day. Women taking part must wear a hat or scarf and an apron. They carry a frying pan with a pancake, which has to be tossed three times before reaching the church. The winner receives a prayer book from the vicar and a kiss from the bell-ringer. Men are not allowed to compete. Perhaps the bell-ringer would not fancy kissing a man!

Like so many other Shrovetide events, it is good fun for those taking part and for the spectators, as it has been for many years. Festivals are fun!

Grant unto me today, O God;
The recognition that all of life is a gift from You;
The desire to use Your gift to the full;
The ability thoroughly to enjoy every moment of the day;
And the wisdom to do this without hurting anyone else.

Early spring (4)

Symbol of new life

How would you like to smash an egg on top of somebody's head and know that the other person would not mind one little bit? You could if you lived in Mexico, for that is what children do to each other during the week before Lent begins. Perhaps it should be said that the eggs are not ordinary eggs but ones that are filled with tiny pieces of paper.

It is just one of many customs to do with eggs that can be enjoyed in early spring. The egg has always been regarded as a symbol of new life and it is not surprising that it is associated with many aspects of spring and Eastertide. In ancient times, eggs were dyed by the Egyptians and the Persians, who then exchanged them with their friends. It was in Mesopotamia that Christians first gave eggs to their friends at Easter to remind them of the resurrection of Jesus.

To Jewish people, too, the egg is a symbol of new life and a roasted egg is one of the foods always on the table for the Passover meal, a reminder of the new freedom they found.

At one time, when Lent was observed more strictly than it is today, eggs were one of the forbidden foods. That is why they were used up to make pancakes on Shrove Tuesday. At the end of Lent, on Easter Sunday, it became customary for people to give eggs as presents to their friends and to servants. These were usually decorated. Nowadays they are not real eggs but chocolate ones.

There are lots of strange and interesting customs. In many places there are egg-rolling events and Pace-egg plays. In the U.S.A., parents hide eggs for children to find. In Germany, eggs are dyed green on Maundy Thursday. In Greece, on Easter Day, people carry red eggs, which they tap together. One person says, 'Christ is risen.' The other replies, 'Truly He is risen.' For Christian people this is indeed the message behind each Easter egg given.

Just now, O God, we think of the new life of spring-time and the rising again of Jesus Christ. Help us to make this a time of new opportunity for His sake.

Maytime (1)

Here we come gathering nuts in May . . .
Nuts in May . . . Nuts in May . . .

How can we? There are no nuts in May! But lots of people used to gather *knots* of May, the blossom of the hawthorn which, in the days before the calendar was changed, was easily found on May Day. This, with other greenery, was gathered by those people who went 'a-Maying', ready for the ceremony of 'bringing in the May'.

The day began very early. Just after midnight, young men and women made their way to the woods to find the branches and flowers. The young women washed their faces in the morning dew, believing that this would not only give them a beautiful complexion but would protect them from certain illnesses. Then all returned home, singing May carols.

Younger children may have been a-maying the day before. With two hoops they made a garland—a kind of cage—which they covered with flowers before seating a doll in the middle. They then carried 'the lady' round the village, collecting money for themselves.

Many May Day customs came from the Roman festival of Floralia (28th April–3rd May) in honour of Flora, Goddess of Flowers and Bride of the West Wind. Others are much older, having their roots in pagan festivals which heralded the coming of spring.

May Day celebrations started early in the day—and still do. In Oxford, it has been the custom, for several hundred years, for the choir of Magdalen College to climb to the top of the tower at 6 a.m. to welcome the sunrise with the May Hymn. There are other hymns and a peal of bells before the festivities begin. It is good to begin a happy day with thoughts of God.

In our carefree moments, in times of joy or pleasure, on days of festivity and celebration, help us to remember You, O God, and begin our day with hymns of praise and thankfulness.

Maytime (2)

May Day celebrations today are small compared with those of the past. For hundreds of years, the May festival was the highlight of the year as people celebrated the passing of winter and the new life of springtime.

People walked in processions with their branches and blossom, pride of place being given to the young tree that would be set up as the Maypole (p. 42). Stripped of its branches, except, perhaps the uppermost, where leaves symbolised new life, it was decorated with flowers and ribbons. Later in the day, people danced around it (p. 54). In some places, a permanent Maypole stood on the village green.

The greatest honour for any young woman was to be chosen as 'Queen of the May'. Usually the prettiest was chosen, for she represented Flora. She spent the day presiding over the festivities from her throne in a leafy bower.

At many of the festivals there was a man covered by a cage of leaves. He was known as the Green Man, or Jack in the Green, or Jack in the Bush. In other lands he was known as Leaf Man, Wild Man or Green George. As part of the celebrations he 'died' to symbolise the death of winter and birth of spring.

Sometimes there was a swordsman, too, who cleared a way for the dancers. His sword also drove away any evil spirits! On the sword was a cake, which was later broken and shared. Even the tiniest crumb was thought to be lucky. So the day passed with fun and revelry, dancing, archery contests and maybe a roasted ox.

Then, in some places, fires were lit on the hilltops at the end of the day. Animals were driven through them to prevent disease and people danced around them—just as had been the custom for centuries.

> Lord, touch our careless eyes;
> New life, new ardour bring,
> That we may read Thy mysteries,
> The wonder of Thy spring.

A. C. Benson (1862–1925)

Maytime (3)

Morris and Country Dancing

To some extent, May Festivals belong to the past. Many of the customs died out as people moved from the country to the towns to work in the new factories. Yet some parts of the festivals, particularly the dancing, are still to be enjoyed because they have been revived in recent years.

May Day is still celebrated in some parts of the country with dancing round the Maypole. Long, coloured ribands are attached to the top of the Maypole, the other ends being held by the dancers. Then, to a lively tune the dancers move in and out, this way and that, until the ribands have been plaited into a colourful pattern. Then, if they have learned their steps aright, they can reverse, undoing the plaiting. These are not the dances that were performed around the old English Maypoles. Plaiting the ribands is a custom that came from Southern Europe.

Dances that are similar to the Old May festival dances are those performed by the Morris men in many parts of Britain. Their dress may vary, but most of them wear hats with ribbons, carry large handkerchiefs or sticks and have bells on their legs. The dances are different, too, but they are all boisterous with stamping and kicking to make the bells jingle wildly.

It is fun to watch and enjoyable for those taking part, but that is not why Morris dancing was popular at May festivals long ago. No doubt the stamping and ringing of bells would awaken the spirits in the ground after the winter. No doubt, too, the noise would drive out evil spirits. Certainly this kind of dancing is a very old pagan custom designed to encourage a good harvest.

Whatever their origin, these, and many other kinds of folk or country dance, form an enjoyable part of many festivals and celebrations, not just at Maytime but throughout the year.

Whether we appreciate the artistry and movement of others or the pleasure of dancing ourselves, make us thankful, O Lord, that we have such things to enjoy.

Maytime (4)

FOLK DANCE

Once the fine weather comes, it is quite common to find teams of dancers enjoying themselves as they entertain others with displays of what are usually called Folk Dances. These are the kinds of dance that have been performed, sometimes for hundreds of years, which have their own particular characteristics.

Morris dancing is one of these, but there are several different forms of this. Most have bright ribbons and bells, but there are unusual ones, such as the Britannia Coconut Dancers at Bacup, Lancashire, who blacken their faces, wear red and black skirts over black breeches and clap wooden discs as they dance. Some dancers are always accompanied by a Betsy, a Fool or a Hobby-horse.

The most famous Hobby-horse, known as 'Oss, is seen in the May Day revels at Padstow, Cornwall. He is an odd creature. His body is hidden by a tarpaulin covering a six-foot hoop. He wears a mask and a tall pointed hat. All day he chases the women, catching one now and then beneath his tarpaulin, which is supposed to bring her luck.

In Minehead, Somerset, is a different kind of Hobby-horse. In fact it is in the form of a ship—a reminder of a shipwreck in 1772. He, too, dances on May Day, but also at other times, teasing holiday-makers at the time of the Minehead Show.

One of the most famous dances is the Cornish Flora or Furry Dance (*Furry* from 'Feria'—a fair). On 8th May, there is dancing in the streets of Helston. Dancing begins at 7 a.m. and continues throughout the day, some dancers dancing through the houses, which it is thought will bring good fortune.

Today, there are many festivals of Folk or National Dancing . . . and they are well worth a visit.

Thank You, O God, for colourful reminders of a world so much different from ours today: and thank You that, no matter what may change, You remain the same, the God of all people of all ages.

Maytime (5)

In many parts of the country, during the early part of the week in which Ascension Day falls, usually during May (p. 199), an old custom is still observed. People gather at the church from whence they walk in a procession around the parish, led by the priest and the choir. Many of the people and children carry wands cut from willow trees, which have been stripped of their bark and perhaps decorated with flowers.

Every so often the procession is halted so that prayers can be offered and also for refreshments, for the perambulations may take a long time. They may also 'beat the bounds' with the wands (p. 57).

This time of year is called Rogationtide. The Sunday of that week is Rogation Sunday and the Monday, Tuesday and Wednesday are Rogation days. The name comes from a Latin word, 'rogare', which means 'to ask', because it is on these days that special prayers are offered, mainly to ask God's blessing on the harvest.

It is a very old custom. Before Christian times there was a festival of *Robigalia*, when people walked in procession through the cornfields and asked their gods to protect the crops from mildew. The Christian Church kept up the custom on 25th April, which they called the 'Major Rogation', but offered Christian prayers instead of pagan ones.

During 5th Century CE, when his diocese was threatened by volcanic eruptions, St. Mamertus of Vienne prepared special prayer litanies asking God's help. These developed into the 'Minor Rogations' preceding Ascension Day, which became days of prayer and fasting. In 1969, the Roman Catholic Church replaced them with periods of prayer for the fruits of the earth, the needs of man and the works of men's hands—to be observed at any time of year.

Hear our prayers, O Lord our God:
For the needs of all Your people throughout the world;
For growing crops and good harvests to meet those needs;
And for all who work to provide for others.
O Lord, in Your mercy, hear our prayer.

BEATING THE BOUNDS

You probably know where your town or village begins and ends, because it is indicated by a sign or a stone by the roadside. Each village has its parish church. A town may have several parishes with churches. Do you know all the boundaries of the parish where you live?

Nowadays we can find this information on a map but, long ago, before there were maps, people wanted to ensure that there were always those who would know; so, once a year, the villagers set out to 'beat the bounds'.

This often formed part of the rogation procession (p. 56) if one was held. On that day, the procession left the church, led by the priest and choir. Many villagers and schoolboys followed, carrying willow wands. Each time they came to a boundary mark, which may have been a bridge, a stone, a tree or some other object, they beat it with their wands.

Then they took one of the boys and beat him too . . . or 'bumped' him against the stone . . . or rolled him in some brambles . . . or threw him in the river. Whichever it was it was painful or uncomfortable and he would be unlikely to forget the spot where it happened. He was probably rewarded with a coin or some other gift.

The custom of 'beating the bounds' may seem strange but, like so many customs, its origins are old. This probably comes from two Roman festivals. *Terminalia* was a festival in honour of Terminus, the god of boundary marks. At the other, *Ambarvalia*, people beat the ground with sticks to drive out the spirits of winter.

Today, in many parts of the country, there are ceremonies of 'beating the bounds', most of them having interesting local customs such as gifts of hot pennies or the scattering of nuts and raisins.

O God
Help us to appreciate the place where we live;
Make us aware of everything that makes it 'special';
Teach us to preserve all that is worth preserving
And do nothing that will spoil our heritage.

Summer (1)

Sun worship

Each year, when the summer is at its height, the 'sun worshippers' come out in large numbers, stripping off most of their clothes and lying in the sun to get nicely tanned. They are not really worshippers of the sun; they just enjoy it.

Worship of the sun is probably as old as mankind. The people of the ancient civilizations of Mesopotamia and Egypt each worshipped the sun and had their festivals in honour of the sun god. Sol, the Latin name for the sun, was one of the Roman gods, popularly known as *Sol Invictus*, 'the invincible sun'. His festival was on 11th December.

Most of the festivals for the sun were held in summer and were intended to try to keep up the strength of the sun. The Incas of Peru had a very sacred ceremony called *Capac Cocha*, in which a sister of the king or a local ruler was sacrificed as a Virgin of the Sun. But the greatest, and most gruesome sacrifices to the sun were those of the Aztecs of Mexico, at whose festivals thousands of people were cruelly sacrificed and their hearts offered to the Sun, many of them willingly allowing their lives to be taken to ensure a place with the sun-god.

In Europe, great midsummer fires were lit. No doubt, originally, these were also used in the sacrifice of humans or of animals. Many superstitions and customs became associated with them, some remaining to this day. Beltane fires, lit at various times from 1st May onwards, reached a peak on Midsummer's Eve, 23rd June, the eve of the longest day and turning point in the sun's career. Huge bonfires were thought to strengthen the sun; torches were carried in procession; and burning wheels were rolled down the hills, believed to help the sun on its journey.

Interesting ideas these are, but we know that nothing we do will affect the sun. So we enjoy it—and thank God for the sun and so many other blessings of our world.

As the sun warms our bodies and Your love warms our hearts, grant, O God, that we may offer to You our best sacrifice—our lives to be lived to Your glory.

Summer (2)

The custom of lighting bonfires and torches, and of rolling blazing wheels down the hills on Midsummer's Eve, has now very largely disappeared, although here and there it has been revived. There are some, for example, which have been re-established in Cornwall, by Cornish Societies, in which the lighting ceremonies are conducted in the old Cornish language.

In the north of England, too, bonfires are still lit in some places, either at Midsummer or on 4th July, the eve of Midsummer in the old calendar. Usually people dance round the bonfire, always in a clockwise (or sunwise) direction.

One of the interesting ceremonies held in midsummer was originally associated with June 21st, the summer solstice, or longest day of the year. Nowadays, at dawn on Midsummer's Day, there is a ceremony at Stonehenge, the ancient temple on Salisbury Plain. No one can be quite sure why and by whom the first part of Stonehenge was built. We do know that it is nearly 4,000 years old and it could well have been a temple for the worship of the sun because it is so orientated that, on 21st June, the rays of the sun break over the Hele (Sun) Stone and shine on the altar stone.

On this day, members of the Ancient order of Druids, in their white robes and carrying their symbolic banners, walk in procession amongst the monoliths and under the great lintels. Hundreds of spectators may watch this dawn ceremony with its ancient hymns and prayers, a link with the oldest ceremonies in the world in which people, in their various ways, have worshipped the Sun God, the giver of life.

There are many other local Midsummer celebrations which have their roots way back in history and folklore and which are both interesting and enjoyable.

An ancient Druid prayer recited at Stonehenge
God, our all-Father, permanent amid all change art Thou. Thou hast ever been and as Thou art so shalt Thou ever be. We seek and find in Thee the glory of the dawn. We seek and find Thee when the darkness of the night has fled. The sleep of faith has ever led through night to dawn.

Summer (3)

Red Indian Summer Festival

People in many parts of the world have their great summer festivals, some of them related, in ancient times, to the worship of the sun when it was at its most powerful stage. Some of the greatest of these festivals have been those held by the Red Indians of the plains of North America, when the whole tribe would gather for the great festival of the summer camp.

The plains Indians had many complicated religious rituals and ceremonies but some practices were common to them all.

When the Sioux assembled, they would first fell a cotton-wood tree and set it up in the centre of the camp (cf Maypole p. 53). Around it was built a circular arbour of branches, the stage as it were, for the great Dance Facing the Sun—known to the white Americans as the Sun Dance. For this there was a complicated ritual, in which every body movement had its meaning.

The Dance usually lasted for four days. The dancers formed a circle and maintained their rhythmic movements for the four days, taking neither food nor drink. They danced facing the sun or the centre pole. Some even pierced their chests with wooden skewers attached to the centre pole by cords and they danced until the flesh broke. The hunger and thirst, the pain caused by the skewers, the fatigue of the dancing, were all endured willingly in the belief that this would bring them nearer to the Great Spirit, who would no doubt reward them, too, with buffalo to be hunted and good harvests.

Other tribes had other dances. The Cherokees, for instance, held a Green Corn Dance, when they danced in a double circle round a drummer in front of a temple mound. There are many ways of making a thank offering to God.

Part of an Arapaho Sun Dance Prayer:

We cannot cease praying to You, my Father, Man-Above, for we desire to live on this earth . . . May our thought reach to the sky where there is holiness. Give us good water and an abundance of food.

Summer (4)

How would you fancy going to a service in a church where there was no heating and no seats, a cold earthen floor and no cushion to kneel on when praying? You would probably say, 'No thank you. I like to be comfortable.'

Perhaps today we are not as hardy as people once were, who had none of the comforts to which we are accustomed. Before the 15th Century, there were no seats and only the rich could afford cushions. To take away some of the cold and damp, the church floors were covered with rushes. Every so often, the old rushes were cleared out and fresh ones put down in their place. This usually happened in summer on the day of the church's wake or patronal festival (p. 130).

Nowadays, rush-bearing is unnecessary, but the old custom is still observed in colourful festivals, mainly in the north of England. At Grasmere, in the Lake District, the ceremony is held on the Saturday nearest to St. Oswald's Day (5th August). In a procession, the clergy and choir are followed by six girls carrying the rush sheet on which are rushes and flowers. Other people carry rushes that have been plaited into shapes.

At Ambleside, Cumbria, the Rush-bearing takes place one Saturday in July (formerly nearest to St. Anne's Day—26th July). It is a colourful procession with rushes woven into patterns and symbols on large wooden frames. In the market place, people sing the special Rush-bearers hymn, then go to church for a service.

Like many old customs, it is no longer necessary—but it is enjoyable and there are still people who like to put all their skill into making something worthy to be taken into the house of God.

Help us, O God, to make good use of all the skills that You have given us; and teach us not to use them selfishly.

Harvest (1)

Some of the oldest festivals to be celebrated are those which give thanks for the harvest. People in ancient times would pray to their gods for a good harvest. Then, when the crops had grown, ripened and been harvested, they said thank-you in the only way they knew, by giving an offering or sacrifice of part of the crops.

When the Hebrew people were journeying through the wilderness under the leadership of Moses, they were given many laws. Some of these related to the offering of the 'first fruits' and the method of so doing was laid down (*Deuteronomy 26; 1–11*).

There were three harvest, or pilgrim festivals, which were celebrated, and still are, by Jews. One of these was *Shavuoth**, also known as Pentecost or the Festival of Weeks. It occurs seven weeks after Pesach* (Passover), at the end of the barley harvest and beginning of the wheat harvest.

Traditionally, this was the time of year when Moses was given the Ten Commandments on Mount Sinai, and so people give thanks, not only for the harvest, but for the Torah. In the synagogue services, there is a reading from Exodus 19 and 20, which tells of the revelation to Moses and the Ten Commandments. There is a special prayer, too, the *Akdamut**, which is a hymn of praise and thanksgiving for the Torah. So Shavuoth is a time when people give thanks to God for two kinds of food—food for the body and spiritual food.

It is a happy festival, with special foods, such as blintzes (fritters stuffed with cheese). In modern Israel, children have baskets of fruit which they sell in aid of the Jewish National Fund. Synagogues are decorated with flowers.

A Jewish prayer:

We thank You, O Lord our God, because, for all time, You gave our fathers a land that is pleasant, goodly and spacious; and because You have given us the Torah, life and food. Blessed are You, O Lord, for the land and for the food You have given us.

Harvest (2)

*Sukkoth**, the second Jewish harvest festival of the year, begins five days after the Day of Atonement and falls at the time of the grape harvest. It is called the Festival of Tabernacles, or Booths, because, during this eight-day festival, meals are eaten, and other family activities take place, in temporary huts or booths set up in gardens or at the synagogue for those with no garden. The roof, with openings to see the sky, is made of branches from which flowers and fruit are hung.

The festival comes from instructions in the Torah: 'You shall dwell in booths seven days . . . so that your generation may know that I made the children of Israel to dwell in booths when I brought them out of the land of Egypt.'

Sukkoth is also called the Feast of Ingathering, when people recall how God has given food in garden and field. During this eight-day festival, the first two and the last two days are holy days. In the synagogue there are symbolic offerings of palm and willow branches, flowering myrtle and an etrog (citrus fruit). These are waved in all directions to remind the people that God is everywhere. Special prayers (*hoshanot**) are offered.

The seventh day is called *Hoshana Rabba**, from the words of Psalm 118, 25: 'Save we beseech thee . . .' On this day the people solemnly process round the synagogue seven times, carrying the palm, willow and myrtle in their right hands and the etrogs in the left.

The eighth day of the festival is a 'day of holy assembly', when prayers are offered for rain and people recall the ancient Temple ceremonies of drawing water (p. 145). The following day is the very joyful *Simchath Torah** (p. 103), the happiest day of the Jewish year.

From a Polish Jewish Prayer Book:

Bless this year for us, O our God, and bless every species of its fruits for our benefit. Bestow a blessing upon the face of the earth, and satisfy us with Thy goodness, O bless our years, and make them good years; for Thine honour and glory.

Harvest (3)

Harvest Festivals

Nowadays we tend to think of harvest festivals as being celebrations to mark the end of harvest, when all the crops have
been safely gathered and stored. Yet many of the celebrations
of the past were held at the beginning of the harvest. The
Jewish people, in the days of long ago, were told to take the
'first fruits' of their produce to the priest as a thank-offering to
God.

In England, it used to be the custom to take to the church, on
1st August, a loaf made from the first grain that was harvested,
to be used in the Eucharist (p. 92). This was the Loaf Mass, or
in the old Saxon language, Hlaf-masse, which gradually
became Lammas.

Lammas Day was important for other reasons too. Some
villages had land known as Lammas land. This was land on
which anyone could put animals to graze, but not before
Lammas Day, by which time any hay growing on this land had
been reaped. In some parts of the country, fairs were also held
at Lammas tide.

But after the Loaf Mass, the work of harvesting continued. It
was especially hard work in the days when harvesting was
done by hand and it was only natural that people would go to
church when the work was completed to say thank you to God
for another harvest.

This was not a harvest festival in the sense that we know
today. The custom of taking into church a fine display of fruits,
vegetables and flowers has developed since just before the
middle of last century. Nowadays, as people in town and
country join lustily in singing 'all is safely gathered in, ere the
winter storms begin', it may not be for food which they personally have gathered but is nevertheless a sincere word of
thanks to God for the harvest and all who helped to provide it.

O God, we say thank you when we see the first fruits of our
labours; we pray for Your strength as we continue in our
work; and we ask You to accept the harvest of our hands and
minds—our special gift to You.

Harvest (4)

Corn Dollies

Harvest Home was always one of the great celebrations for country people in the days before huge machines had been invented for harvesting the grain. A hundred years ago and more, harvesting was a very busy time with everyone giving a hand. Bands of reapers, with their scythes, would move across the harvest fields, cutting the corn, binding it into sheaves and stacking them in the fields to dry. 'Let it stand for three Sundays,' some farmers would say.

Then came the farm wagons, onto which the sheaves were pitch-forked to be carted away. To celebrate, the last wagons were often decorated with ribbons and garlands of flowers. The workers shouted and sang about Harvest Home. That night there was a grand supper in the farmhouse, given by the farmer and his wife for all who had helped bring in the harvest. It was their way of saying thank-you. And what an enjoyable evening it was, with a meal of roast beef and plum pudding, plenty to drink and lots of singing and dancing. (*See also Thanksgiving Day—p. 71.*)

Before this there had probably been an interesting ceremony in the fields. The last of the corn was carefully gathered and twisted, perhaps into the shape of a person or a cross. It was known as the 'Corn Maiden' or 'Corn Dolly'. In other places it went by odd names such as 'The Neck', 'The Old Wife' or 'Granny'. It was an old belief that the last of the corn contained the corn spirit, which had to be kept alive during the winter to be sown with the new corn and ensure another good harvest.

Often the corn dolly was taken into church for the special harvest service before being hung in the barn. Harvest Home may not be celebrated as it once was, but there are many churches in which a Harvest Supper is a time for enjoyment as well as for thanksgiving.

O God our Father, accept our thanks for all Your gifts and for people who have helped us to receive them. Forgive us for when we have taken these for granted.

Harvest (5)

One of the more unusual harvest festival services is held in London one Sunday in October at the church of St. Martin-in-the-Fields, Trafalgar Square. There are the usual fruits, vegetables and home-baked bread. It is the people who attend who look different, for this is the Harvest Festival of Costermongers, who sell from their barrows in the London streets, and all the Pearly Kings and Queens of London will be present. Dressed in their suits, on which thousands of pearl buttons have been sewn, they make a colourful sight. They do not dress like this just for show but to entertain and collect money for charity. So this is more than another offering of food: it is an offering of one's service to others.

Not far away, on the first Sunday in October, in the Church of St. Mary-at-Hill, Billingsgate, fish workers from the famous London market have gathered for many years to give thanks for the 'harvest of the sea'. The church is also decorated with nets and equipment as well as fruit and flowers. Such services are held in many seaside towns too, especially those with a local fishing fleet.

Nowadays there are more people living in industrial towns than there are in country districts. They may hold traditional harvest festivals, using fruit and vegetables bought in the shops, or they may have a special display of tools or pieces of machinery made in local factories. These are just as much a harvest as the fruits of the earth.

In fact, whoever we are, however humble the work we do, however poor we may feel we are, we all have something to offer as a token of our thankfulness.

Thou God of Providence, grant to farmers and keepers of cattle good seasons; to the fleet and fishers fair weather; to tradesmen not to overreach one another; to mechanics to pursue their business lawfully, even down to the meanest workman, even down to the poor; for Christ's sake.

Lancelot Andrewes (1555–1626)

Harvest (6)

Moon Cake Festival

Just as we have our festivals to give thanks for the harvest, so do other people in many parts of the world, some in ways which are similar to ours, others in ways much different, which have their roots way back in history.

When people from Europe first went to America, they discovered that the Indians had many ceremonies in which they prayed to or gave thanks to the Great Spirit. Tribes had their own ways of doing so. The Iroquois, for example, built a Long House, where women performed ceremonies in summer for the growing crops and men did so in winter as thanksgiving for harvest. Delaware Indians held twelve days of ceremonies in October in their Big House, with its massive centre pillar which represented the Creator, Gicelemukaong.

Far away in China, people have celebrated, for many years, a festival similar to our harvest festivals, on the 15th day of their 8th month. It is called Chung Ch'iu and is the festival of the Moon Goddess. It is sometimes called the Moon Cake Festival because special moon cakes are made, some to be eaten and some to be offered to the goddess.

This festival is about six hundred years old. At that time the Chinese people rose up against their Mongol rulers. Being unable to speak openly, they wrote messages on scraps of paper, which were then concealed in the cakes they gave their friends. On this festival, children are allowed to stay up late and go with their parents to a high place, where they light their lanterns and, before eating their cakes, watch the full moon rise.

At the same time, the people of Korea are celebrating their festival of Chusok, on which the day of thanksgiving begins with visits to family graves, where prayers and food are offered. At harvest time there are many good things to remember and there is much for which to be thankful.

As we look back into the past and as we think of today, O God, we are thankful for all who have helped shape our lives and for every blessing received from You. Keep us ever thankful, we pray.

Autumn celebrations (1)

MICHAELMAS

During the late summer, people are very busy on the land, gathering in the harvest, then holding their festivals and celebrations to give thanks for the results of another year's work. But, of course, on the land nothing ever stops. As soon as one harvest has been gathered, the work has to begin again to provide for another year.

It could be said that the date of the new beginnings is 29th September, Michaelmas Day, the Feast Day of St. Michael. In England this has long been one of the 'Quarter Days', on which the rents for a quarter of the year have to be paid. It has been very convenient, too, for most farmers have always had money to do so as a result of gathering in the harvest.

In the past, this used to be the day when contracts officially ended between landlords and tenants or between masters and servants. Some people would be looking for new workers: others would be looking for new jobs. There were no employment bureaux as there are today and so fairs were held in many parts of the country. Known as 'hiring' or 'mop' fairs, they were the places where many new working agreements were made.

Michaelmas fairs are still held in some towns, but today they are just for amusement and 'all the fun of the fair' (p. 131).

But there was more to Michaelmas than business. It used to be a time of feasting and family festivity, when it was customary in many places to have goose to eat. An old saying was

> *Whoso eats goose on Michaelmas Day*
> *Shall never lack money his debts to pay.*

Today, some families still have their meal of goose but most of the Michaelmas customs belong to the past.

Thank you, God, for good harvests, fine food, work to do and money to spend. Hear our prayers for those who lack any of these.

Autumn celebrations (2)

All Hallows Eve

Hallowe'en, the eve of all Hallows or All Saints, is a day that is celebrated in many ways with strange and interesting customs. It is a real mixture of ancient pagan ideas, folklore and religion. Long, long ago, 31st October was the end of the Celtic year with its ceremonial extinguishing and lighting of fires (p. 76). The following day, 1st November, became All Saints' Day (p. 125), which was a very holy day.

It is hardly surprising that the old day of darkness should be a time of mystery, when ghosts, witches and the 'little folk' had to be avoided and evil spirits needed to be driven away. This was their busy night: they would not dare to be around on All Hallows!

No doubt the bonfires helped to scare some away. So did the stamping and shouting in the fields. And what witch or evil spirit would not be scared away by one of those horrible faces cut in a hollowed-out turnip lit by a candle?

There are plenty of apples and nuts at Hallowe'en, too. The Romans added their own festival in honour of Pomana, goddess of fruit, to the old celebrations. Young ladies used to believe that there were all sorts of ways of using apples or apple pips to discover things about the man they might marry. Children enjoyed, and still do, their games of Snap-apple (on a piece of string) or Duck-apple (in a bowl of water).

Today, Hallowe'en is one of the popular festivals for children throughout Britain and in the United States of America. 'Punkies' are made from turnips or pumpkins; party games give much enjoyment; decorations, with witches, bats and spiders, create a 'spooky' atmosphere; and horrid masks can be enough to scare anyone!

Times change. People are no longer afraid of evil spirits. Hallowe'en is no longer a day of fear but a day of fun.

An old Scottish prayer:
From ghoulies and ghosties and long leggety beasties
And things that go bump in the night,
Good Lord, deliver us.

Autumn celebrations (3)

The Fifth of November

> *Guy, Guy, Guy,*
> *Poke him in the eye,*
> *Stick him on the bonfire*
> *And there let him die!*

There are lots of variations of this rhyme that has been chanted by children for many, many years. In the days leading up to 5th November, children take the guys they have made into the streets and ask passers-by for 'a penny for the guy'. On 5th November, or nowadays on a day near to that date, the guy will end up on the bonfire and there will be fireworks that were bought with the money.

The origin of Guy Fawkes' Night is well known, if not in detail. It was a plot devised by certain conspirators to kill King James I, in 1605, by blowing up the Houses of Parliament at the time when he was there. Barrels of gunpowder were placed in the cellars and Guy Fawkes was the man entrusted with lighting the fuse.

Fortunately for the King and Members of Parliament, one of the conspirators sent a warning to a friend to keep away. The building was searched and Guy Fawkes arrested. He wasn't burned on a bonfire! He was dreadfully tortured until he had given the names of his fellows, who were cruelly hung, drawn and quartered.

People were so pleased that the King and Members of Parliament had been saved that they lit their bonfires, as they have ever since with Guy Fawkes on the top. Most people enjoy a good bonfire and this provided an excuse—if one were needed.

Guy Fawkes' Night has, unfortunately, been marred for many by accidents caused by fires and fireworks. It is now more common to have special displays on or nearer the date, which are safer, if maybe not quite as much fun as doing things oneself.

In all our celebrations, O Lord, help us to enjoy ourselves in such a way that we cause no harm to ourselves and no annoyance to others.

Autumn celebrations (4)

United States and Canada

One of the great family occasions in the United States of America is Thanksgiving Day, held each year on the fourth Thursday in November. It is a time when families gather together for feasting on the traditional dishes of turkey, pumpkin pie, and other delicacies. Coming after harvest, it is a kind of harvest festival but many other blessings are remembered too.

Much of the celebrating is like the old-time Harvest Home in Britain (p. 65), for the first people to celebrate Thanksgiving were the Pilgrim Fathers, who left England and made a new home in America in 1619. Conditions were very bad and many of the settlers died. The Governor, William Bradford, was so relieved to see the harvest gathered that he ordered a three-day feast.

An invitation was sent to the local Indians to share the celebrations. They brought turkeys and venison to add to the ducks, geese and fish provided by the settlers. The great feast was eaten outdoors at huge tables.

Gradually, Thanksgiving Day customs spread throughout New England. It was President Lincoln who proclaimed that the day should be observed throughout the United States. The celebration was fixed for the fourth Thursday in November, in 1941. The custom of a Thanksgiving Day National holiday spread to Canada, too, where it is observed on the second Monday in October.

Abraham Lincoln had declared that it would be 'a day of thanksgiving and praise to our beneficient Father'. So Thanksgiving is, as its name suggests, not just a day of feasting but a time for church services, for prayer and for reminding oneself of all the blessings received at the hand of Almighty God.

> For peaceful homes and healthful days,
> For all the blessings earth displays,
> We owe Thee thankfulness and praise,
> Who givest all.
>
> *Christopher Wordsworth (1807–85)*

Light and fire (1)

God is the light of the heavens and the earth, like a niche in which there is a lamp. (Qur'an 24.35)

From earliest times to the present day, people from all parts of the world have associated God, or their chief god, if they believed in more than one, with the light. In ancient times, the great Creator was usually the sky god, perhaps identified with the sun but certainly with the light as opposed to darkness. Similarly, light was inevitably associated with good and darkness with evil. Such beliefs appear time and time again in religious celebrations and festivals. Sometimes the light is represented by lamps or candles and sometimes by fire.

Fires were sacred to many ancient peoples. They were used when offering sacrifices and were the means by which gifts and prayers were sent up to the gods. The Hindu god of fire, Agni, was held in the highest regard. In the Zoroastrian religion, God (*Ahura Mazda**) is light, represented on earth by fire, *Atar*, which came to be called his son. The sacred fire has a central place in all Parsi temples and is never allowed to go out. There is a perpetual light in Jewish synagogues, too. It is a lamp which burns before the ark containing the Torah and is a symbol of God's presence. (*Leviticus 24; 1–4*).

Sometimes the lighting of lamps or candles is a symbol of the light of God coming into the place (p. 75). As he lights the Sabbath candles in his home, a Jewish father offers this prayer:

> *'You are our Light, O Lord, and our Salvation.*
> *In your name we kindle these Sabbath lights.*
> *May they bring into our household the beauty*
> *of truth and the radiance of love's understanding.*
> *On this Sabbath eve, and at all times, "Let there be light" '*

A prayer from the Gelasian Sacramentary
Shed forth, O Lord, we pray Thee, Thy light into our hearts, that we may perceive the light of Thy commandments, and walking in Thy way may fall into no error; through Jesus Christ our Lord.

Light and fire (2)

Light is not only a symbol of goodness but of purity, and one aspect of many ceremonies connected with festivals and worship is the actual or symbolic cleansing that will make the place fit, as it were, for the light which is indicative of the presence of God.

The purity of the light itself is best seen in the kindling of the sacred fire in a Parsi Fire Temple. In the highest grade of temple (*Atash Behram**), fire is brought from no less than 16 different places, such as a king's palace, a priest's house and a blacksmith's forge. These are all blended, purified and unified with elaborate ceremonies when the fire is installed. This is then kept alight by priests, who tend the fire five times a day, offering prayers as they add sandalwood and incense in the *Boi** ('Sweet Smell') ceremony.

In Japan, there are certain rituals observed in Shinto temples called *Oharae* or *Harai*, which are designed to drive away any sins or impurities. These are carried out at the end of each half year (June and December), at any time of trouble and before all festivals. In India it is customary to cleanse temples and homes before any major festival.

In Britain, it has long been accepted that every last piece of greenery should be removed from homes and churches before 2nd February so that everything would be ready for the lighting of the candles at Candlemas. This festival, also known as the Feast of the Purification of the Blessed Virgin Mary, celebrates the presentation of Jesus at the Temple forty days after his birth (*St. Luke* 2; 22–32).

The candles are lit as a reminder of Jesus, who came to bring light to a dark world.

Lighten our hearts we beseech You, O God with the light of Your presence and purify our lives with the refining fire of Your spirit so that in purity and love our whole being may reflect and radiate the glory of God in this world of darkness.

Light and fire (3)

The great Jewish festival of light is *Chanukkah**, an annual reminder of a great triumph of good over evil over 2000 years ago. The Emperor of Syria had forbidden Jews to observe their holy days, destroyed the sacred scrolls and desecrated the temple. A long struggle, led by Judah the Maccabee, led to the overthrowing of the Syrians.

Immediately, people set about cleansing the Temple. They searched for pure oil to relight the Temple lamp but there was only enough for one night. Yet, by some miracle, it kept burning for eight. So Chanukkah is kept as an eight-day festival.

In the home, as well as in the synagogue, there is an eight-branched *menorah** (candlestick). In fact it has a ninth holder for the *shammash* (servant) candle, which is used to light the others. On the first evening of Chanukkah, one candle is lit, on the second, two, and so on until there are eight on the final evening. As each candle is lit, prayers are recited. In the daily service there are special prayers and the reading of Psalms 113 to 118.

Chanukkah is a happy festival with presents being given and games played. One popular pastime is to play with a dreidel—a spinning top with four sides, each marked with a Hebrew letter—N, G, H and Sh. These are the initial letters of *Nes Gadol Hayah Sham* ('A great miracle happened there'). They are also the initials of words which tell whether the player has won or lost any money that has been staked! There is good food, too, perhaps *latkes* (potato pancakes, traditionally made with cheese).

But central throughout the festival is the Chanukkah menorah, placed in the window for all to see—a symbol of light, truth and the triumph of goodness.

Blessed are You, O Lord our God, King of the Universe. You have given victory to Your people in time of distress and You continually guide by the light of Your presence. We praise and thank you for ever.

Light and fire (4)

Light for the world

Most people can find comfort from the light given by even the smallest candle or night-light, for even a small light immediately dispels the darkness. Candles have been used for a long time by people of many faiths as a part of their worship and at their festivals, often symbolically.

It is not uncommon in a Roman Catholic Church to find rows of lighted candles placed before an image of the Blessed Virgin Mary or of a saint, symbolic of a prayer that is being offered to God through that particular person (p. 128). They may also be placed before a crib at Christmastide as a small symbol of adoration.

It is not surprising that candles feature largely in the celebrations of the Christian Church around Christmas, for Jesus said that He had come as 'Light of the World'. Many churches have an Advent wreath with four candles lit on the four Sundays before Christmas. Some churches have a large Christmas candle (like the Easter Paschal Candle p. 109), lit on Christmas Eve at midnight. An old Irish custom is to light a candle to guide the Christ Child on Christmas Eve.

After Christmas, on 2nd February, comes Candlemas, the Festival of Candles. In some churches, candles are blessed and distributed, the light representing Christ as a light to the gentiles (*St. Luke 2;22*).

Jewish people have the Menorah*, the seven-branched candlestick, as their symbol and the eight-branched candlestick for the festival of Chanukkah* (p. 74). Candles are lit each Sabbath (p. 90).

Therevada* Buddhists have a festival called Magha Puja, on the day of the February full moon, recalling how the Buddha ordained 1,250 disciples who were enlightened. In important temples in the east, 1,250 candles are lit on this day.

The light of one small candle may give little light: a lighthouse with a light of several million candlepower shines for miles. Most faiths require each member to lighten the world: collectively they can spread a lot of light.

If, at times, O God, our light should seem small, remind us that each light is but one of many that can bring brightness and cheer into a world of darkness.

Light and fire (5)

Most people enjoy a good bonfire, especially when the weather is cold and the nights are dark. Today we are used to having one on 5th November as part of the fun of Guy Fawkes' Night. But in many of the bonfire nights, held in various parts of the country, we have roots which go back to days long before the Christian era, when the fire was used as part of seasonal celebrations to help or welcome the sun.

The ancient Celts had a festival called *Samhain* ('Summer end'), which fell at the end of October. The sun was then becoming weaker and weaker and it was believed that huge bonfires would help the sun to keep its strength.

At this time, all old fires were extinguished and new ones kindled, not from the dying embers but with a completely new start, using flint sparks and tinder. From this 'need-fire' came not only the huge Beltane bonfires but new fire for the home as well.

Part of the celebration included singing and dancing round the fire as an offering to the gods. This is a common practice elsewhere, too. The Navaho Indians of North America, for example, have their ritual fire dance in which the men with white painted bodies, dance around and very close to the fire, sometimes leaping as high as the flames themselves.

Sometimes fire festivals have been associated with fertility and the next year's harvest. An old superstition said that one should jump over the dying embers and next year's crop would grow as high as one jumped.

In Syria, children listen to the Christmas story on Christmas Eve as they sit around the bonfire. Then they jump over the fire and make a wish. Bonfires form part of Christmas and Easter celebrations in many lands, a link with the ancient spring festivals but now enjoyed by people celebrating the happiest of Christian days.

Almighty God, extinguish in us all that is evil and ignite within us that faith which brings new life and hope in this world of darkness.

YULETIDE

The time for many of the old celebrations was mid-winter, the time of the winter solstice, when the sun is at its weakest and the nights at their longest. Primitive people believed that it was necessary to do what they could to encourage nature to wake up and start all over again. Evergreens were hung on buildings so that seeds in the frozen ground could know that there was still life to be found. Bonfires were lit to give that extra heat that the sun seemed to have lost.

In the countries of Northern Europe there was a mid-winter festival called *Yule*. Where the name originated we do not know. To the Norsemen it was Jol, but it was kept in some of the Teutonic countries too. The central part of this three-day festival was the burning of the Yule log. A huge log was brought in from the forest and kept alight for the three days, during which people remembered their dead and believed that they were sharing in the festival.

It was a time of feasting, drinking, singing and recalling the ancient legends, many no doubt about Odin and Thor, the gods to whom Yule was dedicated and to whom sacrifices were made. Perhaps on the wild nights they would look to the sky, where Odin might be travelling on his eight-legged horse Sleipnir. Sprigs of mistletoe, a sacred plant, were ceremonially cut.

Yule customs later became a part of Christmas celebrations. The greenery and mistletoe are still there but it isn't Odin who travels in the sky at Christmas! Until recently the Yule log was burned in many homes, a symbol of good luck if it could be kept burning for twelve days. A piece was normally kept, too, to kindle the fire the following year.

The beliefs of people today are very different from those of old. We no longer have those winter concerns but we do enjoy the customs we have inherited from the past.

Warm our hearts, O God, with the fire of Your Holy Spirit and enable us to grow nearer to You in love.

Christmastide (1)

Christmas, for many people, is a time for family gatherings, for feasting and drinking, fun and games. It is one aspect of Christmas which has nothing to do with the Christian festival which gave it its name (p. 81). These are customs which were a part of the old Roman mid-winter festival of *Saturnalia*. When the early Christians wanted to celebrate the birth of Christ, they found that this pagan festival, already a holiday, was a good opportunity for them to do so.

Saturnalia was a seven-day festival in honour of Saturn, God of Corn and Harvest. It was a time of excess. Masters feasted with slaves, who were free to do and say what they liked. There was merrymaking and drinking. Houses were decorated. Presents were given and greetings sent. In fact, in Saturnalia we can see the beginning of so many of our present Christmas customs.

If our Christmas dinners seem large today, they are nothing in comparison with those of a few hundred years ago when the meal might last for eight or nine hours. Even the poorer families managed to have a large bird, though not a turkey, which was not then known in England.

Served with the meat was a dish called plum porridge, eaten with a spoon and consisting of meat, broth, raisins, currants, prunes, breadcrumbs and spices. As the years passed, it was made thicker and thicker until it became the Christmas pudding that we know.

Mince pies were originally of minced meat in a cradle-shaped case. It used to be customary to eat a mince pie on each of the twelve days of Christmas to ensure a happy year. Today, few people would be without mince pies, sausage rolls, an iced Christmas cake, fruit, nuts, sweets and lots of other appetising delicacies which help give us our traditional Christmas.

As we enjoy our feasting, we remember the old and lonely—and those people who will go without their own home festivities to provide meals and entertainment for such folk.

O God, in all our festivities, feasting and family fun, keep us mindful of those who are without such things.

Christmas (2)

Santa Claus

Christmas is often described as 'the children's festival' for it has so much appeal to the young—the story of the Baby, the magic of fairy lights, decorations and parties, and, of course, the anticipation of a visit from Father Christmas, or Santa Claus to fill their stockings.

The original Santa Claus was St. Nicholas, a saintly bishop of Asia Minor, whose generosity is recalled in many ways. In Holland he ceremonially arrives in Amsterdam on the eve of 6th December, his feast day, to be welcomed by the Queen. With his servant, Black Peter, he parades through the city. Children hope St. Nicholas, or Sinter Klaas will leave a present in their shoes.

Dutch settlers took the custom of Sinter Klaas with them to America, where he became known as Santa Claus and his visits came to be made on Christmas Eve instead—as they are in most lands today.

A week after St. Nicholas's Day is St. Lucia's Day, 13th December. It is celebrated in Sweden where, very early in the morning, the eldest daughter in the family dresses in a long robe and puts on her head a wreath of greenery in which there are seven lighted candles. Escorted by her brothers, the 'Star Boys', she serves the family, in bed, with Lucia buns, ginger snaps (*pepparkakor*) and coffee. Towns also have their 'Lucias', who visit hospitals and other institutions.

St. Lucia's Day, also known as Little Yule, is a reminder of the pre-Christian festivals of light at the time of the winter solstice (p. 77). From those ancient times, too, came the mimed plays believed to give new life to nature. These plays, performed by groups of actors called Mummers were once very popular at Christmas, as players went from house to house. Today there are few Mummers but there are other forms of entertainment instead, the seasonal pantomime being especially popular with children.

> Be near me, Lord Jesus; I ask Thee to stay
> Close by me for ever, and love me I pray.
> Bless all the dear children in Thy tender care,
> And fit us for heaven, to live with Thee there.

Anon

Christmas (3)

Christmas would not seem complete without the singing of carols, some of them quite old, which tell to music some aspects of the Christmas Story.

Originally a carol was a dance, with singing, enjoyed on festive occasions, but having no religious associations. There are still carols for many occasions but the familiar Christmas carols are mostly songs or hymns of thankfulness and praise to celebrate the birth of Jesus Christ.

One of the best known carol services is the Festival of the Nine Lessons and Carols, held each year on Christmas Eve in the chapel of King's College, Cambridge. The festival was first held in 1918 and first broadcast in 1930. It begins with the first verse of *Once in Royal David's City*, sung as a solo by a chorister, who is not told until shortly before the service is to begin. Each of the nine lessons is read by a different reader. A similar service, also of Nine Lessons and Carols, is held in York Minster at 4 pm on Christmas Eve. Both are now so popular that one has to arrive early to be sure of a seat.

In other churches, the Festival of Nine Lessons and Carols is also used, or perhaps a variation of it. Many take the form of 'Carols by Candlelight', with the church lit only by dozens of candles. Festivals of Carols are also held in public halls and buildings in many towns and cities.

The custom of singing carols around a Christmas tree in the open air is also popular now, especially around large trees such as the one set up in Trafalgar Square, London.

But, for years, there have also been waits, wassailers or carol singers, who have gone from house to house, singing and collecting money either for themselves or for charity whilst relating in song the love of God revealed to man at that first Christmas.

> Still the night, holy the night!
> Son of God, O how bright
> Love is smiling from Thy face!
> Strikes for us now the hour of grace,
> Saviour, since Thou art born!

Joseph Mohr (1792–1848)

Christmas (4)

There may be many trimmings and good things to be enjoyed at Christmas but, as the name of the festival indicates, the one important aspect is that it is the celebration of the birth of Jesus Christ. The name Christmas first appeared in the 11th Century CE in Early English as *Cristes Maesse*, the feast or festival of Christ.

It is almost certain that Jesus Christ was born earlier in the year but his birth was celebrated alongside pagan midwinter festivals which were already holidays. The date was eventually fixed as 25th December, though there are some churches, such as the Russian Orthodox, in which Christmas is celebrated early in January.

For centuries it has been customary to hold a special midnight Mass so that, as Christmas Day dawns, the failthful are meekly bowing in adoration and uniting in the praise of God, remembering how God sent the Messiah, the Promised One, to be the Saviour of the World. Hymns of praise are sung, prayers offered and the familiar story read from St. Luke (*chapter 2, verses 1–20*).

In many churches, during the Christmas season, there will be a simple crib in a corner of the church or chapel with the baby in a manger, watched over by Mary and Joseph, probably accompanied by shepherds and animals. It is a silent reminder that, when the Son of God came into the world, there was no room in the inn. Indeed, from the beginning, He knew hardship and discomfort.

Christmas is the time when Christians open their hearts to make room for Him and to help others in His name.

> O holy Child of Bethlehem,
> Descend to us, we pray;
> Cast out our sin, and enter in;
> Be born in us today.
> We hear the Christmas angels
> The great glad tidings tell;
> O come to us, abide with us,
> Our Lord Immanuel.

Phillips Brooks (1835–93)

Christmas (5)

CHRISTINGLES

One of the enjoyable festivals of Christmas is the Christingle Service, which is held in cathedrals, churches and schools, often to raise money to help children in need through the Church of England Children's Society.

It is a festival which has come to us from Moravia, a part of the present day Czechoslovakia. There, over two hundred years ago, Christingle Services were first held, no doubt the visual aids of their day, for the Christingle was symbolic of the work of Jesus Christ.

A Christingle is an orange that has been decorated with many different symbols. The round orange itself is a symbol of the world. In the top a hole is cut and a candle pushed into it, just as Jesus brought light into the world. Goose feathers or sticks are stuck into the orange so that they point in all directions, for the Light of the World goes in all directions. Attached to the sticks are jellies, sweets, fruits or nuts, a reminder of the fruits of the earth or the good things that are ours through knowing Jesus. A red ribbon tied round the orange represented the blood of Jesus as he died.

In the Moravian Church, the Christingle had to be earned. Children spent time before Christmas in raising money to help buy food for poor families. When they had done so, they received their Christingles, which they took to church for the Christingle Service, where they sang their favourite carols and listened to the old familiar stories.

Afterwards they took their Christingles home and, perhaps, as they ate the oranges, remembered how they had done something to help others because of the love of God in their hearts. That is the real message of Christmas.

> Ah, dearest Jesus, holy Child,
> Make Thee a bed, soft, undefiled
> Within my heart, that it may be
> A quiet chamber kept for Thee.

> *Martin Luther (1483–1546)*

EPIPHANY

January 6th, Twelfth Night, is the day when, traditionally, all Christmas decorations are taken down, for this is the end of the Christmas season. It is also the day in the Christian calendar which is called *Epiphany* ('appearance' or 'manifestation'), when the Church remembers how Jesus was presented for the first time to people who were not Jews.

The people concerned were the three travellers from the East, sometimes referred to as the Three Kings or Wise Men, the 'Magi' who brought their gifts of gold, frankincense and myrrh to present to the young child, who would then have been about two years of age.

The gifts were symbolic. Gold was a gift that would be presented to a king; frankincense was a priestly offering and myrrh a symbol of suffering. They serve as a reminder that Jesus spoke of His kingdom, the Kingdom of God, that He would be like a High Priest who would help people come to God and that He died so that people might be saved from their sin and selfishness.

Today the Wise Men are often shown in Christmas pictures and there may be figures of them in the crib scenes that are put in the churches at Christmas, but the Feast of the Epiphany is not celebrated as much as it once was.

There is, however, an interesting service held in the Chapel Royal, St. James's Palace, attended by the Queen or her representatives, accompanied by the Yeomen of the Guard. For some 700 years it has been customary for the sovereign, at the Royal Epiphany Service, to present three purses, symbolising the gifts of the Wise Men. These are given, at the point where the offertory is taken, by two Gentlemen Ushers of the Royal Household. The gold is later changed into cash and given to pensioners; the frankincense is used in church worship; and the myrrh goes to a hospital.

A prayer for Epiphany (Methodist Service Book)
Eternal God, who by the shining of a star led the Wise Men to the worship of your Son: guide by your light the nations of the earth, that the whole world may behold your glory; through Jesus Christ our Lord.

ADVENT

In the Western world, we are used to thinking of January 1st as New Year's Day. It may seem strange to think that people in some other lands begin their year on a different date. Each religion, too, has its calendar and its own 'new year'.

The Christian Church's year begins at the end of November. This is not as strange as it may seem, for the Christian Calendar follows events in the life of Jesus Christ, beginning, naturally enough, with the festival on which we celebrate His birth. But main festivals are often preceded by a period of preparation and so the Church begins its year four weeks before Christmas, on the nearest Sunday to St. Andrew's Day, 30th November.

This period is known as *Advent* ('coming' or 'arrival'). It is a time when people look forward to the coming of Jesus. Some people also remember how Jesus said that He would come again (*Matthew 24; 29–31: John 14; 28*), and so they look forward to His second coming, also called the *Parousia* (the Greek for 'presence' or 'arrival'). This, of course, is not looking forward to a particular date. Jesus said no one would know when (*Matthew 24; 36–44*).

In many churches, Advent is marked by having an Advent wreath, in which four candles are set. On the first Sunday in Advent one candle is lit, on the second two. On the fourth, the Sunday before Christmas, there will be four to herald the 'Light of the World'.

Some people like to have an Advent calendar. This may be in the form of a card with little windows to be opened, one each day, and each of them giving some guide as to things to think about and so prepare for the wonders of the Christmas story. For, to Christians, Christmas is more than a story of a Baby in a stable: it tells of One who came to help people to grow nearer to God.

> Come, Thou long-expected Jesus,
> Born to set Thy people free,
> From our fears and sins release us,
> Let us find our rest in Thee.
>
> *Charles Wesley (1707–88)*

New Year (Religion) (2)

The Jewish year really begins in springtime on the 1st of the month called Nisan but the great New Year celebration of *Rosh Hashanah** falls early in the autumn on the 1st and 2nd of the seventh month, Tishri (see p. 201). The first of these days is known as 'The day of the sounding of the Ram's Horn', for the Torah commands:

'In the seventh month, on the first day of the month, shall be a solemn rest unto you, a memorial gathered with the blast of horns, a holy gathering . . .'

So, Rosh Hashanah is welcomed with the blowing of the *shofar** (ram's horn), calling to mind Abraham's sacrifice of a ram instead of his son. It is a call to people to remember God and their fellow men, to recall God's act in creating the world, and to think of Him as both Creator and Judge.

The thoughts of God as Judge are uppermost during the first ten days of Tishri. It is a period for self-examination, before God, culminating with *Yom Kippur*, the Day of Atonement (p. 117).

But, although Rosh Hashanah is a time for seriousness and solemnity, it is also a time for happiness and festivity. On New Year's Eve it is customary to eat apples and challot* (twisted loaves) dipped in honey to symbolise hope for a pleasant new year. Cards are sent with the greeting 'L'Shanah Tovah Tikatevu' ('May you be inscribed for a good year'). And, of course, there are sumptuous meals.

Rosh Hashanah offers a time for rejoicing, reflection, and resolution to waste no part of the year ahead.

A Jewish festival prayer:

O Lord our God, grant us the blessing of Your festivals in life and peace, in gladness and joy . . . Make us holy with Your commandments and help us to live according to Your Torah . . . Make our hearts pure that we may worship You sincerely . . We bless You, O Lord.

New Year (Religion) (3)

Islamic New Year

Most people begin their New Year either on a set date or at a particular season. Muslims do not. Their calendar is based strictly on twelve lunar months beginning with the new moon. This means that New Year comes about 11 or 12 days earlier each year (p. 196).

Muslims count their years from the day that Muhammad and his Companions left Mecca to travel to Medina, then called, Yathrib. It was in Mecca that Muhammad first told how he had been given the word which was later to become known as the Qur'an* (p. 102). Some people followed Muhammad but others were afraid that they would lose business if too many accepted the new teachings. So they plotted to kill him.

With the help of friends he was able to escape from Mecca and hasten to Medina, where he and his Companions formed themselves into a religious community which was to spread to many lands under the name of Islam.

The flight from Mecca occurred in the year 622 CE and it is from this date that the Islamic calendar is reckoned. The Arabic word for 'flight' is *Hijrah** and so the Day of Hijrah indicates the beginning of the Islamic year. The letters AH after the number of the year stand for After Hijrah.

Although the flight of Muhammad took place in the month of Rabi 1, the second Caliph, 'Umar, consulted with Muhammad's Companions and it was agreed that 1st Muharram* in the year of Hijrah (15th July, 622 CE) should be the first day of the Islamic calendar. So 1st Muharram is now celebrated as Hijrah Day.

Hijrah Day is one on which Muslims remind themselves of the stories of Muhammad and his Companions and send greetings to their friends.

A Muslim prayer from Al-Hizbul-A'zam

O Lord, I beg of You all the good of this day and all the days hereafter and I seek Your protection from all the evil of this day and the days to come.

DIWALI (DIPAVALI)   *New year festival of light*

Throughout India, and in all parts of the world where people from India have gone to live, one of the highlights of the year is the festival of *Diwali**. For Hindus it is a new year festival and a time of new beginnings.

Diwali is a festival of lights, when people recall the story of how Rama* returned after freeing his wife Sita* from the demon king Ravana* (p. 106). It was a triumph of good over evil, of light over darkness. And so Diwali is a time when lamps and other lights are ceremonially lit. Cities are illuminated with coloured lights—just as seaside towns in Britain may be in summer. House fronts are also illuminated and there are fireworks in the streets.

Inside the home, special pots are made from clay to form the lamps; in Western lands fairy lights and candles are used instead. Houses are cleaned out and special lamps lit to welcome Lakshmi, the giver of prosperity, into every home. Thanks are given for prosperity in the past and prayers offered for the future. In Bengal the people worship Kali* instead of Lakshmi and the festival is called Kali Puja* (worship of Kali).

This festival is of special significance to the Sikhs because it was on this day that the 6th Guru, Hargobind, was released from prison by the Mogul Emperor and welcomed by the Sikhs, who came to meet him carrying candles. The Golden Temple at Amritsar is lavishly illuminated.

Diwali celebrations cover a five-day period, of which the third day is Diwali proper. it is a time for new beginnings. Shopkeepers open new account books; craftsmen dedicate their tools; and members of families remember their particular responsibilities to each other.

Most people love dressing up in their new clothes. They also enjoy the feasting, the exchanging of presents, the music and dancing, all of which help to make Diwali a colourful festive occasion.

A Hindu prayer:
O Lord, lead me from darkness to light, from the unreal to the real, from death to immortality.

BAISAKHI   *Sikh New Year*

The most important Sikh festival in the year is *Baisakhi**, on or about 13th April. It is the beginning of the Bikramì Year in the ancient Indian lunar calendar. It marks the beginning of harvest and the long dry summer.

For the Sikhs it is of special significance, for it was on this day, in 1699, that the last Guru, Gobind* Singh, at a great gathering, called for a volunteer to give his life for the faith. One volunteered and was taken into a tent. The Guru appeared with a bloodstained sword and called for others. The five who volunteered were later produced alive for it was the blood of an animal, and became known as the *panj pyare** ('five brothers'), the first of the *Khalsa** ('Pure ones'), the Sikh brotherhood.

There are great festivities in Amritsar, in and around the Darbar Sahib (The Golden Temple). During the preceding 48 hours there is the Akhand path* (continuous reading of Guru Granth* Sahib) which, on the day, is richly decorated and carried in procession under a *palki** (canopied platform) on a float, whilst bands play and people march. Five men, wearing yellow turbans and robes, represent the panj pyare. Thousands may be fed at the temple *langar* (meal).

Wherever there is a Sikh community, there will be a big celebration in the temple or gurdwara. New members will be admitted to the Sikh Community by the *Amrit** ceremony (p. 180).

Sikh holidays are a blend of worship and festivity. In many places there are fairs with horse-riding, wrestling and mock sword fights. At Baisakhi, presents are given and turbans exchanged to indicate true brotherhood. It is also a time for wearing new clothes and for family gatherings.

A Sikh prayer from the Anand:
O True God, what is there, which is not present in Your House?
Everything exists in Your House; One, to whom You give, shall receive the same.
He will constantly go on singing Your praises and glories, and will fix Your Name (*Nam*) in his heart.

JAMSHEDI NAOROZE AND NAW RUZ

There are two religions which share the same New Year's Day, 21st March, the date of the spring equinox. They are the fairly modern Bahá'í* Faith and the ancient Zoroastrian religion, both of which originated in Persia, now Iran, where the Fasli calendar begins on that day (p. 41).

For the Bahá'ís, Naw Ruz* follows a Bahá'í (19 day) month of fasting (pp. 115, 197). It is a holy day on which no work is done. Zoroastrians (Parsis) celebrate their new year according to the sect to which they belong. Shahenshais* and Kadmis have a New Year's Day in summer (p. 197) but it is not so much of a celebration as Jamshedi Naoroze*, 21st March, which is shared by them all. It takes its name from Jamshed, the ancient Persian king who first celebrated it as a festival.

Parsis begin their New Year by bathing, having a bite to eat and then going to their fire temples to worship. The men will be dressed in white, the women may have coloured clothes, but all will have at least something new for New Year. The year thus begins with *Jashans** (praise), included in which is a prayer for the New Year, which is the same as one used at the birth of a child.

This is the time to greet family and friends with the traditional greeting 'Naoroze Mubarak'* or 'Jamshedi Naoroze Mubarak'—'Happy New Year'. In the home, on this day, the same foods are always eaten. Breakfast is a meal of fried vermicelli or sweetened semolina with nuts (*ravo*). Lunch is always fish (fried), with a kind of vegetable stew and rice with curry, followed by sweets, usually bought in the shops.

Presents are exchanged. These are, according to Parsi custom, nearly always gifts of cash. It is customary, too, for younger people to spend part of the day in visiting the older members of their families to pay their respects and wish good fortune for the coming year.

Some words from the Zoroastrian Kem na Mazda prayer:

Help me, dear God, to overcome hate and envy and fill me with joy in all creation . . . I bow down before You with absolute faith in Your Goodness and Truth. May I always do so and be happy.

Celebration and worship (1)

*Shabbat**, or the Sabbath, is the oldest of the Jewish holidays and sometimes called the 'Queen of Holidays'. It is also the most frequent for, as decreed in the Torah, each seventh day is the day for rest.

Shabbat begins on Friday evening but preparations will have been made earlier in the day, for no work is done on the Sabbath. At the beginning of the Sabbath there is a joyful service in the synagogue with psalms and hymns, one of the most popular beginning, 'Come, my friend, let us welcome Sabbath, the Bride'. There are readings, prayers and the *Kiddush**—a blessing spoken over a goblet of wine.

Afterwards there is the family meal, laid in advance with two candlesticks, a kiddush cup and two *challot** (twisted loaves), which are reminders of manna in the wilderness and are covered with a white cloth.

Father blesses the children at the table and praises his wife in some words from the Bible (*Proberbs 31, 10–29*). She then lights the two candles—reminders of God's power and man's responsibilities. Father says a prayer over the kiddush wine and blesses the bread before the meal, which will be a real feast accompanied by the singing of two *z'mirot** which are special songs in honour of the day of rest. Grace, *Birkhat Ha-Mazon**, concludes the meal.

On Saturday there are three services in the synagogue—Shaharit* (morning), Minhah (late afternoon) and Maariv* (evening). At the end of the Sabbath is *Havdalah**, a ceremony in the synagogue and home, which includes a blessing spoken over wine, spices and the light of the Havdalah candle. The holy Sabbath is thus separated from the working week.

The prayer for the end of the Sabbath.

Blessed art Thou, O Lord our God, King of the Universe, who made a distinction between light and darkness, between the holy and the ordinary, between the Sabbath and the weekday.

Celebration and worship (2)

Worship in God's house

Jewish people observe the Sabbath on the seventh day of the week but in most Christian countries it has been the custom for many years to have the day of rest on the first day of the week. This is sometimes referred to as the Sabbath but more correctly as the Lord's Day, when Christian people recall how Jesus Christ rose from the dead on the first day of the week.

Today, Sunday is observed in many ways. For some it is a day for sport or recreation; for some it is a day for pottering around the home or garden; and for others it is the day on which they like to worship God. For Christian people it is a holy day when they attend churches, chapels or other places of worship to praise God, to offer prayers, to hear readings from the Bible, to listen to sermons, to teach children in Sunday Schools and to take part in very moving celebrations which help people to feel they are near to God.

There is no *one* form of Christian worship. Some, such as Roman Catholics and High Church of England like fine buildings, colourful vestments, ritual and liturgical services with set prayers and wording. Quakers, on the other hand, have none of these things and may spend most of their worship in silence. Some like solemn hymns and a reverent atmosphere: others enjoy hymns with a strong beat and shouts of 'Hallelujah!'

There are many Christian denominations (pp. 22–3), all of which have their own traditions and forms of worship and see these as a means of offering their best to God. There are special festivals in the Christian year but there is a sense in which every Sunday is a festival of praise and worship—a happy day because it is the Lord's Day.

Thank you, O Lord our God, for giving us a day that is different, when we can meet in Your house, sing Your praises, offer our prayers and hear Your word. May it be for us a festive day as we remember Your great love for us and rejoice in Your presence.

THE EUCHARIST   *Holy Communion*

The celebration that is of the greatest importance to nearly all Christians is the *Eucharist*, which takes its name from the Greek word for 'Thanksgiving'. It is called by other names too—the Lord's Supper, Holy Communion, Mass, the Divine Liturgy, the Blessed Sacrament or sometimes simply as The Sacrament.

It is observed by most Christian denominations in response to the instructions which Jesus gave to his disciples at the Last Supper (p. 94) when he said, 'Do this in remembrance of me.' The words of the institution, which form a part of the service in many churches are found in the Bible (*I Corinthians 11, 23–26).*

The breaking of bread and the pouring of wine are recognised by all Christians as symbols of the death of Jesus Christ on the cross. Those taking part in the Eucharist are expected to affirm their beliefs in the words of the Creed, to confess their sins and to come to God in a right attitude of humility. They are then invited to partake of the Holy Communion.

Each communicant receives a wafer, or a small piece of bread, with the reminder that it is, or represents, the body of Christ broken for mankind. This is followed by a sip of wine from a challice (cup), or a small individual glass, as the symbol of Christ's blood, indicating the forgiveness of God and cleansing for all believers.

The interpretation of what happens differs from one church to another. Roman Catholics believe that, after consecration, the bread and wine actually become the flesh and blood of Christ. Other Christians accept them just as symbols and reminders of all Jesus said and taught.

Whichever the belief, all who share in this sacrament agree that Christ is present in one way or another and therefore it is a moving and inspiring celebration.

God our Father, we remember with joy all that Jesus taught and did, how He died for us all and rose to be with You. Help us so to live that we may be His true disciples and fit to be called children of God.

Celebration and worship (4)

Corpus Christi

In the Roman Catholic Church, the Eucharist is usually referred to as the Mass. The name comes from the Latin words of dismissal at the end of the service: *Ite, missa est* (Go, the Mass is ended'). At one time, the whole service was in Latin, as it is in some places today, but, since the 2nd Vatican Council (1962–5), it is now usually in the language of those taking part in the service.

The Order of Mass is in two parts. Firstly there is the Liturgy of the Word, which includes the Creed, prayers, scripture readings and sometimes a sermon. Then follows the Liturgy of the Eucharist, with the offertory, eucharistic prayers and communion.

Mass is a time when people acknowledge the presence and sacrifice of Jesus Christ, then share in the meal, which is symbolic of the unity of Christians, their dependence upon God and their need of spiritual nourishment as they attempt to bring the gospel message to the world.

Roman Catholics are expected to attend Mass and refrain from all unnecessary work on certain days which are known as Holy Days of Obligation. Sunday is one of these. The others may vary from time to time and place to place. In 1918 ten were designated: Christmas, Circumcision (p. 99), Epiphany, Ascension, Corpus Christi, Assumption (p. 99), SS Peter and Paul, All Saints (p. 125), Immaculate Conception (p. 99) and St. Joseph. In Ireland, St. Patrick is kept instead of St. Joseph. The Eastern Church has more such days than the Western.

One of the greatest celebrations of the Mass is on *Corpus Christi* ('Body of Christ'), a festival in honour of the Real Presence of Christ in the Eucharist. It is observed on the Thursday after Trinity Sunday (or the following Sunday, e.g. in U.S.A.) with processions in which the Corpus Christi, the consecrated bread, is carried.

Today, O God our Father, we recall the death of our Lord Jesus Christ, his glorious resurrection, his ascension into heaven and his living presence ever with us. We rejoice and give you heartfelt thanks.

Celebration and worship (5)

Christians celebrate the week before Easter as Holy Week, because it commemorates the last week in the life of Jesus. It begins on a note of triumph with the story of Jesus entering Jerusalem on a donkey (*St. Matthew 21; 1–9*) and the people waving palm branches. Because of this, the first day is called Palm Sunday.

On this day, churches are decorated with palm or with sallow willow, with its large fluffy catkins, which is more readily available. It is customary in some churches to give sprigs of willow or palm crosses to those who worship on that day.

Later in the week comes the special remembrance of the Last Supper which Jesus shared with his disciples and of the events which followed, when Jesus was arrested in the Garden of Gethsemane and taken for trial before the chief priests.

At that meal, Jesus had washed the feet of the disciples and told them that they, too, should undertake the humblest duties toward others. He said, 'I give you a new commandment: love one another.' The Latin word for 'command' is *mandatum* and so the day has come to be known as Maundy Thursday.

An interesting custom that takes place on this day is the distribution of the Royal Maundy by the sovereign of Britain. Special coins are minted for this purpose and given to old people. Long ago, King Edward III, following the example given by Jesus, annually washed and kissed the feet of the poor. Later sovereigns preferred to give the money instead!

But, for Christian people, Maundy Thursday is a time for thought, for Holy Communion (p. 92) and personal preparation for Good Friday (p. 95) and Easter (p. 109).

> Help us, O God;
> To love one another, as You have loved us,
> To serve one another after the example of Christ,
> And in every way to try to please You
> For we know this is Your will.

Celebration and worship (6)

Lots of people like to start Good Friday with a breakfast of hot cross buns—delicious spicy buns, marked with a cross and served hot with butter. Nowadays people eat them before Good Friday too but, not long ago, they were kept as a special symbol of Good Friday.

Like so many customs, hot cross buns originated long before Christianity. The bun, in pagan times, represented the moon and the cross divided it into its four 'quarters'. For Christians, the cross serves as a reminder of the crucifixion of Jesus on this day (*St. John, chapters 18 and 19*). It is not a happy story and one might ask what is 'good' about Good Friday. In one sense it was a black day, yet Christians believe that, because Jesus died, they can be put right with God—and that *is* good news.

It remains, however, the most solemn day in the Christian calendar, as people recall the events of that day. For some it is a day of fasting and abstinence. Many like to spend at least part of the day in church, in some cases for meditation and vigil between the hours of noon and 3 pm (*cf St. Mark 15 v.33–4*).

In many places, there are united services and processions of witness in which a cross may be carried to the church. In some lands, especially the Mediterranean lands, such as Spain and Malta, there are very colourful processions with tableaux of the Good Friday story.

Passion plays, based on the Easter story, may also be performed on Good Friday. The most famous passion play, at Oberammergau, takes place later in the year. Some of the pace-egg customs, celebrated in parts of Britain, are all that remain of olden day passion plays performed by mummers. In some countries, fires are lit late on Holy Saturday as part of an Easter eve vigil.

O Christ, give us patience and faith and hope as we kneel at the foot of Thy cross, and hold fast to it. Teach us by Thy cross that however ill the world may go, the Father so loved us that he spared not Thee.

Charles Kingsley (1819–75)

ASCENSION DAY

(He) . . . was crucified, dead and buried, He descended into hell;
The third day He rose again from the dead,
He ascended into heaven,
And sitteth on the right hand of God the Father Almighty;
From thence He shall come to judge the quick and the dead.

These words from the Apostles' Creed serve as a reminder of the important beliefs of the Christian Church about Jesus Christ: his death on the cross which is celebrated on Good Friday (p. 95), his resurrection on Easter Sunday (p. 109), and his ascension to heaven.

This last aspect is celebrated on Ascension Day, a festival which falls on the Thursday which is forty days after Easter. At one time it was called Holy Thursday. It is one of the Holy Days of Obligation of the Roman Catholic and other churches.

The reason for the forty-day period is found in the Bible, where it is recorded that Jesus Christ, after His resurrection, appeared to His disciples at different times and in various ways over a period of forty days. Then, on the fortieth day, when the disciples were together on the Mount of Olives, at Jerusalem, they saw Jesus for the last time. He told them they were to carry on the work that He had started and they saw Him no more. *(Acts 1; 1–11)*.

People have various ways of interpreting the story but the message behind them is simply that Christians believe in one who still lives and whose spirit guides those who believe.

There are many local customs associated with Ascension Day, such as Rogation processions (p. 56), beating the bounds (p. 57) and well dressing (p. 143), some no doubt conveniently held on Ascension Day because it was a holiday (holy day).

O Lord Jesus Christ, our living Lord and Redeemer, One God with the Father and the Holy Spirit, hear our prayer and grant us the knowledge that You are ever with us to guide us through our earthly life and keep us in Your loving care.

Celebration and worship (8)

The name Whitsun comes from 'White Sunday', so called because it used to be, and still is in some places, a day on which people dressed in white to be baptized into the Christian Church. Whilst this can be done at any time of the year, Whitsun is a favourite occasion because it was on this day that the Holy Spirit came to the disciples and gave them power to continue the work that Jesus had started. Whitsun has been described as the birthday of the Christian Church.

The day is also known as Pentecost, taken from the Jewish feast of that name, for it was on the Day of Pentecost that the Holy Spirit came. The story of that day and of the beginning of the Church are recorded in Acts, Chapter 2.

Today, at Whitsun, or Pentecost, many of the prayers offered in churches are that the power of God's Holy Spirit will continue to come to His people so that they will be guided in all their actions and enabled to serve God well in whatever way He directs.

Unlike Christmas and Easter, this major festival of the Christian Church did not adopt a pagan festival or customs. It simply celebrates a remarkable event.

There are many local customs which take place at Whitsuntide. In the Middle Ages, it was a popular time of year for the performance of Miracle or Mystery Plays, which portrayed episodes of the Bible story. Such plays are still performed at Chester, York and Coventry, though not necessarily at Whitsun.

Whit Monday is a popular day amongst Morris dancers (pp. 44, 54), for fairs (p. 131) and, in the north of England particularly, for parish walks by children. Many of these events are now held instead on the Spring Bank Holiday.

From the Gelasian Sacramentary (8th C)

O God, forasmuch as without Thee we are not able to please Thee, mercifully grant that Thy Holy Spirit may in all things direct and rule our hearts; through Jesus Christ our Lord.

TRINITY SUNDAY

'Go then to all peoples everywhere and make them my disciples: baptise them in the name of the Father, the Son, and the Holy Spirit. . . .'

This, according to St. Matthew (*Chapter 28; v. 19*), was the last command that Jesus gave to his disciples and it sums up the Christian teachings about God, which are known as the doctrine of the Trinity—three in one. The one God is often referred to as God in three persons—the Father, the son and the Holy Ghost or Holy Spirit.

Many people have found it difficult to understand how one God can be three and three be one. St. Patrick once picked up a leaf of shamrock and pointed out that, although it had three parts, it was still one leaf. John Wesley drew attention to three candles in the room but between them they gave only one light.

Others have recalled the actors of long ago who used to play several parts in the same play. To do this they wore different masks so that people could easily distinguish one character from the other. Just as one man could be several 'persons' so God can be seen in three different 'persons'; God the Father, Creator and Supreme Ruler of all things; God the Son, Jesus Christ, God incarnate redeeming His people; God the Holy Spirit, Guide, inspiration and power for His people.

These things are remembered on Trinity Sunday, the Sunday after Whitsun, which is not a major festival but an important celebration in the Church Calendar on which people worship the Three in One.

(It might be interesting, if desired, to make comparisons with the beliefs in other religions of a Triad or Trinity, such as Hinduism with Brahma, Vishnu and Siva, regarded as three personalities of one god.)

May the blessing of God Almighty, the Father, the Son, and the Holy Spirit, be with us and remain with us this day and for ever.

Ave Maria ('Hail Mary'), are words spoken very frequently by some Christians, especially those of the Roman Catholic Church, who accord to the Blessed Virgin Mary, the mother of Jesus Christ, the highest honours and call upon her in prayer to intercede on their behalf.

Apart from main festivals, there are some days on which the Blessed Virgin Mary is especially remembered. The first of these is 1st January, known as the Feast of the Circumcision and Name of Jesus but also the Solemnity of Mary, the Mother of God. It is a holy day of obligation (p. 93).

February 2nd is Candlemas (p. 73), commemorating the presentation of Jesus at the temple. The feast is also called the Purification of the Blessed Virgin Mary.

Lady Day is the traditional name for the feast of the Annunciation of the Blessed Virgin Mary. It is on 25th March, nine months before Christmas, and recalls how the angel Gabriel informed Mary of the forthcoming birth of Jesus (*St. Luke 1; 26–38*).

The feast of the Assumption of the Blessed Virgin Mary falls on 15th August. It is the celebration in certain Catholic traditions of Mary's bodily assumption into heaven. It is an early tradition of the church and is accepted to mean that Mary is now where all Christians will be after the final resurrection of the dead.

On 8th December, there is the feast of the Immaculate Conception of the Blessed Virgin Mary. This should not be confused with the actual conception of Jesus, but is an ancient Catholic belief that, at the moment she conceived Jesus, God granted her the special privilege of being immune from sin and therefore completely pure.

Other Christians, notably non-conformists, place less emphasis on the role of Mary.

> Hail blessed Virgin, full of grace,
> Splendour of all the human race,
> We honour you for Christ your Son,
> Who has for us redemption won.
>
> *Anthony G. Petti (1932 –   )*

Celebration and worship (11)

The Day of Assembly

One of the Five Pillars of Islam is *salat**, the ritual prayer to be offered five times daily wherever the Muslim happens to be. Each prayer consists of a set number of *rakas** (sequences), all of which include the opening words of the Qur'an* (below).

But Friday is *Yaum ul-Jum'a*, the Day of Assembly, when all Muslim men are required to meet together for congregational prayer. It is optional for women. The time for this is mid-day— which is exactly midway between sunrise and sunset. It is not a day of rest in the Jewish or Christian sense. Muslims do not believe that God needed a day on which to rest.

To prepare for congregational worship, the men take a shower or bath, put on clean clothes and avoid any foods such as garlic which could be offensive to others. Ablutions are carried out on entering the mosque.

In the mosque there are no seats. Worshippers stand in straight lines: all are equal before Allah. They face the direction of Mecca, which is indicated by a niche in the wall (*mihrab**). Prayer is led by an *imam** (leader), who is elected from among the congregation.

There is a prescribed ritual for prayer. The raka begins with the words *Allahu Akbar* ('God is most great'). Worshippers stand, bow, prostrate themselves or kneel for the various parts of the raka.

Prayer is preceded by a sermon (*khutbah**) given by the imam. Part may be about current affairs and part in explaining passages from the Qur'an. Sermons should always begin and end with praise of Allah, blessings on the Prophet (peace be on him) and his Companions, and *Du'a*, a prayer for all Muslims.

The opening words of the Qur'an:

In the name of God, the Compassionate, the Merciful. Praise to God, Lord of the Worlds, Most Gracious, Most Merciful, Ruler of the Day of Judgement, You alone we worship; You alone we ask for help. Guide us on the straight path, the path of those whom You have favoured; not the path of those who earn Your anger, nor of those who go astray.

Celebration and worship (12)

People in eastern countries may worship their gods at shrines or in temples, where their worship is usually an individual offering rather than congregational worship. But there are occasions when great numbers of people will gather for temple festivals in honour of the god to whom the temple is dedicated.

Every temple has at least one week-long festival, to which people come in great crowds from neighbouring villages and from further afield, especially to those pilgrim festivals such as Ratha Yatra* at Puri (p. 113). One popular festival is Ganesh* Chaturthi*, in honour of the elephant-headed god of good fortune. Another, especially in Gujarat, is Durga Puja* (p. 106), in honour of the goddess Durga.

*Puja** means worship and this is part of the festival, with offerings being made to the god. Clay statues may be made as places in which the god may dwell. They are treated with great honour during the festival and symbolically thrown in the river or smashed at the end, when the god leaves.

The chief event is usually the public procession of the temple image. Carried on an elephant or on a painted wooden carriage, it is borne round the temple and through the main street to the river, where it is bathed before being replaced in its shrine in the temple.

Buddhists have their temple festivals too. One of the most spectacular is the ten-day festival of Esala Parahera* at Kandy, Sri Lanka. From the Temple of the Tooth, a casket containing a tooth of the Buddha, is paraded in a colourful procession of elephants, dancers, drummer boys and people with torches.

Processions form part of the Matsuri ('festivals') in Japan, such as Sanno Matsuri in Tokyo. Behind the carnival-like rejoicings lie the acts of worship, offerings and sacred meals, aimed at seeking closer union between man and his god—the aim of most religious celebrations.

From the Bhagavad Gita 11:40
All praise be to You . . . God of all, You are the powerful God whose might cannot be measured. You are perfect in every way: You are everywhere.

Holy Books (1)

Scripture festivals

The most important books in the world are the holy books, scriptures or sacred writings upon which people base their religious life. In one sense they may be regarded as text books, for they are the ones which give all the important teachings. In another sense they may be regarded much more deeply than that, for many are considered to be the actual word of God as revealed through his servants or prophets. Indeed the Sikhs regard their book, Guru Granth* Sahib, as a living teacher.

Because of this, the greatest respect is offered to these books. In courts of law it is customary for people to take an oath whilst holding a Bible, for it has long been the belief that no one would take such an oath lightly. Sikhs have the Granth present at all personal celebrations and treat it with the greatest reverence in their services. It must not be touched except when in a state of cleanliness. Muslims, too, must be clean before touching the Qur'an* and would feel it a great insult if the Qur'an were put on the floor. The Jewish scrolls of the Torah are given great honour in synagogues.

People of most religions have one or more days on which they celebrate the receiving of their holy books; sometimes as part of one of their main festivals. Jews give thanks for the receiving of the Torah at Shavuoth* (p. 62) and on Simchath Torah* (p. 103). Sikhs celebrate with a complete reading of the Granth* (p. 104).

During their fast of Paryushan*, Jains celebrate the giving of the Kalpa Sutra by having it read by the monks (p. 119). Muslims recall the revelation of the Qur'an to Muhammad on Lailat ul-Qadr* ('Night of Power') during the last ten days of Ramadan* (p. 118), usually on the 27th day. It is celebrated with readings from the Qur'an and prayers.

So people of many faiths celebrate in differing ways the receipt of what they consider a most previous gift from God.

> Speak now to all Your people, Lord:
> Through sacred books and spoken word
> Your gracious truths You still impart;
> Engrave them on each loving heart.

Holy books (2)

Simchath Torah

The ninth day of Sukkoth*, the Feast of Tabernacles, is the most joyful occasion in the Jewish year, for it is then that the people gather to give thanks for the *Torah* (Law). Throughout the year the Torah will have been read. *Simchath Torah** is the day when the public reading ends with the last part of Deuteronomy. It is followed by the first chapter of Genesis to begin a further year's reading.

The *Torah*, or Law, is given pride of place in the synagogue. It is carefully written on parchment scrolls. It is God's word and therefore there must be no mistakes. Each 'book' consists of a scroll rolled onto two rods. The scroll has a beautiful cover, or mantle, with silver ornaments, bells and a breast-plate similar to that worn by the High Priest in the temple. These are kept in the ark, an ornate wooden case behind embroidered curtains, and taken out with loving care.

When the Torah is to be read, the scroll is carried round the synagogue. The faithful will bow their heads as it passes, some reaching out to touch the tassel of the mantle or to kiss it. The scroll is then opened, and held high for all to see. This is God's word to his people. A pointer, in the form of a closed hand with one finger extended, is used when reading the Law.

At one time the Law was celebrated at Shavuoth* (p. 62), but now the special rejoicing of Simchath Torah comes at the end of Sukkoth. On this day the scrolls of the Law are carried round the synagogue (*Hakafot**), not once but seven times accompanied by singing, led by the cantor, and perhaps dancing too. It is a most happy feast, to which children are called to the very special privilege of the Reading of the Law.

A Jewish prayer for Simchath Torah:
Out of love for us, O Lord our God, You have given us special times for gladness, festivals and seasons for joy, this festival of Simchath Torah, the time of our gladness, a holy gathering—in memory of the exodus from Egypt.

Holy Books (3)

Guru Granth Sahib

In every Sikh temple or gurdwara*, the most important place is reserved for Guru Granth Sahib—not a man but the book which is regarded as the last and permanent guru or teacher (p. 30). Through the Granth God speaks to men. It is held in the highest esteem and treated with the utmost reverence. For the Sikh it is a part of life itself, holding a central place not only in worship but in all personal festivals and celebrations.

At the beginning of worship, Guru Granth* Sahib is carried to its place of honour—a low table on a dais or throne, which is raised above the congregation who sit on the floor. Behind the Granth is a man who waves a *chauri** above the book. The chauri is a short wooden or metal rod with yak hairs set in one end and is a sign of authority. The reader of the book is called the *Granthi*.

In the Sikh Golden Temple at Amritsar, the Granth is read continuously from before sunrise to after sunset every day. The reader, who is dressed in white and wears a blue turban, chants the words aloud for all to hear. A second man sits on his left. Readers take it in turn. The whole reading takes about forty-eight hours and is known as the *Akhand path**.

At all Sikh festivals it is customary for Guru Granth Sahib to be read in temples during the preceding forty-eight hours. It is also read from beginning to end in homes on the occasion of personal festivals, birthdays or deaths. In these cases the reading may be spread over seven days, or 'open time'. At all the happy festivals the reading is started and finished in the morning but for deaths it is in the afternoon.

On certain festivals in India, Guru Granth Sahib is carried in procession through the streets (p. 88).

Some words of Guru Nanak*

I seek only one bounty from my Lord. To bless me with meditation on the Name and then all my tasks would be fulfilled. May I serve God in my childhood and contemplate on Him in my youth and old age.

Holy Books (4)

The first sermon given by the Buddha after his enlightenment, was given to five fellow thinkers in a deer park near Benares. The sermon was entitled 'Dhammacakkappavattana Sutta' ('The discourse which set the wheel of truth turning'). It gave the basic teaching about the Middle Way. Therevada* Buddhists remember this each year at a special festival known as Asala Puja*, or Dhammacakka* Day.

There are two other Therevada Buddhist festivals that are concerned with the proclamation and spreading of the Buddhist teachings. Magha Puja recalls the day on which the Buddha ordained 1250 disciples who were enlightened (p. 75). The other, Poson Perahera*, is commemorated in Sri Lanka, in memory of the time, in 246 BCE, when the Indian Emperor Asoka* sent his son, Mahinda, to teach the Buddhist way to the Sinhalese people. All Buddhist festivals are celebrated on the day of the full moon.

Christians, too, are concerned with the spreading of their beliefs to all people. The last command that Jesus Christ gave to His disciples was 'Go ye into all the world and preach the Gospel . . .' It was in response to that command that Christianity spread, firstly through the near east and into Europe, then in later years, by missionaries, to every part of the world. Many churches have their celebrations or festivals when they remember the work that has been and is being done overseas.

To do this work effectively, people have needed the Bible printed in many languages—a work undertaken by the British and Foreign Bible Society and by other Bible Societies. Today many churches observe the second Sunday in Advent as Bible Sunday, when they give thanks not only for the Bible but for those who have helped to print all or part of it in more than 1500 languages and dialects.

Thanks be to You, O God, for the truth that You have given us in our scriptures. May we learn from them and live by them, helping others to understand not only through our words but by our example.

Triumph over evil (1)

One of the greatest of the Hindu festivals is *Dashara**, the autumn festival that takes place during the first ten days of the month Asvina. The main day of the festival is the tenth day, known as *Durga Puja**, the worship of the goddess Durga. In parts of India, notably Gujarat, the previous days are celebrated as Navaratra* ('Nine nights'), during which sacrifices are offered (p. 119).

In Northern India during this period, a play is performed with elaborate costumes and masks, a different episode each night. *Ram Lila* tells the story of Rama* and Sita*. Whilst Rama was away, Ravana* the demon king of Sri Lanka, carried away Rama's wife Sita. After many adventures Rama was able to overcome Ravana, with the help of the goddess Durga, and return home to great rejoicing. The story is also recalled at Diwali* (p. 87).

Dashara is sometimes called the Festival of Warriors. It has always been popular with the warrior caste and with soldiers, who associate themselves with the fighting aspects of the festival. There are plenty of strenuous activities such as athletics and hunting expeditions.

In those parts of India, notably Bengal and Assam, where the festival is Durga Puja, Durga is worshipped during the nine days. Then there are temple processions and bathing the image (p. 101). In other parts, Durga may be worshipped as Kali*.

However the festival period is celebrated, and by whatever name it is known, there is plenty of merrymaking. The last day may include a carnival procession with huge images of the demon Ravana, filled with crackers and explosives. Fiery arrows are shot into the images which explode—demonstrating the triumph of good over evil.

From the Bhagavad Gita (11.36):
It is right, O God, that peoples sing Thy praises, and that they are glad and rejoice in Thee. All evil spirits fly away in fear; but the hosts of the saints bow down before Thee.

Triumph over evil (2)

It is not often that children attending a place of worship are encouraged to make rude noises. One exception to the usual practice is at the Jewish festival of *Purim*. It is the day on which Jews recall the story of Esther, the Queen of King Ahasuerus.

The story is told in the *Megillah** (Scroll of Esther), the Book of Esther in the Christian Old Testament. Briefly, an official named Haman wanted all the Jews destroyed and he arranged for lots to be cast to decide when it should be done. The word for lots is Purim and this is how the festival came to be named. Haman intended to start by hanging Esther's uncle, Mordecai, but, because of pleas by Esther to the king, all the Jews were saved and Haman was hanged on his own gallows.

Today, the day before Purim is the Fast of Esther, which recalls how she fasted. Purim itself is a day of rejoicing. The story is read in the synagogues on the evening of the festival and again at the morning service. After the reading, the children are encouraged to use graggers and other noise-making instruments whenever the name of the villain, Haman, is mentioned.

In the Scroll of Esther, people are enjoined to make the feast a joyful one: 'make them days of feasting and joy, of sending portions to one another'. So this is a time of celebration in Jewish communities, especially in Israel, with music, plays and carnivals, and, of course, a time for giving and receiving presents. It is also a time for feasting and perhaps eating *Hamantachen* – three cornered pastries filled with poppy seeds.

Behind all the rejoicing is the special thankfulness for deliverance from a tyrant—a triumph of good over evil for God's people.

Blessed are You, O Lord our God, King of the Universe, for all the favours You have shown to us. We thank You, too, for miracles and mighty deeds that have saved Your people from their enemies. For all Your mercies, we praise and bless You.

Triumph over evil (3)

Festival of freedom

*Pesach** (Passover) is an eight-day Jewish festival, celebrated in springtime as a constant reminder of the deliverance of the children of Israel from Egypt in the time of Moses. It is the first of the bread made in haste; parsley dipped in salt, for the people went to Jerusalem to keep the festival.

The Torah decreed that the story of the deliverance should be told each year to the children. So Jewish people have the *Haggadah**, from the Hebrew 'to tell', which is a kind of guide book to the festival. It tells the story (*see Exodus 12*) and contains prayers and songs of thanksgiving.

Before the feast, the house is thoroughly cleaned. No leaven (yeast) must be used and a search is made. Any remaining is swept into a wooden tray with a feather and burned.

On the first evening, the family, dressed in new clothes, come to the table for the Pesach Seder* ('arrangement' or 'order'). There will be candles, a cup of wine for each person plus one for an unexpected guest and certain foods on the Seder Plate.

After *Kiddush** (blessing) has been spoken over the wine, the symbolic foods are eaten. *Matzoh** (unleavened bread) reminds of the bread made in haste; parsley dipped in salt, for the scanty food and tears in Egypt; a roasted shank-bone of lamb, for the paschal lamb sacrifice; a roasted egg, for new life; *maror*, a bitter herb such as horseradish, for the bitterness of slavery and *haroset**, a paste of nuts and fruits, for the sweetness of deliverance.

It is the custom then for the youngest child to ask four questions, which father answers by reading from the *Haggadah*, so reminding of the reasons for celebrating Pesach.

In the home after the meal, as well as in the services in the synagogue, there are special prayers and hymns as well as the reciting of the first two Psalms in the *Hallel* (praise)—Psalms 113–118—in thankfulness to God, not only for past blessings but for those of today.

Blessed are You, O Lord our God, Ruler of the World. We thank You for the deliverance of Your people and for every blessing received in the past and today.

Triumph over evil (4)

Christ is risen, Hallelujah!

It is the custom in many Greek churches for people to meet for worship in the church late in the evening on Holy Saturday. Then, as midnight passes, in the first moments of Easter Day, the priest lights a single candle. It is the signal for all the people to light theirs too so that the church is filled with light. Then the people shout with joy, 'Christ is risen!'

It is a symbol of the triumph of light over darkness, of good over evil; for the message of Easter is that, no matter what man might do, the goodness of God would triumph, that even death would lead to resurrection.

Christ is risen. Hallelujah! These joyful words have sounded from Christians for centuries as they have met to celebrate the most important festival of the year—the new life of Jesus after His death on the cross.

The name Easter is a pagan one. Eostre was the goddess of spring to the people of old. She, it was, who gave new life to the world. It is not difficult to see how the Christian festival of new life tied in with the ancient customs. Easter eggs, too (p. 51), continue a very old custom, using the egg as a symbol of new life. In some lands it is traditionally a time for spring cleaning—a clean sweep, or fresh start, in the home. People also like to wear new clothes for Easter—a custom which has led here and there to lavish Easter parades (p. 133). Churches are bedecked with lovely spring flowers as a contrast to the bareness of Good Friday.

But, for Christian people, many of these things are the trimmings of a joyful festival of worship. Sunrise services are popular in parts of Europe and America and all worship throughout the day is offered with a great sense of thankfulness and joy.

We thank You, O God, for the joy and wonder of Easter, for the story of how Jesus rose from the dead and the knowledge that He lives in the hearts of all who love Him. Help us to understand and to make room for Him in our hearts.

Pilgrimage (1)

People of most religions like to make pilgrimages to places that are of particular importance to their religion. For some it is obligatory. The Muslim, for example, is expected to make the *hajj**, the pilgrimage to Mecca. Others undertake pilgrimages because they want to, because it helps them to improve their religious life or because they believe they will be blessed by God for having done so, especially if the pilgrimage is one that causes hardship. For this last reason, many pilgrims travel on foot.

Every religion has its holy places. For hundreds of years, Christian pilgrims have travelled abroad to such places as the Holy Land or Rome. In Britain, the most famous place to visit was the tomb of St. Thomas à Becket at Canterbury. One of the roads leading to Canterbury is still known as the Pilgrim's Way. Many Christians in recent times have made a pilgrimage to Lourdes (p. 144).

Parsis may make a pilgrimage to the Holy Fire at Udwada*, which has been burning for 1300 years. Buddhists in Sri Lanka visit the Lord's Foot, a footmark in a stone, said to be that of the Buddha.

Some pilgrimages are undertaken at any time. Others are associated with festivals. The Jews of old had three Pilgrim Festivals, Pesach*, Shavuoth*, and Sukkoth*, when they went to Jerusalem (pp. 108, 62, 63).

For many Hindus, pilgrimages are a favourite occupation. They will walk the length of the sacred Ganges and they will travel to many temple festivals. The great Indian pilgrim festival is Kumbha Mela*, the 'Pitcher Fair', which is held every twelve years. An ancient tale tells how gods and demons fought for a pitcher of amrit* (nectar). The successful gods stopped at four places on their way to heaven and the fair is held at these in turn (Prayag (Allahabad), Hardwar, Nasik and Ujjain). Any pilgrimage is an experience never to be forgotten.

O send out Thy light and Thy truth: let them lead me; let them bring me unto Thy holy hill, and to Thy tabernacles.

(Psalm 43; 3)

Pilgrimage (2)

Pilgrimage to Mecca

One of the requirements of a Muslim is that, during his lifetime, he should make a pilgrimage (*hajj**) to the holy city of Mecca. Thousands do so every year.

At Mecca, the pilgrims put on special clothing before going to Bayt ul-haram, the mosque in which the *Ka'ba* is situated. This is a large cube-shaped structure with a black stone set in the side. Tradition says it was built by Abraham.

Pilgrims move round the Ka'ba seven times, if possible kissing the black stone. Afterwards they run or jog seven times between Safa and Marwa, then travel to Mina. On the ninth day is the moving occasion of praying on Mount Arafat. Later, 49 small pebbles are collected for the ceremony of *Jamrat** – stoning the Devil—at Mina. Then pilgrims return to Mecca to encircle the Ka'ba again.

The pilgrimage is over. The pilgrim can now call himself 'al-hajji'. He takes home presents for his friends, such as dates and holy water drawn from the Zam-zam.

At the end of the hajj, on 10th of Dhul-Hijja, is the joyous Muslim festival of Eid ul-Adha*. Known as the Great Festival, or the Festival of Sacrifice, it is celebrated by Muslims throughout the world and lasts for four days.

After prayers in the mosque on the first morning, a sacrifice is made to commemorate the sacrifice of an animal made by Abraham instead of sacrificing his son. Today's sacrifice may be a lamb, a goat, a cow or a camel. Those unable to do so because they live in different cultural surroundings, may send money to relatives overseas, to sacrifice for them. The meat, is sold to provide money for orphans and the needy.

It is customary on Eid ul-Adha* to invite guests to dinner and to send greetings to family and friends.

A prayer of Muhammad:

O Lord! Help me in remembering You, in being grateful to You, and in worshipping You, [*to do so*] in the best possible way.

Pilgrimage (3)

Many of the pilgrimages which people make are to shrines which are the burial places of holy people, perhaps containing the relics of the person concerned. Look around any old cathedral and you will find many tombs, one of which may be the shrine of a saint, for example of St. Cuthbert at Durham or St. Thomas à Becket at Canterbury. Many pilgrims used to go to Compostella, in Spain, to the shrine of St. James, one of the apostles. They then wore a cockle shell to show that they had been there.

People of other religions, too, make pilgrimages. Sikhs and Jains will visit towns that are connected with the founders or other holy men of their religion. Buddhists may not have to travel so far to visit their shrines for there are so many of them, each containing some small relic of a Buddha, perhaps a lock of hair or a tooth. Gautama*, the Buddha, was cremated and his ashes taken to many places, where a pagoda or stupa was built.

In Japan there are many shrines to which people may go to worship the kami (gods). Some are temple buildings but others are very small. Many of the shrines are built on mountain tops, and can only be reached by steep passes or by climbing hundreds of steps. The belief is that the more difficult the journey the more likely that prayers will be answered. Old and sick people, unable to climb, are carried in litters.

One of the most popular places of pilgrimage in Japan is Fuji-yama, the sacred mountain. It has no relics but is said to be the home of a goddess. It is visited each year by over a hundred thousand pilgrims.

Pilgrims may visit a shrine at any time they find convenient but at some shrines there are also great festivals to which pilgrims flock in huge numbers.

O Lord our God, grant us grace to desire Thee with our whole heart; that so desiring we may seek and find Thee; and so finding Thee may love Thee, and loving Thee may hate those sins from which Thou hast redeemed us.

Anselm (1033–1109)

Pilgrimage (4)

Some of the most spectacular festivals to be seen anywhere in the world are those associated with temples and the gods who are worshipped in them. They are attended not only by local people but by pilgrims, some of whom will have travelled hundreds of miles to share in the worship and celebrations. Such festivals last for several days. The famous Esala Perahera* festival (p. 101), at the Dalada Miligawa Temple, the Temple of the Tooth, at Kandy, Sri Lanka, is a ten-day festival.

Few festivals can be more spectacular than Ratha Yatra*, the festival held in honour of Jagannatha, 'Lord of the Universe', a title usually applied to Vishnu and Krishna. The festival is celebrated in various temples but the one to which many thousands of pilgrims go is at Puri, in Orissa, situated on the coast about 480 kilometres south of Calcutta.

The temple of Jagannatha has three huge images, representing Krishna and his brother and sister, Balarama and Subhadra. Every summer these huge brightly painted wooden busts are taken to be bathed (p. 101). They are carried in three huge temple-like chariots (*rathas*), which are pulled through the streets by thousands of pilgrims. It is a time of great excitement as well as a time of devotion. Some pilgrims have been so carried away that they have thrown themselves in front of the huge cars and been crushed to death by the wheels. It is from these incidents at the Jagannatha festival that we get our word 'Juggernaut'.

One popular feature of the festival at Puri is that men of all castes are regarded as equal at the temple. All visitors must also eat a meal that has been cooked at the shrine by men of low caste.

After all, the object of any pilgrimage, regardless of whoever else may be present, is to improve one's relationship with God.

> O God, when earnestly we seek You,
> Please meet us on the way.

Fasting and penance (1)

SACKCLOTH AND ASHES

There are certain times in our lives when we wish to show how sorry or sad we are about something which we have said or done or something which may have happened to us. Sometimes words are sufficient. We apologise and ask the person we may have offended to forgive what we have done. Many of the prayers that are offered are prayers in which we confess our sins and ask God's forgiveness.

There are some occasions when we wish to show our sorrow in other ways too. People in most communities wear black, or some other distinguishing clothing, following a death in the family.

In Old Testament days, it was customary for people to put on 'sackcloth and ashes'. The sackcloth was a coarse uncomfortable cloth made from camel and goat hair. The ashes were put all over the head as a symbol that joy had perished. (*See Esther 4; 1–3*)

Ashes are used symbolically on certain religious occasions to this day. Parsis (Zoroastrians) have their *Matchi** ceremony to give thanks for something special that has happened to them. At the conclusion of the ceremony, the priest brings a ladle of ash so that worshippers can place a pinch of it on their foreheads as a reminder to live a noble, humble life, since one day the body will die and turn to dust, just as does the glowing fire.

One of the Christian holy days is Ash Wednesday, the first day of Lent. At one time it was observed much more than it is today. At present day services, mainly in Roman Catholic churches, ashes from the previous year's palm crosses are put in a bowl and sprinkled with holy water. The priest marks an ash cross with his thumb on the forehead of each participant as a sign of penance.

Prayer offered by the priest at the Zoroastrian ceremony:
From all my sins do I repent and turn back. From every evil thought, evil word and evil deed, which in this world I may have conceived of, uttered or committed, which from me has come forth, or originated through me.

Fasting and penance (2)

Fasting is a practice that has its place in most of the religions of the world. It is a form of self-discipline which helps to strengthen the spiritual life. By denying oneself food or certain other pleasures, one is constantly reminded why one is doing without such things.

Some people have a regular day for fasting. Buddhist monks, for example, may have a fast day (*Uposatha**) once a fortnight. Some Hindus fast on the eleventh day of their month.

There are also certain days on which some people fast to show their sorrow. Jewish people fast from sunrise to sunset on Yom Kippur (Day of Atonement) (p. 117) and on the Fast of 9th Av* (p. 116) as a sign of sorrow or penitence.

In some faiths there are fasts which last for a much longer period than this. For Christians the period that has been regarded for centuries as a fast is the period of Lent, being the forty days before Easter. During this time, people remember how Jesus fasted for forty days in the wilderness to prepare for his work. So people prepare themselves by thinking about the sufferings of Jesus.

Lent was once kept much more rigidly than it is today. Every day was a fast day except Mid-Lent Sunday, when some relief was permitted. Nowadays the only actual fast days observed by Roman Catholics are Ash Wednesday and Good Friday. But there are still many who will deny themselves during Lent, perhaps give to charity, and spend more time in prayer or devotion.

Others who have long fasts are Muslims, who fast during the month of Ramadan* (p. 118). Bahá'ís* fast each year from 2nd to 20th March, the last month of their year, to prepare themselves for a good start to the new year through a better relationship with God.

> Help me not to indulge myself, O God;
> Rather make me ready to deny myself some pleasures:
> And, as I do so,
> May I think of my responsibilities toward others,
> And feel myself nearer to You.

Fasting and penance (3)

Most festivals are happy occasions on which people enjoy themselves as they celebrate something for which they are especially thankful. There are sad festivals too, one of these being the Fast of 9th Av (*Tisha b'Av**), described as 'the saddest day in the Jewish calendar'.

The ninth day of the month of Av really seems to be a black day in the history of the Jewish people. It was on or about this day that Solomon's temple at Jerusalem was destroyed in 586 BCE by Nebuchadnezzar and in 70 CE another temple was destroyed.

It was on the 9th of Av, 135 CE, that the Jewish hero, Bar Kochba, and his men were massacred by the Romans; that Edward I signed a decree, in 1290, expelling the Jews from England; and that, in 1492, 150,000 were driven from their homes in Spain. But it is the destruction of the temples that is especially remembered and the Fast of 9th Av ends three weeks of mourning.

On the evening before the fast begins, people partake of a meal consisting of hard doughnut-shaped rolls (*beigel**) and eggs sprinkled with ashes, as are eaten after funerals. Then they make their way to the synagogue. There they take off their shoes and sit either on the floor or upon furniture that has been overturned.

The morning service is unusual, in that it is the one weekday in the year when neither tallith* nor tefillin* are worn for prayer. They are worn instead for the afternoon service. The mourning candle is lit and the Lamentations of Jeremiah are read.

Some comfort after sorrow is given on the following Sabbath, when the passage is read from Isaiah 40, which begins 'Comfort ye, comfort ye, my people. . .'

From the prayer in Lamentations:

Remember, O Lord, what has happened to us. Look at us and see our disgrace. . . . Bring us back to You, Lord! Bring us back! Restore our ancient glory.

Fasting and penance (4)

The holiest and most solemn day of the Jewish year is *Yom Kippur*, the Day of Atonement, which falls on the 10th day of Tishri (p. 201).

During the previous ten days, people will have been thinking about themselves and God (p. 85), recalling their faults and failings. Yom Kippur is the day for confessing these sins so that a fresh start can be made.

It recalls the ceremonies laid down long ago and recorded in the Torah (*Leviticus, chapter 16*). It was customary for a goat, the 'scapegoat', to be driven into the wilderness, symbolically bearing the sins of the people, then for the High Priest, dressed in simple white garments, to confess the sins of himself and all the people, asking for forgiveness of God.

Today, Yom Kippur is sometimes called the 'Sabbath of Sabbaths' because it is the holiest of days. It is spent in prayer and fasting, seeking God's forgiveness. A good meal is taken on the eve of Yom Kippur, before sunset, and nothing else is eaten until after sunset the next day.

At sunset, as Yom Kippur begins, there is a ceremony of Kol Nidrei* ('all vows'), when people are assured of God's forgiveness for the breaking of vows made between man and God. The fast day is symbolic of God's pardon for those who are truly penitent. The final service, Ne'ilah*, visualises the closing of the temple gates, symbolic of the closing of the gates of heaven, for men's fates have now been decided. The final blowing of the shofar* (ram's horn) brings to an end the ten days of penitence before God.

Part of an old Jewish prayer (Psalm 51)

Be merciful to me, O God, because of Your constant love. Because of Your great mercy wipe away my sins! . . . I have sinned against You—only against You—and done what You consider evil. . . . Create a pure heart in me, O God, and put a new and loyal spirit in me.

Fasting and penance (5)

Every Muslim is required to spend one month each year fasting (*saum**). The month is *Ramadan** and the fast lasts from the sighting of the new moon to the sighting of the next one. It is a time when Muslims remember especially the sending of the Qur'an* as a guide to man. This is commemorated especially on Lailat ul'Qadr* (p. 102).

But Ramadan is also intended as a reminder of the needs of fellow human beings. As Muslims fast, especially on the long days when Ramadan falls in summer (p. 196), they feel the pangs of hunger, such as are felt to an even greater degree by the poor and needy.

All adults who are fit enough to do so must fast between sunrise and sunset each day. Food and drink may only be taken before dawn and after sunset. Extra time during this month is spent in the mosques at prayer and in reading the Qur'an, especially during the last ten days.

Then, with the new moon, comes great rejoicing as people worldwide enjoy the festival of Eid ul-Fitr* (p. 175). The fast is over but people feel closer to God because they have kept it.

Another day which is kept as a fast in Islam is *10th Muharram**. It is a day on which Muslims recall the overthrow of the Egyptians when Moses led the Israelites from slavery. Muhammad kept the day as a fast and directed that others should do so also.

It was on this day, too, that Hussain, the grandson of Muhammad, died in battle and this is remembered especially by the Shi'a*, who mourn his death for 40 days. Meetings are held in the evenings of the first nine days to recall incidents in his life: on the tenth day there are mourning processions with large floats. Religious hymns and ballads are sung. There are no weddings, public performances or television.

A prayer of Muhammad:
Thou art my Lord, I Thy servant. I have wronged myself and I confess my sin. Forgive me then all my sins, for there is none that forgiveth sins save Thee.

PENANCE AND SACRIFICE   *Navaratra; Paryushan*

Fasting serves as a reminder of one's religious responsibilities. Sometimes people wish to do more and suffer discomfort, as by wearing sackcloth and ashes. In some communions and religions, when one has committed a sin, one is required to do penance, which may involve physical pain or hardship or the offering of a costly sacrifice.

The time for doing this often comes before an important festival or before beginning a New Year. The Hindus have a prescribed period known as *Navaratra** ('Nine nights'). It is a period of sacrifice and a major part of religious festivals in many parts of India, leading up to such occasions as Dashara* and Durga Puja* (pp. 101, 106). In Assam and Bengal, particularly, images of Durga are worshipped daily and sacrifices of buffaloes offered.

The Jain year ends in August or September and the last eight days of the old year, known as *Paryushan**, are kept as days of penance. During this time they commemorate Mahavira*, whose birthday falls on the fourth day, and the giving of the holy book, the *Kalpa Sutra*. The Kalpa Sutra is read by the monks to the laity, some of whom may temporarily live as monks (*posadha**).

The last day of Paryushan is a day of fasting, although the very pious will fast for the whole eight days. One of the very important aspects of Paryushan is that of making confession at the meeting house and being determined that no quarrel will be carried forward into the new year.

People may feel a need for fasting, confession, penance or sacrifice, but none of these is of any value without a heartfelt determination to change for the better. The only real and acceptable sacrifice one can offer is a complete dedication of oneself to God.

> I bow in silence at thy feet,
> Hear thou the prayer which I repeat,
> O make my sacrifice complete
> My Lord, my life, my all.
> *James R. Batey 1878–?)*

Special remembrance (1)

If you were asked to make a list of members of your family, no doubt you would include parents, brothers and sisters, grandparents, aunts, uncles, cousins and perhaps a number of distant relatives too. It is doubtful whether you would think to include members who are no longer living. They *were* part of the family.

But in many parts of the world, particularly in the East and in parts of Africa, ancestors are considered to be important members of the family, who may visit from time to time.

In Japan there is a very happy festival called Obon, or Bon, which is held every summer. In Tokyo it is held on 13th July, but elsewhere it is in August. Obon is a Japanese Buddhist festival at which 27 lanterns are lit to guide the spirits of the ancestors on their annual visit to the family home. It is hoped that they will bring good luck with them.

Homes are made bright and happy for the occasion. Candles are lit and special delicacies made to be offered to the ancestors. At the end of the day, the ancestors are entertained with a circular folk dance. It is nice to be able to think of ancestors in this happy way rather than to be sad as some people are.

In China there is a festival called Ch'ing Ming (p. 48), when ancestors are remembered. It is one of many when graves are swept. On the far side of the world, in New Mexico, the Zuni tribes have their mask gods, the Koko, who are dead ancestors from over the Whispering Waters, bringing with them good fortune. Large groups of the masked dances are to be seen in summer.

The Ashanti people of Ghana have special ceremonies known as Adae, when their ancestors are remembered. Stools represent the ancestors and food and drink are placed in front of them. The ancestors are asked to speak to the gods for them and to give them health and good fortune.

Thank you, God, for all members of our family, past and present, for all they have meant to us and all we have inherited from their love and their labours.

Special remembrance (2)

GIFTS FOR THE ANCESTORS

What happens to the spirits of people who die? Are they likely to need help in the place to which they go? People have often thought that they would need help of one kind or another. We sometimes hear people say, of money or other possessions, 'You can't take it with you!' But we know that people, such as the ancient Egyptians, used to put in their tombs all sorts of things that might be useful.

There is a Hindu ceremony, which is held some time after the death of a member of the family. It is known as *Shraddha*. The male descendants of the deceased offer gifts of water, milk and balls of rice (*pinda*). The ceremony is intended to help the dead on their journey to the after life and to keep the link with the living. It is followed by feasting and music.

For hundreds of years, the people of China have had festivals in which they offered help to their ancestors and to others who might be in need. One festival, held toward the end of the year as the weather turned cold, was called Time of Sending Winter Clothes to Ancestors. Graves were swept and sacrifices made. Suits of winter clothes were cut out of paper and addressed personally to the ancestors. These were then burned and it was believed that the ancestors would be warmly clad. At a later period, instead of cutting out clothes, people enclosed 'spirit money' in plain wrappers and burned these instead.

It may be, too, that ancestors could be hungry and in need of offerings of food. Another Chinese festival is Yue Lan, or the Festival of the Hungry Ghosts. It was believed that, on that day in summer, ghosts were released to roam around the world for one day. Obviously they would need food and so small roadside fires were kindled where paper money, fruits and other offerings could be offered to the ghosts.

Although no longer living, the ancestors were considered a part of the family and should be helped.

Today, O God, make us mindful of all who have helped to shape our lives; and give us thankful hearts.

Special remembrance (3)

REMEMBERING THE DEAD

Most people like to remember the members of their family who have died and various reminders may be found in the home, especially on the anniversary of death. In Jewish homes it is customary to light a candle on the anniversary and perhaps to ask for a special prayer to be offered in the synagogue on the nearest Sabbath.

In China and Japan, where people think a lot about their ancestors, it is to be expected that there would be a number of occasions when people would visit and tidy family graves. The Double Ninth Festival (9th day of the 9th month), or Ch'ung Yeung was one of these. It recalls how a man was saved from disaster by climbing to high ground on the advice of a sooth-sayer, whilst everything else perished. People climb to high places and fly kites but they also visit family graves.

A spectacular festival, called Miyazu Toro Nagahi is held in August in Japan in memory of the dead. Thousands of lanterns are set floating on the sea.

The Parsis in India have a special festival for remembering the dead at their dakhmas or Towers of Silence. Their dead are not buried or cremated but placed on the towers. Vultures eat the flesh, and the bones slide into pits of lime. The spirits of the dead—the *Fravashis**—return to God (*Ahura Mazda**) to help in the overthrow of evil. At this festival, *Farvardin*, names of kings, heroes and community leaders are recalled.

All Zoroastrians keep the last ten days of their year as *Farvardegan* Days*, when they remember the Fravashi, the divine essence of God in each man. They may offer gifts of sandalwood and incense to be burned in the Fire Temples. So each family honours the spirits of its own dead and asks them, and the fravashis of other righteous people, to give them protection (p. 128).

Grant unto us, O God, thankfulness for all who have lived good lives and set us an example to follow. Guide us by Your Spirit, so that we may ever walk in Your ways and do Your holy will.

Zoroastrian Fravashi symbol

Special remembrance (4)

FESTIVAL OF REMEMBRANCE

Each year, on the second Saturday in November, the Royal Albert Hall, in London, is filled with people who have gone to take part in the Festival of Remembrance. It is a moving occasion, with military music, hymns, prayers and a procession of flags carried by members of the Royal British Legion. The festival is held in memory of those people who died while serving in the two world wars, 1914 to 1918 and 1939 to 1945.

Among the company will be those who served in those wars, some proudly wearing the medals which they were awarded and others the badges of their particular regiment. They have come to remember their comrades, or perhaps members of their families, who died for their country.

On the following day, Remembrance Sunday, services are held at war memorials in towns and villages throughout Britain. The best known of these is the one held at the Cenotaph in Whitehall, London, at which the Queen and others lay wreaths in memory of the dead. Nearby, in the grounds of Westminster Abbey, are many plots, each for a particular regiment or branch of the armed forces, in which crosses with poppies are 'planted' in memory of individuals. Inside the Abbey, a wreath is placed on the tomb of the Unknown Warrior—an unknown soldier given the honour of burial in the Abbey as representative of all who died.

The two minutes silence at 11 a.m. gives an opportunity to remember those who died:

> They shall not grow old as we that are left grow old;
> Age shall not weary them nor the years condemn.
> At the going down of the sun and in the morning
>   We will remember them.

As time passes, there are less people to remember but we can be thankful that we have peace and freedom in our time—and the best way to show our thankfulness is to buy the poppies which are sold to help those who still suffer or are crippled as a result of war.

For freedom, peace and happiness, and for all who have helped us to have these things, especially those who gave their lives, we give You thanks, O Lord.

Special remembrance (5)

ALL SOULS' DAY

November 2nd is celebrated by the Christian Church as All Souls' Day—the day on which people remember the souls of all the faithful people who have departed this life, and offer prayers for them. The festival was first kept nearly a thousand years ago. A shipwrecked pilgrim was told by a hermit that the souls of the dead who had not yet gone to heaven were crying out because people were not praying enough for them. The pilgrim told Odile, Abbot of Cluny, who set aside the day after All Saints' Day (p. 125) as All Souls' Day.

Later, some people began to believe that, on that day, the souls of the dead actually came to visit their old homes and so they made special 'Soul cakes' from a light dough. They were round, flat, spiced and sweetened. On the previous day, some people went 'souling'—visiting houses, performing short plays, and asking for food, drink or money.

People have long believed that the living can help the souls of the dead (p. 121). They have also been concerned for the orphaned spirits who have no one to pray for them. The Romans used to have a time in May called Lemuria, when they fed the Lemures, the hungry spirits of the dead who had no relatives and were thought to haunt buildings.

There is also a Chinese Buddhist All Souls' Day, held each summer, to remember the spirits who have no descendants to pray for them and especially drowned people who have no resting place. At each temple a large paper 'boat of the law' is made and then ceremonially burned in the evening to help any wandering spirits across the sea of want, hunger, thirst and torment until they reach the final resting place—Nirvana*.

In Mexico, on all Souls' Eve, marigolds are placed on graves as they have been for many, many years. In Britain, and in many other lands, flowers may be laid on family graves on All Souls' Day and special prayers offered for the souls of those who are remembered with love and affection.

May the souls of the faithful, through the mercy of God, rest in peace.

Compline

ALL SAINTS   *Feast Days*

No doubt most people, if asked, could give the names of a number of saints. They might even be able to give the date upon which a few are especially remembered, the day which is known as the feast day. This is often, though not necessarily, the anniversary of the date on which the saint died.

But why are some people called saints? They are men and women whose lives have been very carefully examined because of great work they have done in the name of God. They are then *canonised* and may have a feast day. How many are there? The Roman Catholic Church lists over 4,500. A lot more are recognised by the Eastern Church, Coptic Church and others. And, of course, there are many who do not belong to these churches, who have done equally good work and may be considered saints, though not officially given that title.

Many of the lesser known saints do not have their own feast day and these are remembered each year on 1st November, the Christian festival of All Hallows, or All Saints' Day. On this day, thanks are given for the lives and witness of all holy men and women, known or unknown.

Originally this festival was kept on the first Sunday after Whitsun and it still is in the Eastern Church. The change in the Western Church took place when Pope Gregory III dedicated the Basilica of St. Peter in Rome to 'All the Saints'. The date was 1st November and that date was adopted as All Saints Day.

People entitled 'Saint' are those of the Christian religion. Other religions have their saints too. Hindus give the title *Sri** to holy people; Buddhists have *Bodhisattvas**; Jains have their 24 *Jinas** ('conquerors'); and Jews and Muslims have those who may not be called saint but have spent their lives in the faithful service of God.

On All Saints' Day we give thanks for the lives of all who have helped people to draw nearer to God.

We give You thanks, O God, for all the saints of all ages who have lived good lives, been loyal to their beliefs and worked untiringly to witness for their God. Grant us grace to follow their example.

Patron saints (1)

Patron saints are those who are believed to have a special interest in a particular place or group of people. The custom of having patron saints grew out of the old practice of building a church over the tomb of a saint, who could then be called upon to help the people who visited that church.

Nowadays there are many patron saints (pp. 128–9) but some are thought of as patron saints of a particular country and their feast day becomes a national day of celebration.

ENGLAND: *St. George's Day, April 23rd*

Stories about St. George were first brought to England by soldiers who returned from the Crusades at the end of the 11th Century. There were many romantic tales, especially the one of the way in which St. George killed a dragon, so saving the life of a princess. But it is only a story, first told long after George had died.

In fact we know little about George except that he was a soldier who remained true to his faith, though tortured and put to death on 23rd April, 303 CE.

His flag, the red cross on a white background, was the emblem of the Crusaders as they rode into battle. His day, 23rd April, is not celebrated with the same feeling as are those of the patron saints of Scotland, Wales and Ireland.

SCOTLAND: *St. Andrew's Day, November 30th*

St. Andrew was one of the disciples of Jesus, the brother of St. Peter, and had previously been a disciple of John the Baptist. He is said to have been crucified on an X-shaped cross, although this is doubtful, and this has become his symbol—a white cross on a blue background.

It is said that, long ago, the relics of St. Andrew were taken to Scotland by some monks to give them protection on their journey. At a later date, St. Andrews Cathedral was built over the place where the bones were laid.

The name Andrew means 'manly' and this is sometimes associated with the bravery of the Scots, often evident in times of danger. St. Andrew's Day is a time for celebration by Scots, not only in their homeland but wherever they happen to be.

WALES: *St. David's Day, March 1st*

The patron saint of Wales is Dewi or David, whose feast day is celebrated on 1st March. We know very little about his early life except that he lived in the far south-western corner of Wales in Dyfed, where the present cathedral city of St. Davids now stands.

During his lifetime he founded many churches and monasteries and it is also said that he went on a pilgrimage to Jerusalem. In time he became Archbishop of Menevia, now called St. Davids, and Primate of Wales. He not only led the church in Wales but was able to advise the Kings of Ireland.

Today, on St. David's Day, Welsh people everywhere show their pride in their country by wearing daffodils, and wearing or eating leeks, the national emblems of Wales.

IRELAND: *St. Patrick's Day, March 17th*

There are various stories told about the early life of the boy who was to become St. Patrick, the patron saint of Ireland. He was born late in the 4th Century CE and, as a teenager, was carried off to Ireland as a captive. He escaped to Gaul (France), from whence he returned home.

But, within himself, he knew he must return to Ireland to teach people there the Christian faith. He made his way to Tara, the home of Laoghaire*, the chief king. There he disobeyed the king's orders by lighting a huge fire on the eve of Easter, saying that he had come to light a fire in Ireland that would never be put out.

Later he was given land at Armagh, where he built a monastery and served as Bishop of Ireland. Today Irishmen are proud of their special saint and to wear the Shamrock, the emblem of St. Patrick and Ireland.

Most people are proud of their own country and all the things about it that they have learned to love and enjoy. National days, such as those of the patron saints, give an opportunity for them to express their feelings and show their loyalties.

We give You thanks, O God, for this land in which we live and for all the blessings that are ours. Keep us from doing anything that would spoil it or cause any offence to our fellow citizens.

Patron saints (2)

A long time ago, when people were unable to read and write, religion must have been very frightening, hence many of the strange customs and superstitions that arose. For some people, the only help they seemed to have was in the stained glass windows and statues depicting the saints. These were *real* people and many of them had suffered. If they had suffered, they would be able to understand the sufferings of others. Since they were already safe in heaven, no doubt they would be able to speak to God on behalf of people who prayed to them.

This, of course, is why many prayers are offered to St. Mary, the mother of Jesus. People who had particular problems looked for a saint who might be especially interested and he or she became the patron saint of that group of people. Most of these are so regarded to this day.

There are patron saints for almost every kind of illness. How did they come to be chosen? St. Apollonia, an early martyr of the Christian Church, had all her teeth knocked out. Who better to be the patron saint for those with toothache? And headaches? St. Denis, patron saint of France, had his head chopped off. Few headache sufferers would want a cure like that—but no doubt he would appreciate their sufferings. Others are: Skin disorders and contagious diseases—St. Roch (who caught the plague); Cripples—St. Giles (wounded whilst protecting a deer); Nervous ailments—St. Vitus; Stomach sufferers—St. Elmo; Throat sufferers—St. Blaise.

An interesting custom of Blessing the Throats is still kept on St. Blaise's Day (3rd February) in several churches. Two lighted candles are bound together in the form of a cross and held under the chins of sufferers. The priest touches their throats with the ribbon, says a short prayer and leaves the rest to St. Blaise.

There are saints who are thought to have a special interest in children, notably St. Nicholas and St. Ursula, but also St. Agnes and St. Pancras for those who are a little older. St. Catherine who did not marry is a natural choice for spinsters; St Valentine is renowned as the one for lovers; and St. Dorothy watches over betrothed couples. House hunters can call on St. Joseph, who found no room in Bethlehem!

All trades and professions also have their patron saints, again chosen because of their character or an incident in their life or martyrdom. Some groups of people have several patron saints, chosen for various reasons.

Who better to be the patron saint of postmen than St. Gabriel, the heavenly messenger? Carpenters naturally turn to St. Joseph, who was himself a carpenter. St. Sebastian was shot by archers and left for dead, so he has been adopted by archers, arrowsmiths and pinmakers—as well as by people suddenly struck by sharp pains.

Here are a few others: Air hostesses—St. Genevieve; Architects—St. Barbara; Artists—St. Luke; Bakers—St. Winifred or St. Honorius; Bookbinders—St. John; Booksellers—St. John of God; Brewers—St. Augustine of Hippo or St. Adrian; Butchers—St. Bartholomew; Carpet makers—St. Paul; Cooks—St. Lawrence; Dancers—St. Vitus; Dietitians —St. Martha; Drapers—St. Ursula; Dyers—St. Maurice; Fishermen—St. Peter; Gardeners—St. Fiacre; Goldsmiths and other metal workers—St. Dunstan; Gravediggers—St. Anthony; Hatters—St. William; Hunters—St. Hubert; Librarians—St. Jerome; Masons—St. Thomas; Miners—St. Kieran; Musicians—St. Cecelia; Nurses—St. Agatha; Painters—St. Luke; Physicians—St. Luke; Policemen—St. Michael; Sailors—St. Christopher, St. Nicholas, St. Elmo and others; Shoemakers—St. Crispin; Soldiers—St. George, St. Michael and others; Students—St. Jerome, St. Lawrence and others; Tax collectors—St. Matthew; Wine growers—St. Vincent, Woolcombers—St. Blaise.

[A brief look at the life of the saint will reveal why he or she was adopted and could make an interesting study.]

There are also patron saints for those engaged in sports or various leisure activities, such as St. Bernard for mountaineers. Prisoners can invoke the aid of St. Leonard and those who feel desperate, St. Jude, the patron saint of lost causes. St. Francis is regarded as the patron saint of all animals and birds but St. Blaise is also a patron saint of wild animals, and other saints, too, have a care for wild life.

Almighty and everlasting God, who dost enkindle the flame of Thy love in the hearts of the saints, grant to our minds the same faith and power of love; that as we rejoice in their triumphs, we may profit by their examples; through Jesus Christ our Lord.

Gothic Missal

Wakes and fairs (1)

Most parish churches are dedicated in the name of a particular saint, so we often hear them described as St. Mary's Church, or St. Ann's or St. Peter's. This arose from the custom of building a church over the relics of a saint—but this is true of few churches today. The saint to whom the church is dedicated is the patron saint.

Each year, on the Sunday nearest to that saint's feast day, there is a patronal festival or Wake Sunday. The name wake comes from the ancient custom of holding an all-night vigil before the festival. It was usually a night of prayer followed by the Eucharist. The festival used to be held on the actual feast day and, if a weekday, it was natural that people would not be expected to work after being awake all night. The following day was a public holiday. Stalls were set up in the churchyard for buying and selling. There was food and drink and lots of fun. The word wake came, later, to refer to the feasting and merry-making on the holy day itself and then to the fair held annually on that day.

In the north of England especially, the wake became extended to a week or weeks of public holiday, shared by everyone, when all the local factories closed down.

But here and there the old customs survive. At Marhamchurch, Cornwall, the Sunday following St. Marwenne's Day (12th August) is Revel Sunday. On the Monday, the 'Queen of the Revel' is crowned and there is entertainment for all, with fancy dresses, gymnastic displays, Cornish wrestling, races, dancing, side-shows and refreshments.

By contrast, on a more sober note, Wakes Sunday is celebrated at Eyam, Derbyshire (last Sunday in August) with a special service commemorating the villagers' self sacrifice in preventing a plague from spreading from their village. It was at this time, in 1665, that the first people in the village became ill. It is a proud memory for the village and a cause for thanksgiving.

Thou hast given so much to us, give us one thing more, a grateful heart; for Christ's sake.

George Herbert (1593–1633)

Wakes and fairs (2)

FAIRS

A fair may not be regarded as a festival or even as a celebration in itself, yet a fun fair is often included as a major part of the festivities on such occasions. When the Festival of Britain was held, in 1951, a large fun-fair was set up in Battersea Park but, long before that, fairs developed from local celebrations such as the revels which followed the wakes. One of the most famous of the present-day fairs is St. Giles' Fair at Oxford, which grew from the annual wake of Walton Parish.

Fairs, such as these, were formerly more correctly known as wakes or feasts. The term fair was reserved for the great charter fairs which were primarily for business and could be held only on receipt of a royal charter. Mingling with the traders were the entertainers, who provided the fun of the fair. For people with little opportunity for escape from a hard, boring life, as it was in those days, any fair or wake was a welcome festivity.

Over the years, the fortunes and pattern of fairs has changed considerably. One of the most famous charter fairs, at St. Ives, Cambridgeshire, once lasted for 40 days, from Easter to Whitsun: now it is a one-day market. Some fairs were mainly for the sale of one commodity. At Nottingham Goose Fair in the Middle Ages, 20,000 geese might be sold: now it is just a fun fair.

But there are still fairs at which animals are sold. In Devon, Widecombe Fair, made famous by the song, exists for the sale of Dartmoor ponies and sheep. There are several famous horse fairs, one of the larger ones being at Appleby, Cumbria, where as many as 1,000 gipsy caravans may be seen on Fair Hill for one of their special events of the year. There are other specialised fairs, such as a Pot Fair at Cambridge and a Cheese Fair at Frome.

Many autumn fairs were once statute fairs, known also as hiring or mop fairs (p. 68), at which labourers or servants would be hired but now, like most of the other fairs, they are mainly fun-fairs, with rides and sideshows, bright lights and music, candy-floss and hot-dogs, which all add up to provide a pleasant, carefree time of relaxation and amusement.

Amid the busy-ness of everyday, O God, enable us to 'switch off' from time to time and enjoy our times of relaxation and opportunities for amusement.

Pageantry and processions (1)

PAGEANTRY

There are few things more likely to attract great crowds of people than spectacular displays of pageantry processing through the streets and filling the town with a blaze of colour. Often the music of the bands stirs the emotions as much as the precision with which everything is done and the sheer magnitude of the whole spectacle.

Such pageantry is nothing new. In the ancient world the great triumphal processions of conquering heroes were crowd-drawing occasions. Today some of the greatest displays of pageantry are those concerned with royal or state occasions (pp. 160–5). There are happy festivities as at coronations, jubilees and royal weddings; and there are sad occasions, such as state funerals, with pageantry of a different kind.

The pageantry is not limited, of course, to the outdoor processions. Inside the buildings, such as Westminster Abbey, where ceremonies are held, there is a wealth of colour to be seen in the ceremonial dress of royalty, nobility and clergy with all their attendants, providing a spectacle, the like of which can be seen in few other countries.

On such occasions, the Queen wears her magnificent robes of state and her gold crown studded with jewels. Peers of the realm are there with red robes trimmed with ermine. Members of Orders of Knighthood wear their fine robes and insignia of their Order. The Kings of Arms with their Pursuivants and Heralds are resplendent in their brightly-coloured heraldic tabards. High ranking officers of Army, Navy and Air Force wear full dress uniform bedecked with their awards and medals. And there are many others besides.

Behind the pageantry is a great amount of history. Much that we enjoy began hundreds of years ago when the world was very different from the world we know today. There are some who say it is no longer necessary but most people enjoy the pageantry and the reminder that it gives of our great heritage of freedom and a way of life that is dependable.

Thank you, O God, for our heritage and the freedom of our way of life. May we do our part to maintain all that we consider to be of value in our changing world.

Pageantry and processions (2)

A parade is an opportunity to show off or to draw attention to oneself and there may be all sorts of reasons for doing this. We are familiar with military parades, in which soldiers or members of the other armed forces march through the streets. Often this forms a part of a ceremonial occasion (pp. 160–5) but such parades are also used as a show of strength when a government or conquering nation considers it necessary.

There are various occasions during the year when certain groups of people like to parade—old soldiers on Remembrance Sunday; Scouts on their annual parade to church on or near St. George's Day; and other uniformed youth organizations at their church parades or special celebrations.

Some parades are held to mark a historical event. On July 12th, in Ulster, in large towns such as Belfast, Londonderry and Omagh, there are large parades with bands playing and banners flying as the Orangemen, the members of the Grand Orange Lodges, celebrate a victory at the Battle of the Boyne in 1691.

A different kind of parade is the Easter Parade, held in Battersea Park, London, at 3 p.m. on Easter Sunday. It has no religious, superstitious or military significance. It began in 1829, when a dual was to be fought on Battersea Fields. Society ladies and gentlemen arrived, dressed in their latest fashions. Each year afterwards they met there. Then, in 1858, Queen Victoria herself visited in a new bonnet and dress. So began the Easter Parade a fashion parade with people trying to outdo one another in their elegant fashions. Nowadays it is a kind of carnival (p. 136) with ornamental floats, bands, clowns and even wild animals from a safari park. Easter Parades are also held in America, two of the most famous being in Atlantic City and New York City.

The Annual Harness Horse Parade in Regents Park, London, on Easter Monday, is an opportunity for people to display, and for others to admire, well cared-for horses and equipment.

Sometimes, O God, we like to make a special display of our work and achievements. Keep us humble, remembering that all our abilities are a gift from You.

Pageantry and processions (3)

Each year, on the second Saturday in November, traffic is brought to a halt in some City of London streets for the Lord Mayor's Show, a mile-long procession which introduces the new Lord Mayor to the citizens of London.

The origin of the Lord Mayor's Show dates back to 1215, the year of the signing of the Magna Carta. It was agreed that London should have all its old free customs but on condition that the man elected to be the chief citizen should present himself to the King for royal approval before taking office.

So each new mayor made his way to Westminster on horseback, accompanied by one or two of his officers and a band of citizens, partly to give him support and partly to protect him once he had left the City of London. He travelled thus until 1711 when there was an unfortunate incident in which the new Lord Mayor was thrown from his horse. The citizens decided that their Lord Mayor should have a coach. A second coach, built in 1757, was used until 1896, when a replica was built. It is the one still used today—a magnificent gold coach with elaborate carvings, painted panels and chariot-like wheels, but a most uncomfortable means of travel: it has no springs.

Each year, the new Lord Mayor chooses a theme for his procession. Lorries and floats are decorated, bands play and the Lord Mayor in his coach, flanked by his guard of pikemen, gives the final touch to a colourful pageant.

The Lord Mayor goes first to the Law Courts in The Strand to take the oath before the Lord Chief Justice. The procession then passes through as many wards of the City as can be arranged. In the evening there is a magnificent banquet at the Guildhall, normally attended by many important people including the Prime Minister and the Archbishop of Canterbury. The Lord Mayor of London is a very important person and the Show is one of the highlights of London's pageantry.

Lord, bless our leaders and all who are in positions of authority, that they may carry out their duties wisely in the service and interests of the community.

Pageantry and processions (4)

An important aspect of many festivals and celebrations is the procession through the streets often of spectacular proportions. The great pilgrim and temple festivals of India, when the temple images are taken for bathing (p. 101), are a typical example.

The Japanese, too, enjoy the pageantry of the processions at some of their great festivals. In some, huge floats are drawn through the streets: in others a large palanquin, a portable shrine on long poles, is carried on the shoulders of many bearers. The shrine is the home of the spirit of the local god.

One of the most spectacular of these processions is held at Kyoto, the old capital of Japan, on the occasion of the Hollyhock Festival (p. 138). Huge four-wheeled floats with masts that are 130 ft (39.6 m) high, are accompanied by horsemen and halbardiers, soldiers and priests, dressed as they would have been one thousand years ago when the festival was first held. Another show of pageantry of similar proportion is that at the Gion festival in mid-July, commemorating an appeal made to the gods, over a thousand years ago, for protection from plague.

On a much smaller scale, but none the less interesting, are some of the processions that form a part of local customs and festivals. One of these is the winter celebration of Up-Helly-A', held on the last Tuesday in January at Lerwick, the capital of Shetland. It is a custom handed down from the Norsemen who once lived there and is probably based on sacrifices to the Sun-god (p. 58) as well as the burning of a dead chieftain's boat with his body inside.

A model of a longboat, about 10 metres long, is built complete with a dragon head and shields lining the sides. After dark it is drawn to the seashore at the head of a procession of blazing torches. Bands play and rockets are let off. After singing 'The Norseman's Home', the torches are thrown into the boat which goes up in flames.

Many of the most spectacular processions are those which began as, or still are, part of an offering to God—and an offering worthy of making.

Nothing, O God, is too good to offer to You. Help us never to give less than our best.

Pageantry and processions (5)

Many towns, especially those by the sea, have a carnival week when the town goes gay. Flags and bunting are hung from one side of the street to the other, strings of coloured lights and other decorations festoon the promenade, and many forms of entertainment take place. The climax of the week is the carnival procession with its colourful floats, followed, maybe, by a grand firework display.

Carnivals such as these are usually held at the height of summer when there are many holiday-makers to enjoy them. British weather, of course, has much to do with it too. One of the largest carnivals held regularly in Britain in recent years is the West Indian carnival held at Notting Hill, London, at the end of August. Similar in many ways to the Caribbean Mardi Gras carnivals (p. 137), it is held at this time of the year in preference to February.

The name Carnival comes from the Mardi Gras celebrations. It means going without meat—which is what people had to do in Lent. Nowadays carnivals have no religious meaning and they are not truly festivals, but they are times to celebrate and really enjoy oneself.

Carnivals of many kinds are to be found throughout the world. Many of the eastern festivals, such as Holi (p. 49) and Dashara* (p. 106), as well as the temple festivals, have a carnival-like atmosphere at times. So do some of the celebrations held by the Chinese communities and in Japan.

Carnival processions often form a part of a more general celebration. A town which has a regatta week may end it with a carnival and firework display. Towns, which do not normally have carnivals, sometimes plan them as part of the festivities of a big royal or national occasion or some outstanding local celebration.

Whatever the reason, most people enjoy a carnival—and not just those who take part or watch. Often those who participate collect money for charities to help people in need.

Help us, O God, in all our enjoyments to be thoughtful for the feelings of those around us and mindful of the needs of those less fortunate than ourselves.

Pageantry and processions (6)

MARDI GRAS

Some of the most colourful carnivals in the Western world are those associated with Mardi Gras ('Fat Tuesday'), the day before Lent begins. The custom began with the parading of a fat ox through the streets of Paris on Shrove Tuesday and it developed into a noisy, colourful procession with many opportunities to have a last fling before the forty-day fast began.

Mardi Gras carnivals were introduced to America by the French colonists in 1766. The most famous ones are those held in New Orleans, where the street parades begin about two weeks before Mardi Gras. They are organised by societies or krewes and the king of the Rex krewe leads the procession of several hundred floats. People wearing huge papier maché heads join the procession of colourful tableaux from which riders in bright costumes toss sweets, toys and imitation coins to the crowds lining the streets.

Throughout the Caribbean, carnivals are popular. In some places, such as Haiti, where Christian and African traditions merge, the carnival season lasts from 6th January (Twelfth Night) until Shrove Tuesday. In Trinidad, too, at least all of this time will have been spent preparing for the event, which has been described as 'a madness of colour and throbbing rhythm', which begins at 5 a.m. on the Monday and ends at midnight on Shrove Tuesday.

As many as a couple of hundred people may form one of the bands that present one of the themes of the carnival. Costumes are a pageant of colour and the music of the steel bands echoes everywhere. Carnival here is a mixture of the old Mardi Gras traditions of Europe, the masked characters of Africa, the pageantry and masquerade of slave festivities and the contributions of those from Asia. Singing, dancing, calypso, a festival of arts and all sorts of other activities, combine to make this a happy, carefree festival.

For carnivals of pageantry, costume and colour;
For music and dancing, gaiety and laughter;
And for pleasures of preparation and working with others;
Thank you, God.

Flowers (1)

Many towns and villages have an annual flower festival, at which people like to display their finest blooms and flower arrangements. Some attract visitors from a distance to enjoy the colour and fragrance.

Flower festivals are nothing new. One of the most famous of the old Roman festivals was Floralia, held in honour of Flora, the goddess of flowers. The ancient Chinese, too, had a festival for the goddess of flowers. It became the custom for women to make floral head-dresses to wear at the festival and for children to make their own 'flowers' from paper and silk.

One of the great Japanese festivals is the Hollyhock Festival at Kyoto, the old capital of Japan. Each year, on 15th May, hollyhocks are offered to the gods at two Shinto shrines and there are processions through the streets. The festival was first held about a thousand years ago as an offering to the gods at a time when bad weather was devastating the crops. It has been held ever since.

Not surprisingly, the Japanese, with their love of flowers, have other flower festivals too, such as the Cherry Blossom festival in springtime, when special dances are performed in theatres in Kyoto and Tokyo. Many other countries have flower festivals at the time when certain blossoms are at their best. There are other kinds of festival, such as the well dressings of Derbyshire (p. 143), which arose from a desire to give thanks. And what better way to do so than to 'say it with flowers'.

This is, in fact, what lies behind the flower festivals which are held in churches in many parts of the country. Just as people offer their harvest gifts, so they bring their finest flowers to offer to God as a means of saying thank you for so much beauty. And after the festival the flowers are often given to elderly or sick folk to bring a little brightness into their lives.

All around us, O God, the flowers remind us of the beauty of our world and the wonders of Your creation. Help us to show our thanks by using Your gifts to bring brightness and joy into the lives of others.

Flowers (2)

FLOWER PARADES AND CARNIVALS

Long ago, people discovered that flowers made colourful decorations for any pageant or procession. Sometimes they were given a very special place. One of the greatest of Europe's Mardi Gras Carnivals (p. 137) is the one at Nice, which lasts for twelve days. In the great procession there are many floats and a battle of flowers.

Nowadays the biggest carnival of flowers in Europe is the Jersey Battle of Flowers, held on the last Thursday in July. First held at the time of the coronation of Edward VII, in 1902, it is now enjoyed by thousands of visitors. The procession of huge floats, decorated with millions of flowers, makes its way through St. Helier before the actual Battle of Flowers, for which the flowers have had removed from them anything harmful. Petals are dropped from helicopters too.

Processions and battles of flowers are popular in Italy and in other lands. Holland, known as the 'land of flowers', has its great summer flower pageants at cities such as Rotterdam, The Hague, Leiden and Leersum. One of the greatest parades, popular with visitors at 'tulip time', is the spring Flower Parade with its beautiful floats. Held at the end of April, it processes through the bulb district from Haarlem to Noord-wijk.

The most spectacular event of this kind in Britain is the Spalding Flower Parade, held in May in the bulb-growing area of Lincolnshire. Many bands take part in the parade, which has some twenty floats covered in tulips. It takes almost a year to build the steel frameworks and make the straw mats into which the fresh tulip heads are pinned. These heads are a 'waste product' of the bulb growing industry but help provide a tourist attraction which gives a lot of pleasure to many people.

At many flower parades and festivals the joy given to spectators is shared with others, for the opportunity may be taken to raise money for charitable purposes.

Help us, O Lord, to enjoy the beauty of the flowers and all of creation. May we be mindful of those less fortunate than ourselves and share our joys with them.

Flowers (3)

Many people in summer time like to walk in flower gardens and ornamental parks, where they can enjoy the sea of colour provided by masses of flowers in bloom. Gardeners remove one set of bedding plants as the blooms are fading and replace them with others so that there is a continuous show, changing with the seasons.

Some of the most colourful displays are to be seen in the tulip fields in spring time. The main purpose of growing tulips is to produce the bulbs for people to plant in their gardens or in pots but the flowers make a lovely display during April and May. Holland attracts many visitors in spring, especially to visit Keukenhof, the world's largest flower garden with 70 acres (28.3 hectares) of brightly coloured flowers, and to see the famous Franz Roozen Tulip Show.

Holland is not only famous for its tulips but for other flowers too. There is the Lilliade Flower Show (mostly lilies) at Akersloot, the Rose Show at The Hague and the 'Delta Flora' Gladioli Show in Stellendam.

In Britain, the most famous flower show is the Chelsea Flower Show, staged by the Royal Horticultural Society in the grounds of the Royal Hospital, Chelsea. The Great Spring Show (its official title) has been held since 1913 except during the war years and is attended now by nearly a quarter of a million people during four days toward the end of May.

The Great Marquee is filled with flowers of almost every season, including new varieties. Outside there are colourful patios and rock gardens. There are Floristry Displays and Flower Arrangements as well as exhibitions of furnishings and equipment.

On a much smaller scale, Horticultural Shows are held in most towns by local societies to exhibit the choicest blooms and finest plants. And, of course, there are few brighter displays of flowers in churches than on Easter Sunday, the happiest of all Christian festivals.

As we take pleasure, O Lord, in the beautiful flowers that brighten our world, help us to remember that they are but one of Your great gifts to us.

Flowers (4)

FLOWER ARRANGING   *Ikebana*

Flowers are used for decorative purposes at many festivals and celebrations. No wedding would seem complete without the bouquets and the table decorations. A church would seem very bare without some flowers somewhere, as it does on Good Friday. For special days such as Easter (p. 140), the church may have many such decorations.

These flowers are not just put into vases and spread higgledy-piggledy around the church. They are carefully arranged in the vases or other containers, which are then placed where they will give the best possible effect. Some people have a gift for being able to arrange flowers in attractive decorative shapes and lovely blends of colour.

The art of flower arranging is one that has been learned from the Japanese, who gave it the name *Ikebana*, meaning 'keeping flowers alive'. It came originally from Buddhist worship, in which flowers, and especially the lotus, were offered as a gift to the Buddha. The main room of the house always had a *tokonoma*, or recess, for an image of the Buddha or perhaps a picture with a few flowers.

Ikebana is a symbolic three-dimensional arrangement, always having levels representing Heaven (*Shin*), Man (*Soe*) and Earth (*Hikae*). Modern Ikebana makes use not only of flowers but reeds, twigs, branches, cane and other materials, to make an attractive arrangement.

There are many modern forms of flower arranging, using various kinds of container, wires and supports. A tall display may have tiers of water containers on a pedestal, all hidden by the flowers. Displays often match the occasion or season. White lilies and spring flowers are an obvious choice for Easter. At other times flowers may blend with the Church Liturgical Colours. Posies in pews and strategically placed cushions of flowers give an overall sense of colour and beauty. In fact flowers grace any place of worship, whether they are part of a festival or a simple arrangement in a vase or jar for the Sunday services in a village chapel.

Thank you, God, for the beauty of flowers, the art of arranging them, and the joy they give.

Water and the sea (1)

When on holiday, you may perhaps have come upon a wishing well or a fountain into which people have tossed coins. Perhaps you have done the same, 'just for luck', and have made your own wish.

If so, you have done what people have been doing for thousands of years, except that, for people of the past, it was a much more serious matter than it is today. They depended very much on water, just as we do, but they believed that all water was the home of spirits that needed to be pleased if the water supply were to continue.

Gifts dropped into the wells may not have been coins but bent pins, white stones, broken pottery and even human heads. In ancient Rome, wells were decorated at the festival of Fontinalia and flowers thrown into the water.

In Britain, long ago, many offerings were made to the Celtic goddesses Anu and Brigantia. The Christian Church, anxious to turn people away from ancient beliefs, dedicated wells to St. Anne instead of Anu and St. Bride or Bridget in place of Brigantia. Some became Holy Wells and festivals or annual celebrations were held at them on St. Ann's Day, 26th July, and St. Bride's Day, 1st February, which was the ancient Celtic Spring Festival.

It was believed that rivers, too, had their gods that needed a sacrifice. An old rhyme about the River Dart goes:

> Dart, Dart, cruel Dart,
> Every year thou claimst a heart.

The belief in water gods was common in the Middle East. Some rivers, if not regarded as gods, were sacred (p. 144). Gifts were made to the gods of river and sea.

Parsis, who regarded water not as the home of a god but as one of the sacred elements, have a festival of water in April, when coconuts, sugar and flowers are thrown into the sea, river, lake or pond as an offering.

Whatever our beliefs, water is precious.

O God, to whom love and kindness are more important than sacrifice, grant that these may be our offerings in thankfulness for all Your good gifts.

Water and the sea (2)

WELL DRESSING

In the summer months, many tourists make their way to certain Derbyshire villages to admire the beautiful well-dressings. Perhaps the most famous of these villages is Tissington, where there are five wells, all elaborately decorated for the festival which is held annually on Ascension Day.

The custom goes back to 1350, the year after the Black Death had swept through the country, wiping out large numbers of people. The villagers of Tissington survived because their water had not become contaminated. To show their thankfulness, they made posies or garlands of flowers, which were then tossed into the wells. Years later, in 1615, there was a severe drought. Many wells dried up, but not those of Tissington. Again the villagers were thankful.

The present custom of decorating the wells instead of throwing flowers into them dates from 1818, when pictures were made from flower petals. Many of these well-dressings are very elaborate. There is the main board with its picture, perhaps set within a larger framework or arch. The picture itself usually portrays a story from the Bible, maybe with a brief text.

Well-dressing is the work of a skilled team of people, who take great pride in their handiwork. To make the picture they fill a framed board with clay into which they press any natural objects such as flowers, moss, bark, leaves, cones, stones or feathers. Man-made substances such as glass and plastic are not allowed.

On Ascension Day the villagers assemble at the church for a service before processing to bless each of the five wells – reminiscent of other Rogationtide processions (p. 56). Well dressing is carried out in other villages too, mainly in June and August, some during the local Wakes Week. (p. 130).

Prayer offered at each Tissington well:
May the blessing of God Almighty, the Father, the Son, and the Holy Ghost, be upon these wells and those who use them and care for them, now and for evermore.

Water and the sea (3)

HOLY AND HEALING WATERS

When people of long ago made gifts to the spirits of the waters, it was not always just to ensure a continuing supply. There were interesting beliefs associated with many wells. Some were believed to give healing or special powers to the first to drink from them in the New Year. Some came to be regarded as holy wells because they were used regularly by a holy man who lived nearby. Children who were ill were sometimes dipped in these wells.

Healing waters exist in many parts of the world. In the Bible we can read of the Pool of Bethesda, beside which people waited for the waters to be troubled (*John 5; 1–8*). Probably the most famous of present day healing waters is the spring at Lourdes, France. Since 1858, when Bernadette Soubirous had her visions of the Virgin Mary and a spring appeared nearby, miraculous healings are reported to have taken place. Lourdes, today is a place of pilgrimage to which thousands go each year to seek healing for themselves or to get water to take home for others.

Rivers, too, are regarded by many people as places for healing, cleansing and purification. In the Bible we read how a sick man was cured after bathing in the River Jordan (*2 Kings 5; 1–19*). The same river was used by John the Baptist to baptise people and so cleanse them in a symbolic way (*Mark 1; 1–11*). Water is symbolic of spiritual cleansing to people of many faiths.

Undoubtedly the river that is held in veneration by the greatest number of people is the Ganges, in India. Regarded as a goddess, daughter of the Himalayas, it is said to have absolutely pure water which will give cleansing to all who enter it anywhere along its 1500 kilometre course. Temples line its banks, with *ghats* (steps) from which pilgrims bathe, the most famous being at the holy city of Varanasi[*] (Benares).

Many festivals are associated with holy waters.

Be merciful to me, O God, because of Your constant love . . . wash away all my evil and make me clean from my sin.

(Psalm 51; 1–2)

Water and the sea (4)

Rain dances and festivals

Most of us are probably more used to hoping for a fine day than praying for a wet one. Normally we get enough rain to provide water for all our needs. It is only in times of drought that water supplies run low and farmers begin to wish for rain.

It is difficult for us to imagine what it is like to live in a land where it seldom rains and where people sometimes have to dig deep into the ground to find water. We can understand why people in such lands in the past developed all sorts of ceremonies to ask God (or the gods) for rain.

In modern Israel, there are special ceremonies on the 8th day of Sukkoth*, when people gather at a spring, where they dance and sing songs about water. It is a reminder of an ancient ceremony held on this day because the Rabbis said that this was the time when God decided how much rain would fall during the coming year.

On this day people used to go in procession to a nearby spring, where they drew water in golden pitchers and poured it over the temple altar. Lamps were lit in the courtyard, the shofar* (ram's horn) was blown and people sang and danced all night.

On the other side of the world, in the deserts of Arizona, the Indians had their own ceremonials. Cactus juice was gathered in jars by the women and left for two nights while men and women danced around the jars singing songs about the rain. Then they drank the juice, believing that as they filled themselves with juice so the earth would be filled with rain.

There are many interesting rain dances. The Hopi Indians, for example, have a snake dance, at the end of which snakes are released to ask the rain god to send rain. In many ways and through many prayers, people ask God to provide that most necessary of all commodities—fresh, cooling, life-giving water.

O Lord our God, grant us water enough for our daily needs and a never ending supply of the water of life to satisfy our thirsty spirits.

Water and the sea (5)

GARLANDS FOR THE GODS

If you visit the seaside, it is probably not long before you have thrown a few stones into the sea . . . or maybe played 'Ducks and Drakes' by bouncing flat stones across the waves. It is good fun as long as no-one is hurt. If so there will be trouble!

In the past, in some places, there certainly would have been trouble – not because of hurting someone but because it was thought to anger the spirits of the sea, who might then cause a flood or some other disaster. In ancient times, people were so anxious to please these spirits or gods that they even drowned people as a sacrifice.

Later, it became the custom to offer other gifts instead. In many parts of the world today there are ceremonies in which garlands of flowers or other presents are cast onto the sea.

At Abbotsbury, Dorset, Garland Day is held each year. Children make garlands of flowers which are carried round the village before being placed on the War Memorial in the church-yard. The making of the garlands is a custom that may be a thousand years old. Then, these garlands were made at the beginning of the mackerel fishing season and cast onto the sea to seek the blessing of the gods for the harvest of the sea and the safety of the fishermen.

In later years, when the fishing industry in Abbotsbury declined, the children took their garlands to the church for a special service. The old pagan festival became Christian, for, when the garlands were taken to sea, they were dropped overboard with a hymn and a prayer.

Whatever else their beliefs may be, there are many people who have recognised the vastness of the oceans and the power of the sea. Like the Breton fisherman, they have also realised their need of God.

> *Breton fisherman's prayer*:
> Protect me, O Lord;
> My boat is so small
> And your sea is so large.

Water and the sea (6)

SEA FESTIVALS

Many people who live near the sea, or make a living from the sea, have their own festivals or ceremonies.

Some may commemorate events of the past. The Chinese, for example have a Dragon Boat Festival. In the 3rd Century BCE, a national hero drowned himself in protest against a bad government. The story tells how a kind of dumpling was thrown into the water to feed the fish and the water was beaten to scare the fish so that his body would not be eaten. Today, long, brightly-coloured boats, with dragon heads and tails, race each other with a great deal of noise and splashing, symbolising attempts to rescue their hero.

Racing in boats is quite common around our coasts, particularly yacht racing. Many resorts have their regatta week, in which there may be festivities ashore as well as at sea, perhaps with a firework display or carnival events.

In many fishing ports, there are religious ceremonies of 'Blessing the Boats' or 'Blessing the Waters'. These have their origins in ancient offerings to the gods of the sea (p. 146) and in the Rogationtide ceremonies (p. 56). They are usually held at the beginning of the main fishing season.

In Hastings, Sussex, the custom of blessing the sea is held on or about 26th May. In the evening, a procession wends its way from two churches to the fish market, where the bishop blesses the fishermen and offers prayers. At Whitby there is a service on the quay. At Southampton prayers are offered on the quay and also from a boat as they are in other ports, too.

Later in the year come thanksgiving ceremonies – special ones such as the Whitebait Festival at Southend, Essex, or Harvest of the Sea Festivals held in churches (p. 66) in thankfulness for blessings received.

> *From the Manx Fishermen's Evening Hymn*
> Thou, Lord dost rule the raging of the sea,
> When loud the storm and furious is the gale:
> Strong is Thine arm; our little barques are frail:
> Send us Thy help; remember Galilee.
> *W. H. Gill (1839–1923)*

Music, dancing and culture (1)

EISTEDDFOD, FEIS AND MOD

One of the greatest cultural gatherings in Britain is the Royal National Eisteddfod of Wales, which is held each year in August. It is a festival that has its roots and traditions in ancient times. The ancient Celts had, among their many gods, Ogma, the 'Son of Knowledge', god of poetry and eloquence, who was honoured by the bards.

Today's Eisteddfod, with its Druids and bards, its stone circle and altar, echoes the ancient customs and it is a festival of poetry, music and eloquence with competitions for the coveted bardic crown and chair.

Alternating between sites in North Wales and South Wales, the Eisteddfod attracts thousands of people, who enjoy this great festival of Welsh poetry, singing and culture, all, naturally, in the Welsh language. There are local eisteddfodau too.

The Irish have a similar kind of cultural festival called a Feis*. Originally a Celtic parliament of kings and lords, it met at Tara every third year. Today it is held in different parts of Ireland. Like the Welsh eisteddfod, it is a festival of poetry, music, dancing and ballet, with an emphasis on traditional Irish folk dancing such as lively reels and jigs.

The Highlanders of Scotland have their arts festival called a Mod. This, too, is held annually in different towns in Scotland. It is the Annual Assembly of An Comunn Gaidhealach*, which was founded in 1891 to preserve the Gaelic traditions of the Scots. It is a feast of music, singing and poetry, conducted, as would be imagined, in Gaelic – but it is also an opportunity to promote Scottish Gaelic folk art, crafts and industry.

There is a danger in the modern world for old ways and lore to be lost but it is largely due to societies of many kinds that, far from being lost, such things are interesting more and more people. The Eisteddfod, Feis and Mod are but three of many.

For all that has been handed down to us – a feast of literature, music, crafts, dances, national traditions and customs – we give You thanks, O God.

Music, dancing and culture (2)

Culture is something that never stands still. Many of the arts which we enjoy are those which have been handed down to us from the past but we are continually adding the new creations of artists, writers and composers, the best of which will become part of tomorrow's culture.

People in many parts of the world, as part of their cultural celebrations, have competitions for writing poetry or music. The highest honours of the Welsh Eisteddfod are for writing poetry. In similar vein, the Sikhs have a poetry competition as part of a great festival in June commemorating the death of Maharajah Ranjit Singh.

There are Japanese festivals concerned with culture. Sekiten, on 25th April, is a festival to acknowledge how much Japanese culture owes to the teachings of Confucius. The Bunka-no-hi Culture Day, on 3rd November, is a national holiday, when all government offices and schools close. Its aim is to promote reading and all forms of culture. There are contests arranged by publishers as part of the festival.

In many of the ancient religions and cultures there was one particular god or goddess with especial oversight of crafts, music or learning. The Algonquin Indians of North America had a god of crafts called Manabusch (Big Rabbit). The Hindus look to Sarasvati*, regarded as the wife of Brahma*, the Creator, as the patroness of literature, music and learning.

The festival for Sarasvati is Sarasvati Puja, the date of which varies from one part of India to another. At this festival she is worshipped together with the sacred books of the house. Symbols of learning may be placed before her image, in which she is usually depicted as a cultured lady. Prayers are especially offered by students who are about to take examinations and honours are paid by writers and composers.

Culture and learning, books and music are things often taken for granted but for which we should be thankful.

O God, we have so much for which to be thankful. As we think of our cultural heritage of books, music and all arts, we give thanks for these and all who gave them to us.

Music, dancing and culture (3)

Edinburgh has many tourist attractions. Not only is it the capital of Scotland but it is a city steeped in history with many buildings of interest. In recent years it has had another claim to fame as the centre of one of the greatest Festivals of the Arts in the world.

The Edinburgh International Festival of Music and Drama was first held in 1947 and soon became very popular. For three weeks, at the end of August and beginning of September, there are performances of music of many kinds, orchestral concerts, opera, ballet and drama. The festival includes the military searchlight tattoo on the Esplanade of the castle (p. 161). Music and arts festivals are held in other cities of Europe, Salzburg in Austria being one, but the Edinburgh Festival is probably now the greatest, visited by people from many parts of the world, who not only enjoy the special performances but take the opportunity to visit museums and art galleries too.

Aldeburgh in Suffolk has few of the advantages of Edinburgh. It is a very small town, off the main road, with few tourist attractions, yet it, too, becomes a centre for the arts and music when the Aldeburgh Festival is held each June. People come from far and near to take part in or enjoy the various performances.

The Aldeburgh Festival was first held in 1948, having been planned by one of Britain's best known modern musicians, Benjamin Britten, and his friend, Peter Pears. It was in the church at Aldeburgh that Britten was inspired to write *Noyes Fludde*, a medieval Chester Miracle Play (p. 97) set to music and making use of comedy and drama.

But music festivals do not need to be internationally famous to be appreciated. Many towns have their Arts Week or Festivals of Music which give a great deal of enjoyment to many.

Thank you, dear God, for all those things which we can enjoy, especially for music and drama of so many different kinds: and thank you for all who help bring us these pleasures.

Music, dancing and culture (4)

PLAYWRIGHT AND POET   *Shakespeare and Burns*

There are some writers, poets and playwrights whose names are immortal. As one might expect, there are festivals held in their honour, at which people celebrate, in various ways, the person concerned, with special performances of his works.

For people throughout the world, one of the greatest playwrights is William Shakespeare, the 'Bard of Avon', born at Stratford-on-Avon in 1564 CE. There are 'seasons' for Shakespeare's plays in theatres in many places but at Stratford-on-Avon there is an annual Shakespeare Festival when his plays are performed in the Shakespeare Memorial Theatre. People from many parts of the world visit Stratford to enjoy this festival.

One of the greatest celebrations to commemorate a particular poet is Burns' Night, celebrated by Scots throughout the world on 25th January, the birthday of Robert Burns, in 1759. These celebrations, which began in 1802, shortly after the poet's death, are occasions for feasting and merrymaking.

Pride of place in the feast is the haggis – a sheep's stomach, stuffed with minced heart, liver, oatmeal, suet and seasoning. After being boiled for several hours it is delicious! At the Burns' Night supper, the haggis, the 'King of the Feast', is carried ceremonially into the room to the sound of the pipes. Burns' poem *Ode to a Haggis* is recited before the haggis is cut and shared.

Three toasts are given, the first to the Queen, the second, by an honoured guest, to the immortal memory of Burns, and the third, which is proposed by one of the ladies, is to the lassies, the subject of many of Burns' poems.

Naturally there is a goodly supply of Scotch whisky to wash down the haggis and the rest of the supper. The evening is a festive one with music and dancing, and, of course, the recitation of Burns' poems, ending with the poem that Burns rewrote, *Auld Lang Syne*.

> *A grace of Robert Bruns:*
> Some ha'e meat, and canna eat,
> And some wad eat that want it;
> But we ha'e meat, and we can eat,
> And sae the Lord be thankit.

Festivals of Sport (1)

For many years, the outstanding festival of sport has been the Olympic Games, at which the top athletes, sportsmen and sportswomen of the world have gathered, every fourth year, to compete for the coveted gold medal, which gives them the right to claim to be 'the best in the world'.

When the Olympic Games were first held, in ancient Greece, is not known. There is a record of games held in 776 BCE but they may have existed six centuries earlier than that. The ancient Games were stopped by the Roman Emperor in 393 CE. The modern Olympic Games were inaugurated in 1896, appropriately in Athens, Greece, since when they have been held every fourth year with the exception of years when the world was at war, different countries being hosts for the occasion.

Preparations for the Games have often included the building of a huge stadium in which the main athletics events would be held, besides providing suitable accommodation for swimming, rowing, sailing, football, shooting, riding and other events. It is in the giant stadium that the colourful and spectacular opening ceremony takes place.

Prominent in the stadium is the giant bowl in which the Olympic flame will burn throughout the period of the Games. The flame itself is carried in relays from Greece, the last runner mounting the steps with the torch that will kindle the flame in the bowl. The opening ceremony includes a march-past of all the competitors and team officials, dressed in national colours, one of whom carries the national flag. A similar ceremony opens the Winter Olympics at which the events include skating, skiing, tobogganing and ice-hockey.

For years the Olympics have been a real festival of sport, at which countries have forgotten their differences and have entered into the spirit of competition for the highest awards. Now, alas, politics have marred the games. In recent years some governments have withdrawn their athletes as a protest against the participation of others. It would be a pity if the greatest festival of sport should continue to lose its real spirit.

Grant, O Lord, to the peoples of the world, a right spirit of tolerance, understanding, healthy competition and friendship.

Festivals of Sport (2)

Undoubtedly the most famous annual sporting occasion held in Britain is the Cup Final at Wembley, when thousands of soccer fans and supporters gather to watch the match, televised for viewing by millions, which will decide who will hold the F.A. Cup – the supreme trophy of the Football Association.

Held at the end of the football season, the Cup Final is a climax in every sense of the word. For the players it is a great challenge in a tense atmosphere to play well enough to gain the Cup for their Club and also a coveted cup-winner's medal. For the spectators it is a festive occasion which begins long before the match begins and continues long after the final whistle. It is a colourful event with supporters proudly wearing their team colours, sporting scarves and hats, rosettes and banners. It is a noisy afternoon, too, as rival groups seek to outsing each other, chant slogans and make noises with trumpets or rattles.

Supporters of the winning team go wild with excitement as the final whistle goes and the players mount the rostrum to receive their medals. Soon the winners are running a lap of honour round the stadium holding the Cup aloft for all to see and to receive their acclamation. For the losers it is a moment of disappointment but there are still cheers for them, especially from their supporters, who acknowledge a good effort. Somebody has to lose!

The Cup Final is over for another year but the celebrations are not. On the following day, in the home town of the cup-winners, there is a carnival-like atmosphere as thousands of people line the streets to see the team driven by, perhaps in an open-topped 'bus, on a long route to the town hall for a civic reception. The streets become a sea of colour from the scarves and rosettes, whilst the cry, 'We won the Cup' echoes along the route. It is a weekend that will be remembered for a very long while.

In times of success or victory, O Lord, make us mindful of all who have helped us, our teachers and trainers, fellow players and supporters all of whom, for differing reasons, can truthfully say, 'We won!'

Work and business (1)

May Day is one occasion in the year which has attracted many kinds of festival. The ancient Celtic festival on this day to welcome summer and the Roman festival to Flora developed into the once popular May Festivals.

But times change. Country customs faded as industry grew. People began to think of industrial achievements and the needs of the 'working man'. About a century ago, there were campaigns to get better working conditions. The Congress of the Second International, meeting in Europe in 1889, expressed support for workers in America who were demanding an eight-hour working day. They decreed that May Day should be 'Labour Day'.

In the United States and Canada, Labor Day, in honour of workers, is on the first Monday in September, but in Europe it is May 1st. It is celebrated especially in the Communist or Socialist countries, sometimes with great parades marching past the country's leaders.

It is hardly surprising, in a country such as the U.S.S.R., with its Communist ideals, that the emphasis should be on human achievements or that there should be some recognition of the conquest of space on Cosmonauts' Day, 12th April, the anniversary of Yuri Gagarin's first orbit of the world in 1961.

Workers' celebrations in Britain are associated mainly with the industrial north. The greatest event is the Durham Miners' Gala, held on the third Saturday in July. Started in 1871, it has been described as 'the greatest Trade Union Demonstration in the Free World'. On the day of the Gala the centre of Durham City is closed and bands lead miners from the various lodges who march with their banners. Later they assemble on the riverside race course to enjoy many kinds of amusement. There is also a Miners' Festival Service in the Cathedral.

> Teach us, good Lord, to serve the need of others,
> Help us to give and not to count the cost.
> Unite us all for we are born as brothers;
> Defeat our Babel with Your Pentecost.
>
> *Frederik Kaan (1929–   )*

Work and business (2)

A fore-runner of many of the trade festivals of the present day was the Great Exhibition of 1851, the brain-child of Prince Albert, which was housed in the Crystal Palace, built in London's Hyde Park to advertise British industry to the world. A century later, in 1951, when British morale needed a bit of a boost, the Festival of Britain was planned, through which many aspects of British life, culture and business could be exhibited. A lasting feature of the Festival of Britain is the Royal Festival Hall, on London's South Bank of the Thames.

Large trade exhibitions, or expositions, have been held in many parts of the world, other countries being invited to have a section in which to display their produce. There are also large trade fairs, such as the Frankfurt Book Fair at which publishers from many countries are able to meet.

In Britain, many people enjoy visiting one of the exhibitions in which they have a particular interest. The Ideal Home Exhibition, the Motor Show and the Boat Show are but three of many. At one time most were housed in London at Olympia or Earls Court, but now some are held in the British National Exhibition Centre at Birmingham. Individuals enjoy looking at the latest equipment but international businessmen also conclude deals worth very large sums of money.

For country people, some of the greatest events of the year are the agricultural shows. There are county shows in most parts of the country, including the Royal Show, held early in July at the National Agricultural Centre, Stoneleigh, Warwickshire. At shows such as these, there is much to interest the farmer. Machinery and equipment are on display; salesmen are there to argue about and demonstrate their wares; exhibitions and displays of various kinds are staged and, of course, very important is the judging of the competitions for the finest animal of each class, sparking off friendly rivalry between farmers and stockbreeders. It is an opportunity for people to display and to enjoy the best of everything.

O God, may we take pride in all that we do, to strive always for the very best and not to be satisfied until we have achieved it.

Beginnings (1)

Launching and Stone-laying

Whenever we tackle some new project, we like to give it 'a good start' and believe, in so doing, that we are laying the best possible foundations for the success of the project. In building and construction industries we find special ceremonies to mark the beginning of the work.

In the case of ships, this is usually in the middle of the building process as most are partially built on land and completed when in the water. Once the hull of the ship has been finished, there is a launching ceremony. A platform is erected from which the ceremony is conducted by a distinguished person, who normally does so with such words as, 'I name this ship ". . . .". May God bless her and all who sail in her.' A bottle of champagne is smashed against the ship, and a button pressed, releasing some mechanism and thus allowing the ship to slide into the water for the first time to begin what is hoped will be a long life of sailing.

The ceremonies concerned with a building can begin much earlier, as soon as the ground has been prepared. From earliest times there has been a belief that some kind of sacrifice was necessary to protect the building from all kinds of evil influence. It was not uncommon in ancient times, and in primitive societies more recently, for human sacrifices to be made and people buried by the main corner posts of the house. It is said that the blood of bulls was mixed with the mortar used when building part of the Tower of London.

Nowadays most important buildings have large stones just above ground level, inscribed with the name of the person who laid the stone. They do not have blood under them but possibly a coin or some other memento of the year in which the stone was laid. Foundation stones are usually laid by important members of the organisation for whom the building is being erected, by representatives of groups of people or by those who have contributed financially. At the stonelaying ceremony a prayer may be offered, seeking a blessing for the builders and future users.

Bless, O Lord, the work of our hands that it may prove to be acceptable, useful and of lasting value.

TOPPING-OUT AND OPENING CELEBRATIONS

There are celebrations when a building work begins and maybe others of a minor nature at intervals during the building but probably the most important are those which mark the final completion and opening.

It is an old custom that there should be a 'topping-out' ceremony. In recent years it has been revived by some of the large building firms. Perhaps someone important, such as the Mayor, will shovel the last spadeful of concrete into a small patch left in the roof, after which those who have been working on the building will celebrate with drinks.

From the ground it is impossible to see whether the work has been completed, and so a sign is given. Once it was the custom to hoist a small fir tree or a green branch to the top of the roof and display it. Then flags became more popular. Whatever form the topping-out ceremony may take, it seems the right thing to do. If one seeks a blessing when the foundations are laid, it is reasonable to be thankful for its completion.

Then, of course, comes the official opening if it is a public building. Most opening ceremonies include the cutting of a ribbon which has been tied across the entrance. As with the stonelaying, an important person, or one with a special interest in the activities that will take place there, is invited to perform the opening ceremony. With the words 'I hereby declare this building open', the ribbon is cut with a ceremonial pair of scissors. The party may then retire to a large room in which there will be a service of thanksgiving or a reception for invited guests.

To commemorate the opening, a plaque may have been set in the wall and this is unveiled. Perhaps a tree may be planted in the grounds (p. 158).

Opening ceremonies of a similar nature are performed in respect of bridges, waterways and new constructions of many kinds. They are always occasions for celebration, rejoicing and thanksgiving.

In every task we undertake, O Lord, help us to remember that it is not the beginning that is important but our determination to work at it until it is finished.

TREE PLANTING CEREMONIES   *Tu b'Shevat*

Sometimes, as part of an opening ceremony, a tree may be planted by the person who is declaring the place open. How much of the 'planting' is actually done by the person concerned is questionable. It may be that the hole has already been dug by a groundsman and just a spadeful of earth is scattered over the roots. One would hardly expect the Queen, or the Mayor to do the whole planting.

For many years people will be able to read the plaque that is placed nearby and know who conducted the opening ceremony, for trees live for many years. It is a pleasant custom, too, for trees help to improve the appearance of the grounds of any building.

Tree-planting ceremonies are not new. Long ago, in the Bible Lands, it became the custom to plant a tree when a child was born. The Jewish father would plant a cedar for a boy, because this was a symbol of height and strength. For a girl he would plant a cypress for tenderness and fragrance. The children would care for their trees until the time of their marriage, when branches from their own trees would be cut to support the bridal canopy (p. 185).

It was long ago, too, that the Jewish New Year for Trees was first celebrated. The date fixed for this was 15th of Shevat, or Tu b'Shevat*, which falls about the end of the rainy season on Israel, when the trees are breaking into bud. On this day some people like to eat dates, carob and other fruits and nuts that have been grown on trees in Israel.

But there is a more practical aspect of Tu b'Shevat. Modern Israel is a developing land with many needs, not least of which is a large number of trees – trees to give fruit and trees to give protection to farming land. On Tu b'Shevat, in many lands and communities, Jewish people collect money to buy the trees that are needed in Israel.

O God, as the trees stand firm and lift their arms on high, giving protection to man and beast and joy to those who behold them, so make us strong, dependent upon You, helpful to others and a pleasure to know.

Beginnings (4)

There are many schools, colleges and other institutions which hold festive celebrations on Founder's Day, the day on which they remember the person who was responsible for providing the building or the money to start the work which has continued to this day. Perhaps, in a prominent position, there is a bust or a portrait of the founder.

Few of these establishments will have been founded by a king. One of these is the Royal Hospital at Chelsea, founded by King Charles II nearly three hundred years ago. The Royal Hospital is a hospital in the old sense of the word – a place providing hospitality or a home for people. In this instance it is a home for old soldiers, who wear scarlet-jacketed uniforms and are known as Chelsea Pensioners.

Founder's Day at the Royal Hospital is on Oakapple Day, 29th May, the birthday of King Charles II. Oakapple Day is celebrated in many parts of the country in various ways and commemorates the day when King Charles escaped from his enemies by hiding in an oak tree.

It is hardly surprising that, on this day, the statue of King Charles at the Royal Hospital is festooned with oak leaves and that the old soldiers proudly wear sprigs of oak leaves on their uniforms. The day is celebrated, in true military style, with a parade and inspection. Three cheers are raised for 'our pious founder, King Charles' and another three cheers for 'Her Majesty'. Then the Pensioners enjoy their traditional feast, including plum pudding and beer, before settling down to talk of old times.

Founders' Days are sometimes celebrated with open days, fêtes, sports or concerts. Sometimes they provide a good opportunity for the presentation of prizes and awards. Often they include a service of thanksgiving, not only for the founder, but for the contributions of many people in making it a place in which the present generation can take pride. For such people we should always be thankful.

For those responsible for founding our school;
And for those who have helped make it what it is today;
Thanks be to You, O God.

Ceremonial (1)

Changing the Guard

High on the list of priorities for visitors to London is a view of Buckingham Palace, the London residence of the Queen. The Royal Standard flying at the masthead indicates that she is 'at home' and there may be a chance of seeing her or another member of the Royal Family.

Many people time their visit so that they are there around 11.30 a.m. to see the Changing of the Guard. Each morning the new Guard marches to the Palace from Wellington Barracks or Chelsea Barracks and the band plays in the forecourt as the guard is changed. Then those who have been on guard march away. Usually the guard is mounted by one of the Brigades of Guards, though sometimes, on special occasions, by other regiments. In the summer months, the Guards, resplendent in their bright red uniforms, add a touch of pageantry and colour to the London scene.

Not far away, at Horse Guards Parade, is a similar but smaller ceremony, at which the Household Cavalry – the Life Guards and Royal Horse Guards – are mounted at 11 a.m. (10 a.m. on Sundays). These mounted guards, always popular with visitors, may be seen riding along the Mall on their way to and from Whitehall.

Few visitors would miss a visit to the Tower of London, where guard is mounted by soldiers and Yeomen Warders of the Tower, the 'Beefeaters', in their old-style costumes. There, each night at 9.50 p.m., is the ancient Ceremony of the Keys. The Chief Warder locks the Tower and takes the keys ceremonially to the Resident Governor.

A similar Ceremony of the Keys has, for many years, taken place at Gibraltar. Ceremonial procedures, like this and the Changing of the Guard, can be seen and enjoyed in many countries, most incorporating customs and traditions that have been handed down for many years, adding interest to the colourful pageantry.

Thank you, Lord, for ceremonies and pageantry which add a touch of colour to everyday things and for the heritage that has been handed on to us to be passed on to future generations.

Ceremonial (2)

Some of the most spectacular and moving ceremonial displays to be seen anywhere are those in which large numbers of soldiers are taking part, their full dress uniforms providing a blaze of colour. Military bands and the precision of the marching stir the emotions, and perhaps memories, of many of the spectators.

One of the best known London events is Trooping the Colour, held on Horse Guards Parade on the second Saturday in June. It was first held in 1755, one object of trooping the colour being to show it to foreign soldiers serving the King so that they would recognise it in battle. Each year the Colour of one of the Guards Regiments is paraded before the Queen. There is a display of precision marching, the Queen taking the salute, after which she leads her soldiers back to Buckingham Palace, where she takes a final salute before they march away.

About a month later, there is the Royal Tournament at Earls Court where, in the great indoor arena, displays are given by members of all three services and by some from overseas. It has been held since 1880.

Another spectacular military display is the military searchlight tattoo, held on the Esplanade of Edinburgh Castle each year for three weeks at the end of August and beginning of September as part of the Edinburgh Festival (p. 150). Held at night, the floodlighting gives a somewhat different-from-usual setting for massed bands of pipes and drums, national dancing and other displays, given not only by Scots but by people from other parts of the world.

People living in 'royal', military or naval towns, such as Windsor, Aldershot and Portsmouth have various opportunities to see the services on parade or at special ceremonies or displays.

Help us to remember, O God, that a perfect performance is the result of much training and self-discipline. May this be our approach to the whole of life so that we can give of our best.

Ceremonial (3)

The greatest ceremonial occasions and displays of pageantry are those in which the Sovereign is involved, and none more so than at a Coronation, a spectacle which one seldom has opportunity to witness.

From very early in the history of mankind there have been ceremonies in which kings or rulers have been chosen and installed as leader. Some of these ancient traditions are still found in the Coronation service today. The election and the recognition, now just a formality, date back to Anglo-Saxon times. The annointing with oil comes from the earliest coronations in the Bible. The robes and insignia have developed from Christian and pagan traditions.

The Coronation service itself, conducted by the Archbishop of Canterbury, is an ancient one, framed by St. Dunstan for the coronation of King Edgar in 973 CE. It takes place within the service of Holy Communion, for it is very much a religious ceremony with promises made before God.

The final act is the crowning itself, after which the congregation shouts, 'God save the Queen [*King*]', trumpets sound, bells peal and the Tower guns fire a royal salute (p. 163). Throughout the country, festivities and celebrations are held, which continue far into the night.

Before and after the ceremony, there is a spectacular display of pageantry as the procession makes its way to and from Westminster Abbey. Marching bands, contingents from the army, navy, air force and overseas representatives, cars and carriages with foreign heads of state, and finally the Sovereign in the State Coach, are watched by vast crowds lining the route.

There are, of course, other great royal occasions, such as Jubilee celebrations and royal weddings, all of which provide opportunity for pageantry, though not on the same scale as a coronation, and a good excuse, if one were needed, for many kinds of festivity and celebration.

O Lord, bless our Queen and members of the Royal Family that they may serve our nation well and enjoy the loyalty and respect of their subjects.

Ceremonial (4)

When somebody comes as a special guest to our home, we usually go out of our way to ensure that the visit is one that will be enjoyable and memorable. We ensure that guests are made comfortable and that they are well fed. We take them to see places of interest or to a theatre.

Sometimes the Queen entertains the head of state of another country and, when she does so, she, too, endeavours to make it a memorable occasion. It is another opportunity for ceremonial and pageantry. Usually, after meeting the visitor, there is a state drive to Buckingham Palace, perhaps in an open carriage so that the visitor can see some of the sights of London and be seen by people who line the route. The Queen's escort of the Household Cavalry adds colour to the occasion.

During the visit, there will almost certainly be a banquet to which many important people will be invited. Visits to theatres, or other evening functions are often witnessed by many people who like to see the Queen and her guests with their evening dress, sparkling jewellery and insignia. There are similar occasions when the Prime Minister entertains another head of government.

Sometimes, when the Queen visits another country, she uses the Royal Yacht *Britannia*. She may be greeted, as she enters a foreign port, by the firing of guns as a salute. Similar salutes are fired by visiting warships as they enter foreign ports. It is an old custom to indicate friendship. In olden days, when guns took a long time to load, warships fired all their guns to show they were then empty.

The firing of salutes from guns is another form of ceremonial associated with royal occasions. Guns are taken to the Tower of London and Hyde Park to be fired by the Honourable Artillery Company – 62 shots on very important occasions and 41 on others. Needless to say, live ammunition is not used for this traditional custom.

Grant, O God, that we may always remember those acts of friendship and courtesy which make for good relationships with other people.

Ceremonial (5)

Many of the customs and traditions concerning Parliament are those which have grown out of historical incidents and are carefully retained today as a means of expressing the freedom of Members to govern without interference.

The daily ceremonial begins with the Speaker's procession, in which the Speaker, who controls proceedings in the House of Commons, is accompanied by the Sergeant-at-Arms carrying the mace, and followed by other officials. He makes his way to his seat in the House, where the mace is placed on the table in front of him as a symbol of authority.

The most colourful parliamentary pageantry takes place about the beginning of November or at any time a new Parliament is elected. It is the State Opening of Parliament, in which the Queen addresses both Lords and Commons.

She leaves Buckingham Palace in the Irish State Coach, escorted by the Life Guards and Royal Horse Guards. On arrival at the Houses of Parliament, she is greeted by the Great Officers of State. The Ceremony takes place in the House of Lords, where peers and law lords are assembled. Wearing the Imperial State Crown and the Robe of State, over 18 feet long, she is escorted to the throne.

An officer known as Black Rod then summons the Commons to the Bar of the House. When they are assembled, the Lord Chancellor takes from an embroidered purse the speech which outlines the policy for the coming session of Parliament and hands it to the Queen who reads it.

Before the Queen arrives, another interesting ceremony has taken place. Members of the Yeomen of the Guard, the Queen's official bodyguard, in their Tudor style red and gold uniforms, will have searched the cellars, as has been done since the Gunpowder Plot (p. 70).

Parliamentary pageantry and procedures are part of the British heritage of which people are rightly proud.

Thank you, O God, for the great heritage and traditions of freedom which, as a nation, we treasure. Grant that we may never take such things for granted but may be thankful for all that we hold dear.

Ceremonial (6)

Scotland also has its proud traditions in respect of Parliament and the monarchy, with colourful and historic ceremonies. When there are royal proclamations, these are made, at the Mercat Cross in Edinburgh, by Lord Lyon King of Arms, who is supported by three heralds and three pursuivants, all of whom are dressed in multi-coloured tabards, bearing the royal arms of Scotland. The proclamations are made to the accompaniment of fanfares of trumpets.

The Lord Lyon King of Arms holds one of the oldest offices in the world. In ancient Celtic times, one of his duties was to make a proclamation at coronations. He is now responsible, among many other duties, for all state ceremonial in Scotland.

When the Queen visits Scotland, she has her own body-guard—looking very different from the English Yeomen of the Guard. They are members of the Royal Company of Archers, dressed in green uniforms and having a tall feather in their caps. They are present on all royal occasions and take precedence over all royal guards.

Parliamentary ceremonial is to be found elsewhere in Britain, in Northern Ireland and in such places as the Channel Islands and the Isle of Man, which have their own governments.

On the Isle of Man, the main ceremony takes place on 5th July. The two houses of the Manx Parliament, when they meet together, are said to be assembled 'in Tynwald'. Each year people gather around Tynwald Hill, at St. John's, to hear read out all the laws passed during the past year. They follow the tradition begun eleven hundred or so years ago by the rulers of Man.

Before the proclamation by the Lieutenant-Governor, the party processes along an avenue of flag poles from the church, where prayers have been offered, as is the custom on most British parliamentary occasions.

Almighty God, bless our Queen, all Officers of State and Members of Parliament that they may govern our people wisely and well.

Ceremonial (7)

ORDERS OF KNIGHTHOOD

One of the finest church buildings to be found anywhere in the world is St. George's Chapel, Windsor Castle. Not only is it finely constructed but it is filled with history, for over the stalls (seats) are the swords, helms and banners of those who use them, the Knights of the Order of the Garter, the highest and perhaps oldest order of Knighthood in Great Britain.

Founded in 1348, it arose from an incident at a court ball, when a lady lost one of her garters. To save her embarrassment, the King picked it up, put it on his leg, turned to the laughing company and said, 'Honi soit qui mal y pense' (Shamed be he who thinks evil of it). Then he added that he would make it the most honourable garter ever to be worn.

So the Most Honourable Order of the Garter came into being, limited to the King and twenty-five knights—the most honourable men in the land. Later the number was increased to include some other royalty but the number is kept small and new Knights can only be elected to replace those who die.

Each year in June, there is a Garter Day celebration. After a formal banquet, the Queen, members of the Royal Family and Knights of the Garter process in their full regalia from the Castle apartments to St. George's Chapel for a service, the Knights wearing the blue garter on the left leg below the knee and the ladies a blue sash.

There are other important Orders of Knighthood, the well known Scottish one being the Most Ancient and Most Noble Order of the Thistle, consisting now of the Sovereign and 16 Knights, who meet in the Thistle Chapel of St. Giles' Cathedral, Edinburgh.

The honour of being invested as a Knight of these and other orders is reserved for those who have given great service to their country.

Almighty God, we are thankful for men and women of honour and integrity, who have given great service and loyalty to our land. May we follow their example.

Ceremonial (8)

On the evening of the Thursday after July 4th, an unusual procession moves along Upper Thames Street in the City of London. In front are two wine porters in white smocks and top hats, sweeping the road so that those walking in the procession 'slip not on any foulness'. This is hardly likely to happen today but it could well have done 700 years ago when the custom began.

This is the procession of the Worshipful Company of Vintners, who have just elected their new Master and Wardens and are going to church to attend a special service. In the procession are the Company's Barge Master and Swan Markers. The Vintners, Dyers and the Queen own all the Swans on the Thames between Henley and London Bridge.

Towards the end of July, the Barge Master and Swan Markers take to the river for the ceremony of 'Swan Upping', that is marking the cygnets to indicate to whom they belong. The Queen's Swan Keeper is dressed in scarlet, the Vintners' in green and the Dyers' in blue. The beaks of swans belonging to Vintners have two nicks, the Dyers one and the Queen none.

The Vintners and Dyers are two of the Livery Companies of the City of London, so called because of their livery, or dress, which distinguished them. In the 15th and 16th Centuries, they were powerful guild organisations which controlled their particular trade. Some of the other more important Companies were the Fishmongers, Goldsmiths, Mercers, Grocers, Drapers, Merchant Taylors and Skinners.

Today these City Livery Companies may still have some control over apprenticeships and standards. They support charities and education. Modern Companies are also included in the 81 that exist today. It is the representatives of these Companies that meet on Midsummer Day to elect two Sheriffs for the City of London and on Michaelmas Day to elect the Lord Mayor—again very colourful occasions with traditions steeped in history.

For all the interesting customs that add colour and interest to life today we praise Your name, O God.

National festivals (1)

Some of the greatest national celebrations and holidays are the Independence Days on which people recall, with great festivity, how their country became free to govern itself and become a fully independent nation. In some countries, such as India, many people regard these as of greater importance now than the traditional religious festivals.

Israel celebrates Independence Day, Yom Ha-Atsma-ut*, in April or May and Jews throughout the world join with the Israelis to commemorate the setting up of the state of Israel. It was a long struggle and many lives were lost. The previous twenty-four hours are observed as Memorial Day with the flags flying at half-mast. Then, in the evening, as Independence Day begins, the flags are hoisted and celebrations get under way with dancing in the streets and firework displays. On the following day there are military parades and events which stir a feeling of national pride.

Perhaps the most famous Independence Day is that celebrated on 4th July in the United States of America. It is the most important day in the national history of the U.S.A. for it was on that date, in 1776, that the Americans declared themselves independent of British rule. The day itself is a day of great festivity with parades, barbecues, picnics, pageants and firework displays. Nowadays it is probably celebrated more enthusiastically in small towns than it is in the large cities but, throughout the country, the United States flag is proudly flown and there is an intense mood of patriotism. On the previous Sunday, many Americans will have attended thanksgiving services in their churches.

The Americans had fought to gain their independence from Britain but since then the countries have grown closer together, both of them proud of their stand in the world for freedom and the help they have been able to give to others.

> Lord, while for all mankind we pray,
> Of every clime and coast,
> O hear us for our native land,
> The land we love the most.
>
> *J. R. Wreford (1800–81)*

National festivals (2)

Most people have days we call Red Letter Days, on which they have something special to celebrate. Countries have their Red Letter Days too, when people remember an important happening in their history. Some are Independence Days (p. 168) or Liberation Days on which their country was freed.

Sometimes people celebrate an event which prevented their country from being overrun. Long ago, when Napoleon was making himself master of much of Europe, one of the decisive battles to keep Britain free was the Battle of Trafalgar, in 1805. That was a long time ago, but Trafalgar Day is still celebrated, particularly in naval circles, on 21st October. Similarly, on 15th September, Battle of Britain Day commemorates the victory in the air in 1940, which prevented an invasion of Britain.

There are days, too, when people may celebrate the overthrow of evil in their own land. French people, for example, enjoy a national holiday on Bastille Day, 14th July, the anniversary of the day in 1789 when the great fortress-like prison in Paris, symbolic of evil, was destroyed.

Happily, some Red Letter Days are those on which people can celebrate because they have learned how to work together for the good of others. Commonwealth Day is a reminder of the co-operation of countries throughout the world that were once the British Empire. Europe Day celebrates co-operation in Western Europe and United Nations Day the efforts of that body to work for peace and the good of people throughout the world.

People of most religions also have their Red Letter Days, many being their major festivals. There are commemorative days, too. In Scandinavia, Reformation Day is a reminder of Martin Luther's stand, which led to the formation of Protestant churches. Happily, there are other times, such as Christian Aid Week, when Christians of all denominations work together for the good of deprived people in many lands of many creeds.

As we look back with thankfulness, O Lord, teach us to look around us at the concerns of others and to work for a happier future for all mankind.

Gatherings and assemblies (1)

Most people like to do things in company with others. It is often more interesting to be able to share experiences and interests than it is to do everything alone. That is why many people like to worship God in a church, where they can be part of a congregation that likes to worship in a particular way, where there is a sense of belonging and where members obviously care for one another. Usually the weekly congregational worship takes a set form but most churches have their anniversaries and other festivals which highlight some of their activities.

There are times, too, when local churches hold special events such as Choir Festivals in which they all take part. One of the best known events in England in which many local churches unite is the Keswick Convention. First held in 1875, it has been held regularly since then for a fortnight during July. A great marquee is set up on the Convention site. Over 6000 people can be seated there and in a neighbouring tent to hear fine speakers and enjoy meetings to suit both young and old. Events are held in local churches, too, and the street leading to the tent is lined with stalls, on which useful literature, pictures, records and other commodities of a religious nature are for sale. People come from all over the world to share in the convention.

Occasionally, too, there are great religious crusades, at which evangelists and singers seek to pass on the Gospel message to any who will attend. Some of the greatest of these, held in many countries of the world, have been those led by the American evangelist, Billy Graham. A crusade lasting several weeks may attract hundreds of thousands, many of whom have their religious life deepened as a result of the experience. Sometimes, too, people of one particular religion or denomination will hold a mass meeting in a large public hall or open space.

Perhaps the most important aspect of such large gatherings is the inspiration, not only of great speakers but of sharing worship, devotion and prayer with so many others.

O God, as we assemble together, may our contribution be such that others may benefit and we shall be blessed.

Gatherings and assemblies (2)

People living in remote areas or in small communities sometimes like the opportunity to meet with other people in much larger groups, if only for a short time. In the Highlands of Scotland there are lots of these small communities, sometimes many miles from their nearest neighbours. Long ago families settled in a particular area. They were known as Clans, each having its own leader. Each also had its distinctive dress or tartan.

In certain parts of Scotland, during the summer, members of local clans would gather together for the Highland Gathering or Highland Games, members living far away sometimes coming back for the occasion. Today these Highland Gatherings are popular with holiday-makers as well as with the Scots themselves. Some of them attract thousands of people.

One of the most famous is that held at Braemar on Royal Deeside. After Queen Victoria had attended a modest gathering there in 1848, it grew and grew. Organised by the Braemar Royal Highland Society, it is now held in a vast natural amphitheatre, Princess Royal Park. Thousands of people come from all over Britain and from overseas. Apart from the sporting events, running, jumping and 'heavy events' such as tossing the caber, throwing the hammer and putting the stone, there are displays of Scottish dancing, as well as the colourful spectacle of the pipe bands and the pageantry always associated with royalty.

Another Highland occasion is the National Mod (p. 148). It is a Gaelic festival of music, drama, poetry and singing but it is also a time for Scots to get together. The town where the Mod is held becomes very colourful with the mingling of many tartans of Scots in their national dress. Perhaps to many of them the informal part is at least as important as the competitions. The festival ends with a Ceilidh*, an enjoyable social gathering with singing and dancing which extends well into the night as the Scots sit around the fires exchanging folk tales and stories before returning, in many cases, to far-away homes.

For all the enchantment of Highlands and islands;
For pipers and tartans; for gatherings with kinfolk;
To You, O God, be the praise and the glory.

Family festivals (1)

Most people would agree that a happy home and a loving family are two of the greatest blessings one can have in life. Yet they are things which are so often taken for granted.

Have you any brothers and sisters? If so, do you love them? Enough to wish to take care of them? In India there is a delightful festival called *Raksha Bandhan**, held each year in August. Raksha means 'to protect': bandhan means 'to tie'. On that day, girls tie a *rakhi**, a red and gold thread, around the wrists of their brothers with the prayer that it may protect the men from all evils. The brothers, in turn, promise to protect their sisters. It is a custom which has its roots in the ancient Hindu stories in which Indra's wife was given such a thread by the God Vishnu to tie on her husband's wrist and so protect him from the strong demon-king, Bali. Nowadays, girls without brothers may 'adopt' a man from outside the family.

And what about parents? How much thought do we give to them? One of the Ten Commandments in the Bible says, 'Honour your father and mother'. It has been the custom in many lands and religions for people to honour and respect their parents—and to care for them when they become old.

The popular Hindu festival of Dashara* (p. 106) is a family festival with reunions and feasting (p. 174). It is a special holiday for brides and engaged couples, who receive presents. It is also a kind of Mothers' Day, for mother holds a special place in Hindu families.

In the Western world we are familiar with Mother's Day. In Britain it began as Mothering Sunday (p. 174) but some of the American customs have become attached to it. Recently people have also begun to celebrate Father's Day in June. It is nice to have an opportunity to be able to make little gifts to parents on these occasions—just to say thank you for so much: it is better, of course, not just to limit this to one day in the year.

Dear Father, who in Your love has set us in a family: give us a real love and concern for the well-being of one another.

Beryl Bye

Family festivals (2)

Most festivals, naturally, are celebrated by adults, often for religious reasons. Children may not appreciate the meaning behind the festival but they certainly enjoy the presents that may go with it, or the new clothes, or the special food. There are, however, in some lands, special festivals for children.

In Japan, on March 3rd, there is the festival of *Hina –Matsuri,* sometimes called the Girls' Festival, the Dolls' Festival or the Peach Festival. It is called the Dolls' Festival because it is the time when special sets of dolls are unpacked and displayed on a tiered stand in the guest room of the house. The set includes, on the top tier, the emperor and empress. Below them are 3 ladies-in-waiting, 2 pages, 5 musicians and 3 guards. Food and wine are placed there for them and they remain on show for a month, after which they are packed away for another year. Hina Matsuri is a happy day with party games, fancy dress, balloons and tasty food—a real children's festival.

The boys have their turn a couple of months later, on 5th May. *Tango-no-seku* is a national holiday with an emphasis on the qualities expected of young men. Bamboo poles outside each house have a cloth streamer on them for each boy, in the shape of a carp. It is hoped that the boys will be like the carp—strong and courageous. Iris leaves are also displayed because the name of these, when spoken, sounds the same as the words for 'striving for success'. On display in the home are Samurai dolls and copies of the armour worn by Samurai warriors. For the boys this is a happy day.

But parents do more than just hope. A very old festival, held on 15th November is called *Shichi-go-san*. These are the Japanese numbers seven-five-three, for, on this day, parents have taken their children—girls aged seven, boys aged five and all children at the age of three—to the temple to express their happiness that their children have reached these ages and to pray for their future health and happiness. Good parents really care.

Thank you, O God, for our parents and for all the love and care they have given us. Help us to grow to be the kind of people of whom they can feel proud.

Family festivals (3)

Families the world over inevitably become split with some members perhaps living a long way from home. Some have to leave home to find work: others may marry and set up their own homes. But there are very happy occasions when family reunions can take place and festivals often provide an opportunity for this. For many people, Christmas is one such occasion.

Mothering Sunday, the 4th Sunday in Lent, used to be time for family reunions. It was the one day in Lent when people were allowed to ease up on their fasting and to have a bright cheerful day. It received its name from the fact that, on that Sunday, people in little villages went to the mother-church of their parish to offer gifts. A couple of hundred years ago, it became the custom for girls, who were working as servants, to go home and take trinkets, flowers or a cake for mother.

The cake was a Simnel cake, of which there were various kinds. They were rich cakes, well baked, which would last until Easter, when they were normally eaten. No doubt the girls hoped mother would be pleased with their special efforts at baking. Boys, who were apprenticed, would also be given time off to return home with presents on this day.

People in other lands, too, have had similar occasions when they have been able to return home for festivals. The Indian Dashara* is very much a family festival when daughters return to their father's home and gifts are exchanged. The Muslim festival of Eid ul-Fitr* (p. 175) is also a happy time of reunions and present giving. The old Chinese festival Ch'ing Ming (p. 48) was a family occasion. Those unable to return home would make a small sacrifice in the hope that the 'spirit' of the offering would reach the ancestral home.

Families are important and it is sad when members of a family lose touch with each other.

As we remember our families, O God, we say thank you for those with whom we live, and we remember those far away. Grant Your blessing to us all.

Family festivals (4)

Festival of Fast-breaking

People of most countries and religions have their own special celebrations when the whole family gathers to enjoy the festivities. The highlight in most Western countries is Christmas (pp. 78–82). In Scotland it may also be Hogmanay (p. 38) and, in the U.S.A., Thanksgiving (p. 71).

The great family festival of Islam is Eid ul-Fitr*, the Festival of Fast-breaking, which is celebrated on 1st Shawwal, at the end of Ramadan*, the month of fasting. Having fasted for a month, it is easy to imagine the joy with which the new moon is sighted, heralding the day of festivity.

Festivity should not be confused with frivolity, over eating or other excesses. It is a time of joy because of the spiritual fulfilment of the fast. With the sighting of the moon, greetings are exchanged—*Eid Mubarak**—'Happy Eid'.

The day always begins with prayer (*salat**). The men take a bath, put on their new clothes and go to the mosque for prayers. The imam* usually reminds them that they should be praying for those who are not as fortunate as they are.

In the home, decorations will be hung to give a festive atmosphere. Eid cards, greetings and presents are exchanged. Special dishes are prepared—spicy meat and potato pastries (*samosas*) are often eaten and the table is spread with all sorts of delicacies.

Eid ul-Fitr is a time for family reunions, for visiting relatives and friends, for forgetting quarrels and for almsgiving or charity.

And as people put on their new clothes they no doubt remember that this is a time for a new start in other ways too, in a spirit of peace and forgiveness.

A prayer from Al-Hizbul-A'zam :
O Lord, send down to us food from heaven so that it becomes a day of rejoicing for the first and last among us and a sign from You. Grant us Your sustenance: You are the best of sustainers.

Birth and naming (1)

One event that gives rise to celebration in most families is the birth of a new baby. For the parents it is an event for which they have planned and prepared and to which they have looked forward for a long time. Relatives and friends are delighted, too, and send congratulations to the new Mum and Dad as well as a present for the baby.

Most parents do not mind whether the baby is a boy or whether it is a girl but in some countries a son is especially celebrated because he will keep the family name alive and one day become head of the family.

Parents are always happy to show the new baby to their neighbours. Many also like to present him before God as a very early introduction to the religious community in which he will grow up.

A Muslim father will welcome his child into the Muslim faith by whispering in the right ear the *Adhan**, the great call to prayer, and in the other the *Iqaamah**, the second call to prayer. Then the first chapter of the Qur'an* is recited and prayers offered. So the baby first hears the words which will be so important during his lifetime.

Sikh parents take their babies to the gurdwara* to present them before Guru Granth* Sahib. Some *amrit** (p. 180) is prepared and five verses from the Japji* are recited. A little amrit is dropped into the baby's mouth and the mother drinks the rest. At this ceremony the baby is named (p. 177).

A Jewish boy child is initiated into the faith, normally on the eighth day of his life, when he is circumcised in accordance with the commands found in the Torah. Muslim boys are also circumcised. In some religions it is customary to clip off the first growth of hair.

Christian parents take their children to a church to be baptised, christened or dedicated (p. 181). It is sometimes looked upon as a naming ceremony but it is much more than that. It is a time when the parents can say thank you to God for the baby and promise to bring up their little one in the Christian faith.

Teach us, O God, to care for the little ones entrusted to us so that we may help them to learn Your ways.

Birth and naming (2)

How did you get your name? Most people have at least two, one of these is the surname or family name: the others are the names that our parents chose for us. Perhaps your names were chosen simply because your parents liked them. Maybe you were named after one of your grandparents or somebody else of whom your parents were very fond.

In the early books of the Bible we read how children were sometimes named according to circumstances in which they were born or in the hope of what kind of person they might become. Muslim children today might be given a name such as Abd Allah (Servant of God) or the name of Muhammad or one of the Prophet's family. Christian parents may sometimes choose the name of a person from the Bible, such as Mary or Timothy. Many names have a meaning. You may like to look up the meaning of yours and see whether they really describe you.

Most religions have their naming ceremonies. Although Christian children are named by their parents soon after birth, the name is officially given in church at the time of their christening. Jewish boys are named on the day of circumcision and girls when the father is called to the Torah on the Sabbath following their birth. Sikh children are named on the day when they are presented before Guru Granth* Sahib. The Granth is then opened at random and the first letter of the first hymn on that page is declared to be the initial of the child's name.

For Hindus the naming ceremony is one of the samskaras (ceremonies), which are considered of great importance. Like the Christian christening, it is conducted by a priest, who gives the baby its name and offers prayers. Muslims usually name a child on the seventh day after birth, the name being announced by the father after the recitation of verses from the Qur'an* in the presence of family and friends, who then celebrate with a great feast.

Grant, O God, that we may live in such a way that we will do nothing to tarnish our good name but make it one that will be honoured and respected.

Initiation (1)

Initiation ceremonies

For young people growing up in Britain, the age of 18 is considered very significant. That birthday is usually a time of special celebration, for the person is now classed as an adult, able to please himself without needing his parents' consent, able to vote and expected to make his own decisions. We say that he has 'come of age' or 'has the key of the door'. Most 18th Birthday cards have a key on them to mark the occasion.

In religion, too, there is a time when a young person is received as a member of that religion. It is usually much earlier than the age of 18, in some cases when the person himself decides to enter into the full life of his religion but in others, as in the case of Judaism (p. 179), when he reaches a certain age. In some religions, parents decide when the time is right.

Sometimes this involves receiving a symbol that will remain a constant reminder for the rest of life. A Hindu boy, for example, once received the Sacred Thread which hung from his left shoulder to his right hip. The origin of this was to invest him as a member of one of the castes, indicated by the colour of the thread.

Zoroastrians (Parsis) have a ceremony called *Naojote** to initiate a child into the religion some time between the ages of 7 and 14. After bathing and prayers, the priest puts on the child a white garment called a *Sudreh** and a thin girdle called a *Kusti**. This has 72 strands of lamb's wool to represent the 72 chapters of *Yasna** (prayer book). It is tied three times round the waist, as prayers are offered, symbolising good words, good thoughts and good deeds (p. 33).

The Sudreh and Kusti are worn throughout life. The Sudreh is a constant reminder to follow a straight and right path and the Kusti to gird up the loins to fight all evil and falsehood.

Part of the prayer in the Naojote ceremony:
Help me, Lord, to do the good work I have set out to do. I want no reward or gain. All I need is the help of Your Good Mind, and Faith to get divine knowledge to spread Your word.

Initiation (2)

BAR MITZVAH

The proudest day in the life of any Jewish boy is the day on which he becomes *Bar Mitzvah*, a 'Son of Commandments'. The Bar Mitzvah ceremony takes place at the age of 13, at which stage the boy is regarded as having 'come of age' in his religion. He can now count as one of the ten men (*minyan*) necessary to form a congregation for worship. The fixing of the age of 13 probably came from an old saying, 'At five a child is brought to the Bible, at ten to the Mishnah*, at thirteen to the Commandments'.

Before the great day, he will have attended Hebrew classes so that he knows how to read the scriptures in that language. In the synagogue he will be required to read from the Hebrew Torah.

On the morning of his special day, the boy is taken by his father to the synagogue, where, for this service, he will be called by his Hebrew name. He receives his *tallith** (prayer shawl), which he will wear at weekday morning prayers, on Sabbaths and at festivals for the rest of his life.

He also puts on his silk-embroidered *cappel* or *yarmulka* and the *tefillin** (phylacteries), one box bound on to his forehead and one on the left arm, each containing a strip of parchment with words from the Torah.

Called to the *bimah* (platform), he reads from the Torah, using the silver pointer to indicate the place. His reading is commended by the Rabbi, who then blesses him with the ancient priestly blessing (below).

No doubt there will be a big celebration party to mark this great occasion, attended by family and friends but the greatest memory will be that of the moment when he was regarded as a fully grown member of a great people.

(*In Reform Synagogues there is a similar Bat Mitzvah for girls, who may also read from the scrolls.*)

The priestly blessing of Aaron

The Lord bless thee and keep thee; the Lord make His face to shine upon thee and be gracious unto thee; the Lord turn His face unto thee and give thee peace.

Initiation (3)

When a Sikh boy is old enough to know what he is doing, he is initiated into the Sikh brotherhood, the *Khalsa**, at an important ceremony in the gurdwara, where Sikhs meet to worship God. It is known as the *Amrit** ceremony, that being the name of the nectar, sweetened water, which is used.

Five Sikhs stir the amrit in an iron bowl, using a double-edged sword (*Khanda**). The senior one reads Guru Nanak's* famous poem, the *Japji** and another a poem by Guru Gobind* Singh. This is followed by the *Anand**, an important hymn.

The five, when not reading, squat with one knee on the ground—a position from which they could spring quickly into action. After the Anand, the young man to be baptised joins them. He then recites: 'The Khalsa is of God and the Victory is of God'.

Five times he drinks amrit that is poured into his hands; five times amrit is splashed onto his eyes; and five times it is sprinkled on his hair after his turban has been slightly moved. He is then reminded that, as a member of the brotherhood, he has to keep certain vows. If he does not do so, he will have to take Amrit again.

At the end of the service, everyone shares the Karah Prasad* (p. 31). Those who have been baptised, or initiated, will now proudly wear the five Ks (p. 30) and, of course, the turban. As boys they will have fastened their uncut hair under a *rumal* (like a small handkerchief): as men they wear the turban, by which members of the brotherhood are easily recognised.

Verses from the Japji (29):
Make divine knowledge your food and mercy your steward; and listen to the Heavenly music that exists in the heart.

I salute God again and again. God is primal and pure with unknown beginning, Who cannot be destroyed, and Who remains the same in all ages.

Initiation (4)

BAPTISM AND CONFIRMATION

One of the important sacraments of the Christian Church is Baptism. A sacrament is a religious service with a symbolic meaning. In the case of baptism, the water is a symbol of the cleansing of the inner person so that the Holy Spirit of God can work in that person.

In many of the Christian denominations, babies or small children are taken to be baptised 'in the name of the Father and of the Son and of the Holy Ghost' (*Matthew 28; 19*). The means of doing this varies from church to church. The ceremony is usually conducted at the font. In some churches the minister dips his fingers in the water and marks the baby's forehead: in others the priest may pour water from the font using a shell or small jug. In the Orthodox Church the baby is dipped completely three times in a tub of consecrated water.

In other churches there is no infant baptism. Baptists, for example, argue that baptism should only take place when a person is old enough to decide for himself. In such churches, adult baptism is by total immersion in a large tank or baptistry, in which the believer is lowered into the water by the minister. It is a very moving service because the person to be baptised often speaks beforehand, telling how he came to the decision for baptism.

In the Orthodox Church there is no further service but in others there is a later commitment. In some churches it is called Confirmation: in others it is being 'received into membership'. It indicates that the person has decided to follow the Christian way and to confirm the promises made by his or her parents at the time of baptism. There are classes leading up to Confirmation so that candidates for Confirmation know what they are doing. In the Roman Catholic Church, Confirmation may be at the age of seven but in most churches it is thought preferable that it should not be before teen-age. Confirmation is conducted by a bishop who places his hand on the head of each and prays that God's Spirit will work in that person. It is followed by the sacrament of Holy Communion (p. 92).

Help us, O God, to know how You would have us to live and then to offer ourselves to You so that our lives may be lived to Your glory.

ORDINATION OF CLERGY

Most denominations of the Christian Church have people who are especially responsible for the spiritual life of the members of the church. They may be known as bishops, priests, deacons, ministers or by other names. Usually they are people who undertake these responsibilities and no other but some are part-time ministers following other occupations too.

In many of the churches, a man, or in some churches, a woman, may be accepted on completion of a course of training. He is then recognised as a clergyman. In some churches he is then said to receive Holy Orders, a sacrament by which he receives the gift of the Holy Spirit to enable him to perform well all the duties required of him. The service is called *ordination* and the clergyman is *ordained.*

The offices of bishop, priest and deacon are based on the early practices of the Christian Church (*Acts 6; 1–7*). It is believed that the power of the Apostles of Jesus has been passed on by laying hands on the heads of their successors. This is always done at ordination services by a bishop.

In the Roman Catholic Church, the bishop is the man with authority for teaching and governing in a certain area of the church. He has the authority to confirm, to ordain and to ensure that all the sacraments of the church are available to his flock. The priest may offer the sacrifice of the Mass and forgiveness of sins. The deacon may assist at the Mass. They all have many other duties too. In the Orthodox and Anglican Churches there are also bishops and clergy who are ordained for their work by the laying on of hands.

The tradition of Roman Catholics has long been to ordain only single men, who take vows of celibacy (not to marry) so that they have no distractions from their work. Other communions happily accept married men as ordained priests or ministers. In either case, ordination indicates a full commitment to the work of God in His Church.

For all who are ordained to administer the sacraments and to give spiritual help to Your people, we give You thanks, O God, and pray Your blessing on their work.

Initiation (6)

Honours and awards

Great interest is aroused in Britain twice a year with the publication of the Honours Lists—the New Year Honours in January and the Queen's Birthday Honours in the middle of the year. These are awards ranging from Knighthoods to lesser awards, such as the OBE and MBE, which have been made in respect of some outstanding service to the country or the community. The list includes politicians, civil servants, military personnel, entertainers, sportsmen and others. There is recognition of long service as well as bravery.

Such awards are actually presented at ceremonies held about twelve times a year, known as investitures. Awards, made in the name of the Queen are, whenever possible, bestowed by her in person, usually in the ballroom of Buckingham Palace. About 200 recipients will be at each investiture, together with members of their families. Music is played by Guards in their scarlet uniforms and the Queen is accompanied by her personal bodyguard, the Yeomen of the Guard.

Names of recipients are read out by the Lord Chamberlain in court dress and the award is passed on a red velvet cushion to the Queen by a gentleman usher. Knights are always first to be invested. A prospective knight kneels on the investiture stool to be 'dubbed' by the Queen. She touches him lightly on each shoulder with a light sword, known as receiving the acolade, then hangs his order round his neck and says, 'Rise, Sir . . .'. They exchange a few words, then the new knight backs away to be followed in turn by others.

For those receiving their various awards it is a day that will always be remembered—the visit to Buckingham Palace, with all its dignity and formality, the personal meeting with the Queen herself, but perhaps most of all the feeling of pride in having been granted an award in respect of services that have been given, possibly without thought of reward.

Teach us, good Lord, to serve Thee as Thou deservest; to give and not to count the cost; to fight and not to heed the wounds, to toil and not to seek for rest; to labour and not to ask for any reward save that of knowing that we do Thy will.

St. Ignatius Loyola (1491–1556)

Marriage (1)

Sooner or later, most young people begin to think of marriage and of the person, or kind of person with whom they would like to live. Long ago, in Britain, young ladies would try to find out who they might marry. There were various ways in which they believed they could do this by baking cakes or arranging apples or nuts on the eve of certain saints' days—St. Mark's, St. Faith's, St. Thomas's, Michaelmas, Hallowe'en and others.

It is interesting to read about these strange old customs—but it seems a very chancy way of discovering who one's partner might be! The Chinese believed that the gods might be able to help. On the 7th day of the 7th month they had a Festival of Maidens, when unmarried girls made offerings to the gods and asked for a happy marriage to a husband of their choice.

In many parts of the world, young people do, in fact, choose their partners but in others, particularly in Muslim, Hindu and Sikh communities, it is customary for parents to choose a suitable partner for their son or daughter. Usually the partner chosen is acceptable, but the young people can refuse if they so wish.

An engagement or betrothal is a time for great rejoicing as members of both families give presents to the young couple 'for their bottom drawer' and wish them well. Sometimes an engagement party is held. In Jewish families the betrothal is of great importance and, at this time, a document is drawn up giving details of all the wedding arrangements. In some countries a dowry is still required before a girl can marry.

Usually the boy and girl becoming engaged share the festivities but not necessarily so. Sikhs make the announcement at the bride's home but she may not be present. Members of both families offer their best wishes and give presents such as a kameeze or shalwar for the girl and a turban for the boy. Prayers are always said before Guru Granth Sahib to ask the blessing of God upon the forthcoming marriage.

Grant, O God, your blessing upon those who are engaged to be married that, as they prepare themselves and plan for their future, they may make wise decisions.

Marriage (2)

The most important day in the lives of many people, and one which they will always remember, is their wedding day, the day they began a new life with someone very special.

Marriage customs vary from one country to another and according to differing religious customs—so many that we can mention only a few. Brides marrying in a Christian church will often decide upon a 'white wedding', since white is a symbol of purity. Jewish brides do likewise. But a Sikh bride will be dressed in a deep red dupatta, shalwar and kameeze, embroidered in gold.

In the Christian marriage ceremony the bride and groom make certain promises, or vows, and give rings as a token of their marriage. Rings are given at Jewish weddings, too. Ceremonies need not be held in a synagogue but in any building, or in the open air, as long as they take place beneath a canopy (chuppah), symbolising the home they will set up together.

Sikh marriages always take place in the presence of Guru Granth Sahib (p. 104). After prayers have been offered, the bride's father places a garland of flowers on the holy book and one on each of those to be married. The bridegroom leads his bride four times round the Granth, each holding the end of a scarf, before they are showered with flower petals for luck. Hindu couples take seven steps together round a holy fire, making promises at each step.

Muslims do not require anyone to officiate at a wedding but there must be two adults present as witnesses. Marriage for them is a civil contract—an agreement of two people before God and man. In Britain, people need only be married in the presence of a civil Registrar, but many prefer to marry in a place of worship so that they can ask God to bless their married life together.

Then comes the reception—a great feast, presents galore and the good wishes of families and friends. At the end there are many happy memories . . . and promises to be kept!

O God, help us never to make or to take promises lightly, but to honour all the promises or vows we make to other people and before You.

Death and burial (1)

It might be said that death is hardly a festive subject and would not be regarded as a celebration, yet it is, nevertheless, inevitable, coming sooner or later to everyone and there are customs which are observed by the families and friends of those who are left to mourn the loss of their loved one.

In one sense death is the end of life but people of most religions believe that, in another sense, it is just a beginning. This life is seen as a short introduction to a long life in a spirit world. The body may die but the soul lives on. Death is described by some people as being 'called home to God'. A Muslim, when he first hears news of a death, will quote words from the Qur'an*: 'Verily, unto God we do belong and, verily unto Him shall we return' (*Qur'an 2: 156*).

Muslims do not normally make a show of their grief. Jews, on the other hand, make their grief more obvious. Their first words are: 'Blessed be the true judge.' They tear part of their clothes as a symbol of their grief and go into strict mourning for seven days, staying at home except on the Sabbath, wearing no shoes and sitting on low stools. There follows a long period of mourning until after the stone has been placed on the grave.

In many cases, especially in hot lands, the funeral (p. 187) has to take place very soon afterwards. It is customary for many people to see the body in the coffin to pay last respects to the departed. In the case of important people, kings or queens, rulers and political or religious leaders, there may be a 'lying in state', when the coffin is placed in a large building so that people can file past as a sign of respect.

These are sad occasions for the mourners but there is a brighter side too. A Christian funeral service may well be a time for singing happy hymns of praise and thanksgiving for the life of the person who has died and rejoicing that he has gone 'to a better world'.

We praise You, O Lord our God, for Your servant(s) now departed from us. Receive [*him*] unto Yourself and give comfort to all who mourn.

Death and burial (2)

Funeral customs vary from one country to another and according to various religious beliefs. For most people, the end is in the form of burial or cremation, though the Parsis in India have their Towers of Silence (p. 122).

In hot countries, the funeral takes place without delay. Muslims will wrap the body in sheets and carry it to a mosque, where a funeral prayer is offered before the body is buried. Cremation is customary for Hindus, who, in India, burn the body on a funeral pyre. The ashes may then be scattered on the holy waters of the river Ganges.

In Britain, it is customary for bodies either to be laid in a coffin, which is buried in a cemetery, or in one which will be burned in a crematorium. In the latter case, the ashes may then be scattered in a Garden of Remembrance. In the case of people who have a belief in a God, prayers are offered beforehand.

No longer do people consider it necessary to bury with someone such things as he may need for his future life, but there are customs observed in some faiths which suggest a continuation of life. A Sikh is buried wearing the Five K's (p. 30) which have meant so much to him as a member of the Khalsa*. A Jew is buried wearing the tallith* that was presented at his Bar Mitzvah and worn all his life when at prayer. The fringes on the tallith, the life-long reminder of God's commands in the Torah, will have been cut off.

Servicemen who have been killed may be buried with 'full military honours', having the coffin draped with the national flag and being escorted by their colleagues. Very important people may be given a State Funeral with an impressive service, a long slow-moving funeral procession and a lot of pageantry of a sombre nature.

Roman Catholics celebrate a Requiem Mass, a musical setting of the Mass (p. 93) for the dead. The name comes from the opening words 'Requiem aeternam dona eis Domine'—Give them eternal rest, O Lord.

To all Your faithful servants departed this life, grant eternal rest, O Lord.

Anniversaries (1)

Most of us have certain anniversaries that we like to celebrate each year. As children, our birthdays are no doubt the most important and we look forward to receiving our cards and presents. Perhaps we invite our friends to a party for games and a tea at which we have a birthday cake with one candle for each year of our age. We begin to feel quite grown up as the number of candles increases.

As people get older, they are not quite as anxious to have birthdays and do not let on how old they are—but secretly they still enjoy the greetings from relatives and friends because they know they are remembered. Old folk often take great pride in their age and each birthday is another mile-stone. As soon as someone has reached, say, his 80th birthday, he will say he is 'getting on for 81'.

As life passes, we have other anniversaries to remember. For many people, Wedding Anniversaries are the most important for they are a time to celebrate many happy years of living together as husband and wife. The special landmarks are the Silver Wedding, Golden Wedding and Diamond Wedding at 25, 50 and 60 years respectively.

We have other personal anniversaries, too, that we may like to celebrate: 'the day I first met my wife', 'the day we moved to this house', 'the day I started work in this place' or 'the day I retired'. These are the happy days but there are sad ones too, as when we recall the death of people we have loved. We all have many memories, and anniversaries are annual reminders of these.

So, too, we find that organisations and religions have their festival anniversaries, when members recall people or events of the past which provided them with something today which they enjoy or find very important. As with personal festivals, some are happy and some may be sad but all of them are times when people like to celebrate in a particular way, usually with thankfulness.

O God, as we recall the many events of the past that have influenced our lives, sad ones or happy ones, we give You thanks for every blessing received.

Anniversaries (2)

It is only natural to expect that Buddhists would celebrate events in the life of their founder, Gautama* Siddartha*, (p. 14), who became known as the Buddha*, the enlightened one. These are the dates of his birth, his enlightenment and his death. Some also keep the anniversary of his first sermon, Dhammacakka* Day (p. 105).

In the Mahayana* tradition, Bodhi Day is celebrated as the day on which Gautama became enlightened, which made him the Buddha Sakyamuni*—the first Buddha. At the festival kept to celebrate the Birthday of Buddha Sakyamuni, images of the Buddha are covered with pink flowers and devotees bow in veneration before the shrine. Then tea made from hydrangea leaves is poured over the head of the image. In Japan this is known as Hana Matsuri—a festival of fresh flowers brought to the temple, where the image is bathed in *amacha** (sweet tea).

When the Buddha died he passed to *Nirvana** (Nibbana), or slipped into a state of restfulness or bliss, which is referred to as Parinirvana or The Great Decease, now kept as a festival.

According to the Therevada* tradition, all three of these events in the life of the Buddha happened to fall on the full moon day of the lunar month Vaisakha* (April–May). The anniversary is therefore one of the greatest celebrations that can be imagined. Known as Wesak* (or Vesakha Puja*), it is a three-day festival in which buildings are decorated with flowers and lanterns and there are spectacular processions. Captive birds are set free in memory of the compassion of the Buddha and rows of candles are lit.

People gather for meditation and worship in homes and in shrine rooms in the temples. Gifts of flowers are offered to the Buddha, presents are exchanged and gifts left on the doorsteps of the poor.

This is the main Buddhist festival kept in Britain. Buddhists in many countries remember thankfully the one whose life and teachings have helped lots of people.

The Buddhist Triple Refuge (freely translated)
I go to the Buddha to become confident.
I find help in the teachings of the Buddha.
I am inspired by the monks who live by these teachings.

Anniversaries (3)

HINDU ANNIVERSARIES

Hindus, with their many gods and temples, have so many festivals that it would be quite impossible to mention them all. There is probably a festival somewhere on most days of the year. Two of the most important festivals are ones which could be regarded as anniversaries of people whose stories have come from the distant past and are recorded in the holy books.

The most important of these is Janmashtami* (or Janam Ashtami) the birthday of Lord Krishna. Of all people in the Hindu religion there is probably no one that means more to such a large number of people, to whom he is known as Lord, the child of the god Vishnu, the warrior hero of the *Mahabharata**, a champion of justice and one with a great sense of fun, fond of music and dancing. To different people he can represent any or all of these, and even more. The words and teachings of Krishna are in the *Bhagavad Gita** ('Song of the Lord').

Janmashtami, or Krishnashtami, occurs at midnight, the time Krishna is said to have been born. It is celebrated mainly in North and Central India, where thousands keep night-long vigils in the temples after a day of fasting. Sometimes there is an image of Krishna in a cradle in the temple. After midnight, gifts of sweetmeats are placed in the cradle and others eaten. The festival usually includes singing and the enactment of stories from the life of Lord Krishna.

In springtime there is a festival called *Ramanavmi**, which celebrates the birth of Rama*. The story of Rama, the King of Ayodhya, and his struggle against Ravana* is told in the Hindu epic poem, the *Ramayana** and is enacted at such festivals as Diwali* (p. 87) and Dashara* (p. 106).

Festivals such as these may be celebrated by Hindus living in Britain but they are unable to do so on the same scale as they keep them in their homeland.

He who offers to me with devotion only a leaf, or a flower, or a fruit, or even a little water, this I accept from that yearning soul, because with a pure heart it was offered with love.

(Bhagavad Gita 9:26)

Lord, accept such gifts as we offer to You, humble though they may be, because we offer them in love for You.

Anniversaries (4)

Many paths to God

People of many religions celebrate the birthdays of great teachers who contributed greatly to their religion or to the community at large. Hinduism is a very old religion with no one person who might be regarded as founder but in fairly recent times there have been great Hindus whose birthdays are celebrated, though not necessarily as festivals.

One of the greatest was Sri Ramakrishna (1836–86). Born a Brahman*, he became chief priest of a Kali* Temple in Calcutta. He also spent time living as a Muslim and as a Christian. He became convinced that there is Universal Truth in all religions. Today his teachings are followed by people in the Ramakrishna Vedanta Movement and he is regarded as a saint. It was another Hindu, Swami Vivekenanda, who introduced the Ramakrishna Movement to the U.S.A. Another great Hindu of modern times was Mahatma Gandhi, whose life and teachings had such an effect upon modern India that his birthday, Gandhi Jayanti*, is celebrated as a public holiday.

Mahavir* Jayanti is a day celebrated by the Jains in remembrance of the birth of their great teacher who, during thirty years of teaching, gathered many followers. His real name was Vardhamana but he took the name of Mahavira* (Great Hero), the twenty-fourth Jain 'conqueror' (p. 32).

Zoroastrians keep two festivals in honour of their founder, Zarathustra (p. 33), Khordad Sal* is the day on which they celebrate his birth and Zarthostno Diso* the anniversary of his death. Both are celebrated with great veneration and special services in the Fire Temples.

There is no doubt that the teacher who had the greatest influence on the people of China was Confucius (p. 17). His birthday is celebrated in some Chinese communities and also at the Japanese festival of Sekiten (p. 149), commemorating his great contribution to national life.

As one can ascend to the top of a house by means of a ladder or a bamboo or a staircase or a rope, so divers are the ways and means to approach God, and every religion in the world shows one of these ways. (Sri Ramakrishna)

Thank You, God, for all who have pointed a way to You.

Anniversaries (5)

Guru Anniversaries

There are many Sikh festivals, some of which are much more important than others. Baisakhi* (p. 88) and Diwali* (p. 87) are celebrated generally and Holi-Mohalla (p. 49) at Anandpur. *Melas** (fairs) are popular celebrations.

There are also festivals which mark the birth, accession and death anniversaries of the ten Gurus. These are known as Gurpurbs*, four of which are perhaps of greater importance than the others. The date of these celebrations varies from year to year because the Indian Bikrami Calendar is used. Full anniversary celebrations may last for three days. On two days there is the Akhand Path*, the continuous reading of Sri Guru Granth* Sahib.

Very important is the Birthday of Guru Nanak*, generally in November. He was the founder of the Sikh religion (p. 30). On the day preceding, a great procession is held (as on p. 88). On the day, the *Diwan** (religious session) begins about 4 or 5 a.m., continuing with various activities until about 1.20 a.m. the next day, the time of Guru Nanak's birth, followed by praise for the Guru and reading the Holy Word, finishing about 2 a.m.

Guru Gobind* Singh was the tenth Guru and his birthday is celebrated in December or January. It was he who founded the Khalsa* (p. 30–1) and declared the Granth to be the only Guru after him (p. 30). Celebrations are similar to those for the Birthday of Guru Nanak.

Guru Arjan Dev was the Guru responsible for compiling the Adi Granth* and building the Golden Temple (p. 31). He was put to death on the orders of the Emperor. Guru Tegh Bahadur was beheaded for refusing to change his religion. Anniversaries of both these martyrdoms are celebrated.

Another Sikh anniversary celebration is that of the setting up of Sri Guru Granth Sahib as the permanent Guru. On this day, Sikhs rededicate themselves to follow the teachings of the Gurus as contained in their Holy books.

Affirmation of a humble leader—Guru Gobind Singh
     I am—and of this let there be no doubt—I am but a slave of God as other men are, a beholder of the wonders of creation.

Anniversaries (6)

Islam and Bahá'í

For Muslims, the most important person ever to have lived is the Prophet, Muhammad (peace be on him). These words are expressed whenever his name is mentioned. Through him came the words of the Qur'an* and the religion of Islam was established. The anniversaries of his birth and his death are important Muslim festivals.

The birthday of Muhammad, Meelad ul-Nabi*, sometimes referred to as Prophet's Day, is celebrated throughout the Muslim world with assemblies at which the Prophet's birth, life, words and triumphs are related. There are ceremonial readings and prayers as well as many forms of rejoicing. The actual birthday is 12th of Rabi ul-Awwal but the whole month is celebrated as the 'birth month'.

Other events in the life of Muhammad are celebrated at various festivals (see p. 204). His death is remembered on Lailut ul-Isra, 'The Night of the Journey', when it was said, 'Muhammad (peace be upon him) is dead but God is alive.'

A Muslim prayer from Al Hizbul-A'zam
O Allah (God) grant us that we be listeners to and obedient to Thy commands and become sincere friends and companions among ourselves.

Many years later another religion was 'born'. The Bahá'í* Faith (p. 29) was the outcome of the teachings of the Báb* and later of Bahá'u'lláh* regarded as the great prophet of whom the Báb had spoken. Not surprisingly, Bahá'ís celebrate the birth and martyrdom of the Báb and the birth and death of Bahá'u'lláh. These, like all Bahá'í holy days, are religious in nature generally with scripture readings and prayers, followed by a social occasion with refreshments.

The most important Bahá'í festival is the Feast of Ridván*, described by Bahá'u'lláh as 'the Lord of Feasts'. It marks the anniversary of the twelve days during which Bahá'u'lláh declared his mission in the Garden of Ridván near Baghdad. All work is suspended on the 1st, 9th and 12th days. The first day of Ridván is the day on which all Bahá'í administrative bodies are elected worldwide.

Pronunciation guide

This is a general guide to the pronunciation of words marked *
in the book. There are many variations both in the spelling and
pronunciation of Jewish, Arabic and Indian words, according
to country and dialect.

Stress marks⁄ follow the main syllable.
Where not otherwise indicated, a vowel is short, otherwise ā as
in bar; ē, ī as in feet; au͞, ō as in rope; au as in taut; ū, o as in
boot; a, e, ae, ai, ei as in maid; āī, āy as eye; ch, kh, h as in loch;
c̄ as ch; s̄ as sh; q as k; v often as w; ḥ, e not sounded; ( ) not
sounded in some dialects.

JEWISH WORDS
Some words ending in th may be written as ending in s.
There are different endings for plurals, e.g. challot is feminine
plural of challah. B and V are sometimes interchangeable.
    Akdamū⁄t; Āv (or Āb); Bei⁄gel; Birkha⁄t Ha-mazo⁄n; Challo⁄t;
Cha⁄nukkāh; Hagga⁄dah; Hakafo⁄t; Harō⁄set; Havda⁄lāh;
Hōsha⁄na Rabbā⁄; Hoshano⁄t; Ki⁄ddūsh; Kol Ni⁄drei; Māā⁄riv;
Maimo⁄nides; Ma⁄tzoh; Megi⁄llah; Mezū⁄zah; Mish⁄nāh;
Ne'ī⁄lah; Pesach; Rōsh Chō⁄desh; Rōsh Hasha⁄nāh; Se⁄der;
Shabba⁄t; Sha⁄harit; Shavū⁄oth; Shemā⁄; Shō⁄fār; Simcha⁄th
Torā⁄h; Sūkkoth;Ta⁄llith; Tefi⁄llin; Tisha b'Āv; Tū b'Sh(e)va⁄t;
Yom Ha⁄'A⁄tsma'ū⁄t; Z'miro⁄t.

MUSLIM WORDS
Adhā⁄n; Allāh⁄; Ayyā⁄t; Eid (Id) Mubā⁄rak —ul–Adhā⁄
—ul–Fi⁄tr; Ha⁄jj (Ha⁄ji); Hi⁄jrāh; Ibā⁄dis; Imā⁄m; Iqāā⁄māh;
Ismā⁄īlīs; Jamrā⁄t; Khar⁄ijis; Khū⁄tbar; Lai⁄lat ul–Qadr; Mahdi⁄;
Ma⁄sjid; Meelu⁄d ul–Nabī⁄; Mihrā⁄b; Mūha⁄rram; Qur'ā⁄n;
Rakā⁄; Ram(a)dā⁄n; Salā⁄t; Saum; Shahāda (Shahīa); Shī⁄a;
Sūfi; 'Ūthmān; Wahhā⁄bi; Zakā⁄t.

BAHÁ'Í WORDS
Akkā; Bāb; Bahā'ī; Bahā'u'llāh; Naw Rūz; Ridvān; Tabrīz.

JAPANESE WORDS
Sound all letters separately including final vowel.

INDIAN WORDS

Although grouped according to religion, some words are common. South Indian names, such as Rama and Ratha may lose final 'a' in North India. South Indian Siva and Sri become Śiva and Śri in North.

HINDU Ātman; Bhāg(a)v̲ād Gitā'; Brahmā'; Brahmā'n; Brah'man(a)s; Chā'tūrthī; Dasha'ra (Dūs(h)e'ra); Diwā'li; Durgā'; Gane̲'sh; Jan(a)māst(a)mi; Jaya'nti; Kālī'; Kū'mbh(a) Me'la; Mah(a)bhā'r(a)ta; Mandā'la; Nat(a)rā'ja; Nav(a)ra'tra; Pū'ja; Rākhī'; Ra'ksha Ba'ndhan; Rām(a); Rām(a)na'vmi; Ramāy̲'(a)n(a); Ravanā'; Ra'th(a); Rig–Ve̲'da; S(a)rasv̲ā'ti; Sītā'; Sī'va (Śī'va); Sri (Śri); Ūp(a)nī'shads; Vāranā'si; Ve̲'das.

SIKH A'di (or Ādi̲) Granth̲; Akha'nd pā'th̲; A'mrit; Ana'nd; Baisakhi (*Visā'khī*); Cha'kra; Ch̲a̲uri'; Diwā'n; Gūrdwā'ra; Gūrpūr'bs; Gōbi'nd; Japjī; Kaçchā'; Kanghā'; Kārā'; Kar̲āh Prasā'd; Kha'nda; Khā'lsa; Kīrpā'n; Mūl ma'ntra; Nām; Nān'ak; Pal'kī; Panj Pyare (*piā'rī*); Punjā'b; Tak'khat.

JAIN Āg(a)mā'; Ahi'msa; Jāīn; Jaya'nti; Jinas (*Jāīnas*); Karmā'; Mah(a)vīra; Pār'śva; Paryu'shan; Po'sādha.

PARSI Ahrīma'n; A'hūra Ma'zda; A'ngra Mai̲'nyu; Ā'tash Behrā'm; Boi (*boy*); Fārv̲ārdegā'n; Frav̲ashī; Jamshe'di Na̲o̲r̲ōz̲e̲; Ja̲'shan; Ka'dmi; Khordad Sal'; Kū'sti; Mā'tchi; Naojō'te̲; Ohr'mazd; Sha'henshā̄ī; Sū'dreh̲; Ūdwa'da̲; Ya'sna, Zārtho'stnō Dī'sō.

BUDDHIST WORDS

A'maċha; A'sālā Pū'ja; Asō'ka; Bōddhisa'ttvās; Bū'ddha; Bū'ddha-rū'pa; Dha'mma Vijay̲'a; Dha'mmaċa'kka; Dū'kkha; Gāū'tama; Hīnayā'na; Ma'gga; Mahayā'na; Man'dala; Nīrv̲ā'na; Nīrō'dha̲; Perahe'ra; Pō'sadha; Poso'n; Samūdā'ya; San'gha; Śākyamū'ni; Siddār'th̲a; Therev̲ā'da; Upō'satha̲; V̲esā'kha; Wesa'k.

CELTIC AND GAELIC WORDS

Feis (*Fesh* or *Fash*) Laoghaire (*Leary*)
Ceilidh (*Kayly*) Gaedhealach (*Gaelic*)

Calendar of Festivals

This calendar of festivals is intended as a guide so that festivals can be anticipated and incorporated to advantage in assemblies or R.E. themes. It can only be a guide because so many festivals are variable as a result of the differing calendars of the world. Where it has not been possible to give a definite date, there is an approximation. Dates shown in italics are the first and last dates upon which the festival could fall. Muslim festivals have not been included as these fall earlier each year (see separate table on page 202). It is strongly recommended that reference be made to an up-to-date Calendar of Festivals, such as that compiled and edited by Desmond F. Brennan, Religious Education Centre, West London Institute of Higher Education, Isleworth, Middlesex TW5 5DU on behalf of the SHAP Working Party, published annually by the Commission for Racial Equality.

The *Gregorian Calendar*, in use in most Western lands and in Japan, is a *solar* calendar, based on the time taken for the world to encircle the sun. Most others are *lunar* calendars, timed from the appearance of the new moon. All need some adjustment if they are to cover a full solar year. Most of the festivals and celebrations in countries using the Gregorian Calendar are fixed, though some of the Christian festivals, such as Easter, are lunar based and known as movable feasts.

The *Jewish Calendar* is a lunar calendar, normally having twelve months alternately 30 and 29 days long, a lunar month being $29\frac{1}{2}$ days. Years are calculated from Rosh Hashanah, which falls in the autumn. The months are Tishri, Heshvan, Kislev, Tevet, Shevat, Adar, Nisan, Iyar, Sivan, Tammuz, Av and Elul. To adjust the lunar calendar to the solar year, an extra (embolismic) month is added seven times in each 19-year period. Known as Ve-Adar, it follows Adar, which in those years is given an extra day.

The *Islamic Calendar* is strictly lunar, with twelve months alternately of 30 and 29 days, giving a year of 354 days. In each cycle of 30 years, eleven are leap years but, even so, each year begins earlier, moving a complete year cycle in $32\frac{1}{2}$ years. Islamic months are Muharram, Safar, Rabi ul-Awwal, Rabi ul-Akhir, Jumada al-Awwal, Jumada al-Akhir, Rajab, Sha'ban, Ramadan, Shawwal, Dhu l-Qi'da, Dhu l-Hijja (30 days in leap years).

The *Bahá'í Calendar* is a solar based calendar with 19 months of 19 days and 4 or 5 extra 'intercalcary days' between the 18th and 19th months. Festival dates are therefore fixed.

Zoroastrians (Parsis) follow three calendars so their festivals may fall on different days according to the calendar used by each of the sects. The *Fasli Calendar* has a Leap Year, so festival dates remain constant. The *Kadmi Calendar* is said to be the most ancient (*Kadim*) and dates are a month earlier than the same festivals in the *Shahenshai Calendar*. Neither of these has a leap year and festivals fall one day earlier every four years. Those dates marked 1984 will therefore be one day earlier in 1988.

In *India* several calendars have been in use. In 1957 the government adopted the *Saka Calendar* of Southern India, to be used alongside the Gregorian Calendar, but festival dates may be governed by the other calendars such as the *Bikrami Calendar* of Northern India or by other factors.

In China the Gregorian Calendar was adopted in 1912 but festival dates remained largely based on the old lunar calendar which began with the first full moon after the sun had entered into the constellation of Aquarius. With successive anti-religious governments, many of the Chinese festivals indicated below have largely fallen into decline; a few being kept by Chinese overseas communities.

Major festivals indicated thus ǀ require absence from school or work.

JANUARY

(see also December/January—p. 202)

1	New Year (Gregorian Calendar)	38, 39
	Ganjitsu (Japan)	39
6	Epiphany *Christian*. Twelfth night	83
—	Plough Sunday/Monday. Sunday/Monday after Epiphany	43
6–7	Christmas Eve/Christmas Day *Russian Orthodox*	118
18–25	Week of Prayer for Christian Unity *Christian*	23
17	Wassailing the apple trees, Carhampton, Somerset	42
19	Epiphany *Russian Orthodox*	—
25	Burns' Night, Scotland	151
—	(*Last Tuesday*) Up-Helly-A', Shetland	135
—	Birthday of Swami Vivekananda *Hindu*	191

JANUARY/FEBRUARY

Chinese New Year (Yuan Tan) *21/1:19/2*	40
Tu b'Shevat (New Year for Trees) *Jewish* (15th Shevat) *16/1:14/2*	158

FEBRUARY

2	Candlemas *Christian*	73, 75, 99
15	Parinirvana *Mahayana Buddhist*	189
—	Sarasvati Puja *Hindu*	148
—	Shiva Ratri *Hindu*	47
—	(Full moon day) Magha Puja *Therevada Buddhist*	75
—	Birthday of Sri Ramakrishna *Hindu*	191

FEBRUARY/MARCH

Shrove Tuesday (Mardi Gras) *Christian 3/2:9/3*	50, 137
Ash Wednesday *Christian*. Day after Shrove Tuesday	50, 115
Lent *Christian*. 40 days—Ash Wednesday to Easter	115
Mothering Sunday *Christian*. 4th Sunday in Lent	173–4
Purim (Lots) *Jewish* (14th Adar or Ve-Adar) *25/2:25/3*	107
Lantern Festival (Teng Chieh) *Chinese* End of New Year	48
Holi (Spring Festival) *Hindu*	47, 49
Hola-Mohalla (Spring Festival) *Sikh*	47, 49

MARCH

1	St. David's Day, Wales	126–7
3	Hina Matsuri, Japan	172
17	St. Patrick's Day, Ireland	126–7
11–20	Farvardegan Days (Fasli) *Zoroastrian* (10–19 in leap year	
	+ extra day, Rozevahizak 20/3)	122
21	Spring Equinox	41
	Fasli New Year *Zoroastrian*	41
	Jamshedi Naoroze *Zoroastrian*	89
	Khordad Sal (Birth of Zarathustra-Fasli) *Zoroastrian*	191
	Naw Ruz *Bahá'í*	89
25	Lady Day: Annunciation of BVM *Christian*	99
—	Ramanavmi (Birthday of Lord Rama) *Hindu*	190
—	(*2nd Monday*) Commonwealth Day	169

MARCH/APRIL

Palm Sunday *Christian*. Sunday before Easter *15/3:18/4*   94
Holy Week *Christian*. Week from Palm Sunday to Easter   94–5
Maundy Thursday *Christian*. Thursday of Holy Week   95
Good Friday *Christian*. Friday of Holy Week   95
Holy Saturday *Christian*. Day before Easter   95–6
Easter Sunday *Christian 22/3:25/4*   109
Pesach (Passover) *Jewish* (15th–21st Nisan) 1st day *27/3:24/4* †   108

APRIL

4 or 5 Ch'ing Ming (Festival of Pure Brightness) *Chinese*   48, 120, 174
8   Buddha Sakyamuni's Birthday *Mahayana Buddhist*   189
12   Cosmonauts' Day, U.S.S.R.   154
13   (*usually*) Baisakhi *Sikh*   88
21   1st Day of Ridván *Bahá'í*   193
23   St. George's Day, England   126–7
25   Sekiten *Japanese Confucian*   149
30   Zarthostno Diso (Death of Zarathustra-Fasli) *Zoroastrian*   191
—   Mahavir Jayanti (Birth of Mahavira) *Jain*   192

APRIL/MAY

Ascension Day *Christian*. 40 days after Easter *30/4:3/6*   96
Well Dressing in some Derbyshire villages   143
Rogationtide *Christian*. Sunday–Wednesday before Ascension Day   56–7
Yom Ha'Atsma'ut (Israel Independence Day) *Jewish* (5th Iyar)
   16/4:14/5   168

MAY

1   May Day—Festivals   52–5
              —International Labour Day   154
2   12th Day of Ridván *Bahá'í*   193
              (1984) Zarthostno Diso (Kadmi) *Zoroastrian*   191
5   Europe Day   160
              Tango-no-seku, Japan   172
8   Flora Day, Helston, Cornwall   55
10   (*or nearest Saturday*) Spalding Flower Parade   139
15   Hollyhock Festival, Kyoto, Japan *Shinto*   138
23   Declaration of the Báb *Bahá'í*   193
29   Oakapple Day   159
              Ascension of Bahá'u'lláh *Bahá'í*   193
—   (*last Monday*) Spring Bank Holiday   97
—   Christian Aid Week *Christian*   169
—   (*Full moon day*) Wesak (Vesakha Puja) *Therevada Buddhist*   189
—   (*near end*) Chelsea Flower Show   140

MAY/JUNE

Whit Sunday *Christian*. 7 weeks after Easter *10/5:13/6*   97
Trinity Sunday *Christian*. Sunday after Whit Sunday   98
Corpus Christi *Christian*. Thursday after Trinity   93
Shavuoth (Pentecost) *Jewish* (6th & 7th Sivan)—1st day *16/5: 13/6* †   62
Martyrdom of Guru Arjan Dev *Sikh*   192

Dragon Boat Festival (Tuan Yang Chieh) *Chinese* (5th day of 5th
   month)   147
Father's Day. Sunday after Trinity   173
Morris Dancing   44, 55–6, 97

JUNE

1   (1984) Zarthostno Diso (Shahenshai) *Zoroastrian*   191
21   Summer Solstice (Longest Day)   58–9
24   Midsummer Day   58–9
—   (*Full moon day*) Poson (Dhamma Vijaya) *Therevada Buddhist*   105

JULY

4   Independence Day, U.S.A.   168
5   Old Midsummer Day   59, 165
   Tynwald Day, Isle of Man   165
—   (*First week*) The Royal International Agricultural Show   155
9   Martyrdom of the Báb *Bahá'í*   193
12   Orange Day, Ulster   133
13   Obon *Japanese Shinto/Buddhist*: Tokyo (elsewhere in August)   120
—   (*third Saturday*) Durham Miners' Gala   154
16–25   (1984) Farvardegan Days (Kadmi) *Zoroastrian*   122
26   (1984) Kadmi New Year Day *Zoroastrian*   89
—   (*last Thursday*) Battle of Flowers, Jersey   139
31   (1984) Khordad Sal (Birth of Zarathustra—Kadmi)
   Zoroastrian   191
—   (*Full moon day*) Asala Puja (Dhammacakka Day)
   Therevada Buddhist   105

JULY/AUGUST

Tisha b'Av (Fast of 9th Av) *Jewish* (9th Av) *17/7:15/8*   116
Festival of Maidens *Chinese* (7th day of 7th month)   184

AUGUST

1   Lammas Day   64
   (*Sunday after 12th*) Revel Sunday, Marhamchurch, Cornwall   130
15   Assumption of Blessed Virgin Mary *Christian*   99
15–24   (1984) Farvardegan Days (Shahenshai) *Zoroastrian*   122
25   (1984) Shahenshai New Year Day *Zoroastrian*   89
30   (1984) Khordad Sal (Birth of Zarathustra) (Shahenshai)
   Zoroastrian   191
—   (*last Sunday*) Plague Sunday, Eyam, Derbyshire   130
—   Royal National Eisteddfod, Wales   148
—   Raksha Bandhan *Hindu* (Full moon day of Sharavan)   173
—   Anniversary of Guru Granth Sahib *Sikh*   104
—   Yue Lan (Hungry Ghosts) Festival *Chinese Tao*   121
—   Chung Yuan (All Souls' Day) *Chinese Buddhist* (15th day
   of 7th month)   124

AUGUST/SEPTEMBER

Janmashtami (Janam Ashtami) (Birth of Lord Krishna) *Hindu*   190
Ganesh Chaturthi *Hindu* (4th day of Bhadrapada)   101

Paryushan (Penance) *Jain*   119
Edinburgh International Festival of Music and Drama   150, 161

SEPTEMBER

—   (Monday after 4th) Abbots Bromley Horn Dance,
         Staffordshire   44
13   (1984) Farvardin *Zoroastrian*   122
15   Battle of Britain Day   169
29   Michaelmas   68

SEPTEMBER/OCTOBER

Harvest Festivals   62–7
Rosh Hashanah (New Year) *Jewish* (1st & 2nd Tishri)—1st day
   6/9:5/10 †   85
Yom Kippur (Day of Atonement) *Jewish* (10th Tishri) *15/9: 14/10* †   117
Sukkoth (Tabernacles) *Jewish* (15th–22nd Tishri)—1st day
   20/9:19/10 †   63
Simchath Torah *Jewish* (23rd Tishri) *28/9:27/10* †   103
Chung Ch'iu (Mid Autumn Festival) *Chinese* (15th day of 8th
   month)   67
Birthday of Confucius *Chinese Confucian*   192
Navaratra (Nine-night sacrifice before Dashara) *Hindu*   106, 119
Durga Puja *Hindu*   101, 106, 119
Ch'ung Yeung (Double Ninth) *Chinese* (9th day of 9th month)   122

OCTOBER

20   Birth of the Báb *Bahá'í*   193
21   Trafalgar Day   169
24   United Nations Day   169
31   Hallowe'en   69
31   Reformation Day, West Germany and Scandinavia   —
—   Dashara (Autumn Festival) *Hindu*   106, 119

OCTOBER/NOVEMBER

Diwali (Dipavalli or Kali Puja) Indian New Year *Hindu/Sikh*   87

NOVEMBER

1   All Saints' Day *Christian*   125
2   All Souls' Day *Christian*   124
3   Bunka-no-hi Culture Day, Japan   148
5   Guy Fawkes (Bonfire) Night   70
—   (*Second Saturday*) Lord Mayor's Show, London   134
—   (*Second Sunday*) Remembrance Sunday   123
12   Birth of Bahá'u'lláh *Bahá'í*   193
15   Shichi-go-san, Japan   172
—   (*Fourth Thursday*) Thanksgiving Day, U.S.A.   71
30   St. Andrew's Day, Scotland   126–7
—   Birthday of Guru Nanak *Sikh*   192
—   Time of Sending Winter Clothes to Ancestors *Chinese*
         (1st day of 10th month)   120

Advent Sunday *Christian*. Nearest Sunday to 30/11   84
Chanukkah *Jewish* (25th Kislev–2nd/3rd Tevet)—1st day
    28/11:27/12   73
Martyrdom of Guru Tegh Bahadur *Sikh*   192

DECEMBER

6	St. Nicholas f.d.	79
—	(*Second Sunday in Advent*) Bible Sunday	105
8	Immaculate Conception of B.V.M. *Christian*	99
8	Bodhi Day *Mahayana Buddhist*	189
13	St. Lucia's Day	79
24	Christmas Eve *Christian*	81
	Festival of the Nine Lessons and Carols	80
25	Christmas Day *Christian*	82
31	New Year's Eve. Hogmanay	38
31	Joya no kane *Japanese Hindu/Shinto*	39

Birthday of Guru Gobind Singh *Sikh*   192

TABLE OF ISLAMIC FESTIVALS

These fall about 11–12 days earlier each year. The dates given are only approximate: the Muslim day begins in the evening and is dependent upon the actual sighting of the new moon. Years marked ø are Leap Years.

HIJRI YEAR (AH)	1403	1404	1405ø	1406	1407	1408	1409ø	
	1982	*1983*	*1984*	*1985*	*1986*	*1987*	*1988*	
Day of Hijrah (1st Muharram)	19/10	8/10	27/9	16/9	6/9	26/8	14/8	86
10th Muharram	28/10	17/10	6/10	25/9	15/9	4/9	23/8	118
Mawlid ul-Nabi (12th Rabi ul-Awwal)	28/12	17/12	6/12	25/11	15/11	4/11	23/10	193
	1983	*1984*	*1985*	*1986*	*1987*	*1988*	*1989*	
Lailut ul-Isra (27th Rajab)	10/5	29/4	17/4	6/4	27/3	16/3	4/3	193
Ramadan begins	12/6	1/6	21/5	10/5	30/4	18/4	8/4	118
Eid ul-Fitr † (1st Shawwal)	12/7	1/7	20/6	9/6	29/5	18/5	7/5	175
Eid ul-Adha † (10th Dhu l-Hijja)	19/9	7/9	27/8	16/8	6/8	26/7	15/7	111

Lailut ul-Bara'h (Night of Forgiveness), when special prayers are offered for forgiveness in the belief that this night determines the destiny for the coming year, is the night of the full moon a fortnight before Ramadan begins.

Index

Abraham, 9, 18, 85, 111
Adi Granth, 30
Advent, 21, 75, 84, 105, 202
  calendar, 84
Agama, 32
Agriculture, 8, 155 (*see Harvest*)
Ahimsa, 32
Ahriman, 33
Ahura Mazda, 9, 33, 72, 122
Akdamut, 62
Akhand Path, 88, 104, 192
Aldeburgh Festival, 150
All Hallows, 69, 125, 201
All Saints' Day, 21, 69, 93, 124–5, 201
All Souls' Day – Chinese, 17, 124, 200
  – Christian, 124, 201
Almsgiving, 27, 175
Altar, 4, 45, 59, 145
Amaterasau, 8, 11
Ambarvalia, 57
Amrit, 88, 110, 176, 180
Amritsar, 31, 87–8, 104
Anand, 31, 88, 180
Ancestors, 7, 17, 40, 46, 48, 120–2
Angakok, 46
Anglicans, 22–3, 182
Angra Mainyu, 33
Anniversary, 1, 122, 125, 170, 188–93
Annunciation, 21, 99, 198
Apostles' Creed, 21, 22, 96
Arafat, Mount, 27, 111
Arts Weeks, 150
Asala Puja, 105, 200
Ascension Day, 21, 56, 93, 96, 143, 199
Ash Wednesday, 114, 115, 198
Ashanti, 120
Ashes, 114, 116
Asoka, 105
Assumption of BVM, 93, 99, 200
Atheism, 10, 34
AUM, 12–3
Autumn, 8, 68–71, 85, 106
Avesta, 33
Aztecs, 8–9, 58

Báb, The, 29, 193, 199, 201

Bahá'í Calendar, 89, 197
Bahá'í Faith, 29, 89, 115, 193
Bahá'u'lláh, 29, 193, 199, 201
Baisakhi, 30, 31, 88, 192, 199
Bands, 132–3, 135, 137, 161–2, 171
Banquet, (1), 78, 134, 163, 166
Baptism, 21, 24, 97, 144, 176–7, 180, 181
Baptists, 23, 181
Bar Mitzvah, 179
Bards, 148
Bastille Day, 169
Bathing temple image, 101, 106, 113, 135
Battle of Britain Day, 169, 200
Battle of Flowers, 139, 200
Bayt ul-haram, 111
Beating the bounds, 56–7, 96
Becket, St. Thomas, 110, 112
Bells, 38, 39, 52, 54, 162
Beltane, 58, 76
Bessie; Betsy; Betty, 43–4, 55
Betrothal, 184
Bhagavad Gita, 12, 101, 106, 190
Bible, 20, 24, 102, 105
  Jewish, 18, 20, 179 (*see Torah*)
  Societies, 105
  Sunday, 105, 202
Big House, 67
Bikrami Calendar, 88, 192, 197
Birkhat Ha-mazon, 90
Birth, 158, 176
Birthdays, 104, 176, 178, 188
  (*see under names of individuals*)
Blessed Virgin Mary, 75, 99, 144
Blessing, 37, 75, 90, 108, 110
  boats or waters, 146–7
Bodhi Day, 15, 189, 202
Bodhisattvas, 15, 125
Boi ceremony, 33, 73
Braemar Highland Gathering, 171
Brahma, 12, 47, 98
Brahman, 7, 12–13
Brahmins, 12
Bread, 3, 64, 92
Britain, Festival of, 131, 155
Britannia Coconut Dancers, 55
Britten, Benjamin, 150
Brothers and sisters, 172

Buddha, 14, 75, 105, 110, 112, 189, 199
Buddhism; Buddhists, 2, 4, 14–5, 75, 125, 141, 189
    Chinese, 11, 124
    Japanese, 120
    missionaries, 105
    monks, 115
    pilgrims, 112
    temple festivals, 75, 101, 110
Bunka-no-hi Culture Day, 149, 201
Burial, 187
Burns' Night, 151, 198

Calendar of festivals, 196–202
Calendars, 1–2, 27, 29, 37, 41, 196–7; Bahá'í, 29, 197; Bikrami, 192; Chinese, 40; Christian, 83, 84, 95, 98; Fasli, 41, 89, 197, 198–9; Jewish, 37, 196; Muslim, 27, 37, 86, 196; Zoroastrian, 197
Calling for help, 42–7, 75, 128–9, 135, 145
Calvin; Calvinists, 22–3
Cambridge, King's College, 80
Canada, 71, 154
Candlemas, 21, 73, 75, 99, 198
Candles, 3, 72–5, 79–80, 82, 84, 87, 90, 108–9, 120, 122, 128, 188–9
Canterbury, 110, 112
Caribbean, 136–7
Carnival, 49, 50, 106, 107, 133 136–7, 139
Carols by candlelight, 80
Ceilidh, 171
Celtic cross, 20
    – customs, 69, 142, 165
    – deities, 8, 148
    – festivals, 76, 154
Celts, 148
Ceremonial and pageantry, 132, 160–7
Ceremony of the Keys, 160
Challot: challah, 3, 85, 90
Changing the Guard, 160,
Chanukkah, 19, 74, 75, 202
Charity, 80, 82, 111, 115, 136, 167, 175, 189
Chassidic Jews, 19
Chelsea Flower Show, 140, 199
Cherry Blossom Festival, 138

Chester, 97, 150
Chicomecoatl, 8
Children's Festivals, 173
China, 15–7, 34, 48, 67, 120–2, 124, 136, 138, 147, 184, 191, 197
Chinese New Year, 17, 40, 48, 198
Ch'ing Ming Festival, 17, 48, 120, 174, 199
Choir festivals, 170
Christadelphians, 24
Christening, 176–7
Christian Aid Week, 169, 199
Christian Scientists, 25
Christian Unity, 23, 93, (169), 198
Christianity, 9, 20–3, 34, 45, 51, 84, 95–7, 99, 105, 109, 176, 181–2
    beliefs, 20–3, 96
    calendar, 83, 84, 95, 98
    denominations, 22–4, 91, 169, 181–2
    devotions and worship, 36, 91–3
    festivals, 2, 51, 78–84, 91, 93–9, 109, 196
    missionary, 105
    observances, 185–7
    pilgrims, 110
Christingle service, 82
Christmas, 2, 21, 45, 75, 76, 77–84, 174, 198, 202; – cake, 78; – candles, 75, 84; – carols, 80, 82; – cribs, 75, 81, 83; – decorations, 83; – Eve, 75, 76, 79, 80–1, 198, 202; – pudding, 78; – tree, 2, 80
Chung Ch'iu, 67, 201
Ch'ung Yeung Festival, 17, 122, 201
Chung Yuan, 124, 200
Church of England, 22–3, 91
Church of God, 23
Church of Scotland, 22–3
Circumcision, 176–7
Circumcision of Christ, 93, 99
City of London Companies, 167
Cleansing, 39, 40, 73, 109, 144, 181 Ritual – 3, 100, 108
Coming of Age, 178
Commonwealth Day, 169, 198
Communism, 17, 34, 154
Confession, 50, 114, 117, 119
Confirmation, 181–2
Confucius; Confucianism, 17, 149, 191, 201

Congregational worship, 100–1, 170
Congregationalists, 23
Conventions, 170
Corn dollies; corn maiden, 65
Coronation, 132, 162, 165
Corpus Christi, 21, 93, 199
Cosmonauts' Day, 154, 199
County Agricultural Shows, 155
Coventry, 97
Creator God, 7–9, 12, 18, 47, 67, 72, 85, 98
Creed, 21, 92–3
Cremation, 187
Cross, 3, 20, 95, 109, 123
Cultural festivals, 148, 149, 150
Cup Final, 153
Cuthbert, St., 112

Dakhma, 122
Dance drama, 3, 44, 45, 47
Dance Facing the Sun (see Sun Dance)
Dance of Shiva, 47
Dancers, 4, 44, 101, 120
Dancing, 2, 6, 11, 47, 53–5, 138
    Celebration –, 76
    Ceremonial –, 11, 45, 60
    Country –, 54–5
    Festive –, 38, 40, 87, 130, 137, 148
    Folk –, 44, 54–5, 120, 148
    Horn –, 44
    – in worship, 103
    Maypole –, 42, 53
    Morris –, 2, 44, 54, 55, 197, 200
    National –, 55, 148, 161, 171
    Ritual –, 43, 46, 59, 76, 145
    Street –, 49, 55, 168
    Symbolic –, 44
Dashara, 13, 106, 119, 136, 172, 174, 190, 201
Day of Assembly, 100
Day of Atonement, 19, 63, 85, 115, 117, 201
Day of Hijrah, 27, 86, 203
Day of Judgement, 26
Dead, 77, 120–5
Death, 7, 9, 104, 109, 114, 120, 186–7
    Symbolic –, 2, 44, 53
Dedication, 1, 38, 176
Derbyshire, 130, 138, 143, 200
Dervishes, 46
Dhamma Vijaya, 15, 200

Dhammacakka Day, 15, 105, 189, 200
Dipavali (see Diwali)
Displays, 39, 161
Diwali, 13, 31, 47, 87, 106, 190, 192, 201
Diwan, 192
Dolls' Festival, 173
Double Ninth Festival, 122, 202
Dragon Boat Festival, 17, 147, 200
Dreaming, The, 7
Druids, 59, 148
Dukkha, 14
Durga Puja, 13, 101, 106, 119, 201
Durham, 112
    Miners' Gala, 154, 200
Dyers' Company, 167

Easter, 2, 21, 45, 51, 76, 94, 95, 109, 115, 133, 140–1, 174, 196, 199;
    – candle, 75, 109; – eggs, 2, 51, 109; – Eve, 95–6; – Monday, 133; – parades, 109, 133
Eastern Church (see Orthodox)
Edinburgh, 150, 161, 165, 166
    – Festival, 150, 161, 201
Egg rolling, 51
Eggs, 2, 50–1, 108–9, 116
Egypt, 18, 58, 63, 108
Egyptians, 8, 51, 118, 121
Eid ul-Adha, 27, 111, 202
Eid ul-Fitr, 27, 118, 174, 175, 202
Eightfold Path, 14–5
Eisteddfod, 148–9, 200
Elim Four-Square Alliance, 23
Engagement, 184
Enlightenment, 14–5, 105, 189
Eostre, 109
Epiphany, 21, 43, 83, 93, 198
Equality, 3, 31, 100, 113
Esala Perahera, 15, 101, 113
Eskimos, 7, 46
Eucharist, 3, 64, 92, 93, 130
Europe Day, 169, 199
Evil spirits, 41, 42–3, 53–4, 69
Exhibitions; Expositions, 39, 155
Eyam, Derbyshire, 130, 200

F.A. Cup, 153
Fair, 1, 49, 64, 68, 88, 97, 130–1, 192

Family festivals, 39, 40, 48, 68, 71, 78, 88, 172–5
Farvardegan Days, 33, 122, 198, 200
Farvardin, 33, 122, 201
Fasli Calendar, 41, 89, 197, 198–9
Fast of Esther, 107
Fast of 9th Av, 19, 115, 116, 200
Fast-breaking, Festival of, 175
Fasting, 1, 27, 39, 50, 56, 60, 89, 95, 114–9, 174, 175
Father's Day, 172, 200
Feast; feasting, 1, 3, 65, 68, 71, 77–8, 85, 87, 107, 121, 130, 151, 172, 174, 177, 185 (see Banquet)
Feast Day, 1, 125–6, 130
Feasts, movable, 196
Feis, 148
Fertility, 2, 6, 8, 42, 44–5, 67, 76
Fête, 1, 159
Fire, 33, 72–7, 110
Fire temples, 33, 72–3, 89, 122, 191
Fires: – bonfires, 49, 53, 58–9, 70, 76–7, 95, 127 (see also Yule)
  Ceremonial –, 33, 38, 49, 59, 69, 122
  New Year 38
  – ritual lighting, 3, 38
Fireworks; Firecrackers, 40, 48, 70, 87, 106, (135), 136, 147, 168
First fruits, 62, 64
Fish symbol, 20
Fishermen; fishing, 66, 146–7
Five Ks, 3, 30–1, 180, 187
Five Pillars of Islam, 27, 100
Flambeaux procession, 38
Flora: Floralia, 52, 53, 138
Flora Day, Helston, 55, 199
Flower arranging, 140–1
  – festivals/shows, 138–40, 199
  – parades, 139, 199
Flowers, 48, 52–3, 62, 65, 124, 138–41, 185, 189
  as offerings, 142–3, 146, 189
Fontinalia, 142
Food, 3, 27, 31, 50, 62, 63, 66, 71, 74, 89, 90, 108, 113, 118, 124, 175
Fool, 2, 44, 55
Football, 152, 153
Foundation stones, 156
Founder's Day, 159

Four Noble Truths, 14
France, 144, 169
Fravashi, 33, 122
Fuji-yama, 11, 112
Funeral rites, 7, 187
Funerals, 116, 132, 186–7
Furry Dance (see Flora Day)

Gaelic festivals, 148, 161
Gandhi Jayanti, 191
Ganesh Chaturthi, 13, 101, 200
Ganges, 2, 110, 144, 187
Ganjitsu, 39, 198
Garland Day, Abbotsbury, 146
Garter Day, 166
Gautama, 14–5, 112, 189
Gayatri Mantra, 13
Genuflexion, 4
Ghats, 144
Gibraltar, 160
Gion Festival, 135
Gipsies, 131
Girls' Festival, 173
Gobind Singh (see Guru)
Gods:Goddesses, 6–9, 11, 26, 40, 43, 45–7, 52, 67, 69, 77, 101, 110, 112–3, 138, 142, 144, 147–8, 184, 190
Golden Temple, 31, 87–8, 104, 192
Good and evil, 8, 26, 42–45, 72, 106, 109
Good Friday, 21, 94–5, 109, 115, 141, 199
Gospel, (21), 93, 105
Graham, Billy, 170
Granth (see Guru)
Granthi, 104
Graves, 48, 67, 120–122, 124
Greece, 9, 51, 152
Greek Orthodox Church, 22–3, 109
Green Corn Dance, 60
Guards, Brigade of, 160, 161, 183
Gun salutes, 162–3
Gurdwara, 3, 31, 88, 104, 176–8
Gurpurbs, 192
Guru, 30–1, 104, 192
  Arjan Dev, 31, 192, 199
  Gobind Singh, 30–1, 49, 88, 180, 192, 202
  Granth Sahib, 30–1, 88, 102, 104, 176–7, 184–5, 192, 200

Hargobind, 87
Nanak, 30–1, (104), 180, 192, 201
Tegh Bahadur, 31, 192, 202
Guy Fawkes Night, 70, 76, 201

Hadith, 26
Haggadah, 108
Hajj, (2), 27, 110, 111
Hakafot, 103
Hallowe'en, 69, 184, 201
Hanamatsuri, 189
Hanukkah (see Chanukkah)
Harai, 73
Hargobind, Guru (see Guru)
Harness Horse Parade, 133
Harvest, 6, 42, 49, 56, 60, 62–8
 – Festivals, 45, 64, 66, 67, 201
 – Home, 65, 71
 – of the Sea, 66, 147
Hastings, 147
Havdalah, 90
Healing waters, 144
Hebrew, 19, 74, 108, 179
Henotheism, 9
Highland gatherings, 171
Hijrah, Day of, 27, 86, 202
Hina-Matsuri, 173, 198
Hinayana Buddhism, 15
Hinduism:Hindus, 2–3, 12–3
 ceremonies and observances 115,
   119, 121, 125, 177–8, 184–5,
   187
 dancing, 4, 47
 festivals, 48–9, 87, 149, 161, 172,
   190–1
 gods, 7, 9, 47, 72
 pilgrimages, 110
 prayer and worship, 36, 47
 shrines, 39
 symbols, 3, 178
Hobby-horse, 44, 55
Hogmanay, 38, 175, 202
Hola-Mohalla, 31, 49, 192, 198
Holi, 13, 48–9, 136, 198
Holidays; Holy Days, 1, 78, 96, 130
Holland, 79, 139, 140
Hollyhock Festival, 135, 138, 199
Holy Books, 102–5, 119, 149
Holy Communion, 3, 92–4, 162, 181
Holy Days of Obligation, 93, 96, 99
Holy Land, 2, 110
Holy Saturday, 95–6, 109, 199

Holy Spirit, 21, 23, 97–8, 181–2
Holy Thursday, 96
Holy waters and wells, 142–44, 187
Holy Week, 94–5, 199
Honours Lists, 183
Horn Dance, 44
Horse Fairs, 131
Horticultural Shows, 140
Hoshana Rabba, 63
Hoshanot, 63
Hot Cross Buns, 95
Houses of Parliament, 70, 164
Huitzilopochtli, 8
Humanism, 10, (17)
Hungry Ghosts Festival, 17, 121,
   200

Ibadis, 28
Icons, 3
Id Festivals (see Eid)
Ikebana, 141
Imam, 27, 28, 100, 175
Immaculate Conception, 21, 93, 99,
   202
Incas, 58
Incense, 40, 73, 83
Independence Days, 168–9, 199, 200
India, 12–5, 28, 30–2, 49, 73, 87–8,
   101, 104, 106, 110, 119, 144,
   149, 168, 172, 174, 187, 190–2,
   197
Industrial harvest, 66
Ingathering, Feast of, 63
Initiation, 176, 178–81
International Labour Day, 154, 199
Investiture, 166, 183
Iran, 28, 41, 89 (see Persia)
Ireland, 75, 93, 127, 133, 148
Isangoma, 46
Islam, 26–8, 46, 86, 100, 118, 193
   (see also Muslim)
Islamic Calendar 27, 196–7, 202
Isle of Man, 165
Isma'ilis, 28, 29
Israel, 45, 62, 107, 145, 158
   Independence Day, 168, 199

Jagannatha, 113
Jainism:Jains, 3, 32, 36, 102, 112,
   119, 125, 191
Jamshedi Naoroze, 33, 89, 198

Janmastami (Janam Ashtami), 13, 190, 200
Janus, 39
Japan, 6, 8, 11, 15, 36, 39, 41, 46, 73, 101, 112, 120, 122, 125–6, 138, 149, 173, 189, 191, 196
Japji, 36, 176, 180
Jehovah's Witnesses, 24
Jersey Battle of Flowers, 139, 200
Jerusalem, 22, 96, 108, 110, 116
Jesus Christ, 3, 20–1, 73, 78, 80–1, 83–4, 91–6, 98–9, 115
Jews (*see Judaism*)
JHVH, 9, 18
Jinas, 32, 125
Jinja, 11
Jordan, River, 144
Joya no Kane, 39, 202
Judah the Maccabee, 74
Judaism, 2, 18–9, 20, 51, 62, 63, 64, 74, 108, 115
  calendar, 37, 197
  ceremonial, 72,
  – old, 45, 145, 158
  creed, 18
  customs, 122, 158
  festivals, 37, 62–3, 74, 85, 90, 103, 107–8, 115–7, 158, 168
  food, 4, 107, 108
  New Year, 85, 201
  observances, 3–4, 115, 117, 176–9, 184–7
  people, 125
  prayer, 36
  symbols, 3, 18–9
  Torah, 102

Ka'ba, 2, 27, 111
Kaccha, 31
Kadmi Calendar, 33, 89, 197, 200
Kali Puja, 87, 201
Kalpa Sutra, 102, 119
Kami, 6, 11, 112
Kami-dana, 11, 36
Kandy, 15, 101, 113
Kanga, 31
Kara, 31
Karah prasad, 31, 180
Karma, 32
Kesh, 30
Keswick Convention, 170
Key of the Door, 178

Khalsa, 30–1, 88, 180, 192
Khanda, 30, 180
Kharijis:Kharijites, 28
Khordad Sal, 33, 191, 198, 200
Khutbah, 100
Kiddush, 90, 108
Kirpan, 30–1
Knights, 132, 166, 183
  – of the Garter/Thistle, 166
Kojiki, 11
Koko, 120
Kol Nidrei, 117
Korea, 15, 67
Krishna, Lord, 12, 49, 113, 190, 200
Krishnashtami, 190
Kumbha Mela, 110
K'ung Fu'tzu (*see Confucius*)
Kusti, 178
Kyoto, 135, 138

Labour Day, 154
Lady Day, 99, 198
Lailat ul-Barah, 27, 202
Lailat ul-Isra, 27, 193, 202
Lailat ul-Qadr, 27, 102, 118
Lakshmi, 87
Lammas, 64, 200
Lamps, 72, 74, 87, 145
Langar, 31, 88
Lantern Festival, 17, 40, 48, 198
Lanterns, 40, 48, 67, 120, 122, 189
Lao-Tze:Lao-Tzu, 16
Last Supper, 92, 94
Launching ceremony, 156
Lemuria, 124
Lent, 21, 50–1, 114–5, 137, 174, 198
Life and death, 2, 6, 8, 44, 109
Light, 33, 48, 72–7, 79, 87, 109
Light and darkness, 3, 8, 72, 75, 109
Light of the World, 75, 82, 84
Livery Companies, 167
Loaf mass, 64
London, 66, 80, 123, 131, 132–4, 136, 155, 160, 163–4, 167
Long House, 67
Longest day, 58–9, 200
Lord Lyon King of Arms, 165
Lord Mayor's Show, 134, 201
Lord of the Dance, 47
Lord's Day, 91
Lord's Supper, 92
Lots, Feast of (*see Purim*)

Lotus, 13, 14, 141
Lourdes, 110, 144
Lunar Calendars, 27, 37, 40, 86, 88, 196–7
Luther:Lutherans, 22–3, 169
Lying in State, 186

Magga, 14
Magha Puja, 75, 105, 198
Mahabharata, 12, 190
Maharajah Ranjit Singh, 149
Mahavir Jayanti, 32, 191, 199
Mahavira, 32, 119, 191
Mahayana Buddhism, 15, 189
Mahdi, 28
Maidens, Festival of, 17, 184, 200
Maimonides, 18
Malta, 95
Mana, 6
Mandala, 12, 15
Mantra, 13, 15
Mardi Gras, 50, 136–7, 139, 198
Marhamchurch Revel, Cornwall, 130, 200
Maror, 108
Marriage, 158, 184–5
Marx, Karl, 34
Masjid, 27
Masks, 2, 69, 106, 120, 137
Mass, 3, 81, 92–3, 182, 187
Matchi Ceremony, 33, 114
Matins, 36
Matsuri, 11, 101
Matzos, 3, 108
Maundy Thursday, 51, 94, 199
May Day/Festival, 52–5, 154, 199
Maypole, (2), 42, 53–4
Maytime, 52–7
Mecca, 2, 26–7, 86, 100, 110, 111
Medicine man, 6, 46
Medina, 27, 86
Meditation, 4, 15, 95, 189
Meelad ul-Nabi (*see Prophet's Day*)
Megillah, 107
Melas, 110, 192
Menorah, 3, 18–9, 74–5
Methodists, 23
Mexico, 51, 58, 124
Mezuzah, 18
Michaelmas, 68, 167, 184, 201
Mid Lent Sunday, 115
Mid Winter, 77–8, 81

Midsummer Day/Eve, 58–9, 167, 200
Mihrab, 27, 100
Military occasions, 150, 161
  parades, 133, 154, 168
Miners' Festival, 154
Miracle Plays, 97, 150
Mishnah, 18, 179
Missionary, 25, 105
Miyazu Toro Naghi, 122
Mod, 148, 171
Moll, 44
Monks, 14–5, 32, 36, 102, 119
Moon, 8, 67, 95
  Full –, 48, 49, 67, 105, 189
  New –, 37, 86, 118, 175, 196
Moon Cake Festival, 17, 67
Moon Goddess, 67
Moravians, 22–3, 82
Mormons, 25
Moses, 18, 62, 108, 118
Mosque, 27, 100, 111, 118, 175, 187
Mothering Sunday, 172, 174, 198
Mother's Day 172
Movable feasts, 196
Mourning, 114, 116, 118, 186
Muhammad, 26–8, 86, 102, 111, 118, 193
Muharram, 27, 86, 202
Mul Mantra, 30
Mummers, 44, 45, 79, 95
Music, 40, 87, 132, 148, 150, 170
Muslim, 2, 9, 26–9, 86
  Calendar, 37, 196, 202
  Fasting, 115, 118
  Festivals, 111, 118, 174–5, 193
  Holy people, 125
  Observances, 4, 176–7, 184–7
  Pilgrimage, 110–1
  Worship and prayer, 36, 100
Mystery plays, 97

Nam, 30
Names; Naming ceremonies, 176–7
Nanak, Guru (*see Guru*)
Naojote, 178
Nataraja, 47
National Agricultural Centre, 155
National Exhibition Centre, 155
National festivals, 126–7, 168–9
Nature gods and spirits, 6–7, 11–2, 42, (65)

Nature worship, 47
Navaratra, 106, 119, 201
Naw Ruz, 29, 89, 198
Ne'ilah, 117
New clothes, 40, 87-9, 108-9,
    172-3, 175
New Day, 36
New Life, 45, 48, 51, 53, 109
New Moon Festival, 19, 37
New Start, 36-41, 87, 109, 115,
    117, 119, 175
New Year, 38-41, 119, 198; Bahá'í,
    89, 115; Chinese, 40, 48, 198;
    Christian, 84; Fasli, 41, 89;
    Hundu, 87; Islamic, 86; Jain,
    119; Japanese, 39, 198; Jewish,
    19, 85, 201; Kadmi 89, 200;
    Nature, 41; Shahenshai 89, 200;
    Sikh, 88; Zoroastrian, 33, 89
New Year Customs, 38, 144
New Year Festivals, 39
New Year for Trees, 158, 198
New Year's Eve, 38-9, 202
Nine Lessons and Carols, 80, 202
Nirodha, 14
Nirvana (Nibbana), 15, 32, 124, 189
Nonconformists, 22-3, 99
Norsemen and gods, 8, 77, 135

Oakapple Day, 159, 199
Oberammergau, 95
Obligation (see Holy Days of . . .)
Obon, 120, 200
Odin, 77
Ogma, 148
Oharae, 73
Ohrmazd (see Ahura Mazda)
Olney Pancake Race, 50
Olympic Games, 152
OM, 12-3
Opening ceremonies, 157-8
Orangemen, 133, 200
Order of the Garter, 166
Order of the Thistle, 166
Ordination of clergy, 182
Orthodox Church, 3, 22, 93, 125,
    181-2
Orthodox Jews, 19
'Oss, 55
Oxford, 52, 131

Pace eggs, 51, 95

Pageantry and processions, 132-7,
    160, 171, 187
Pageants, 134, 137, 139, 168
Pagoda, 15, 112
Palm Sunday, 94, 199
Pancake Day, 50, 51
Panj pyare, 88
Parades, 3, 133, 137, 139, 154, 159,
    161, 168
Parents, 172-4
Parinirvana, 15, 189, 198
Parish walks, (56-7), 97
Parliament, 70, 164-5
Parsis (see Zoroastrians), 33, 72-3, 89,
    110, 114, 122, 142, 178, 197
Parsva, 32
Parties, 69, 173, 179, 184-5, 188
Paryushan, 32, 102, 119, 201
Passage rites, 7
Passion plays, 95
Passover, 3, 19, 51, 62, 108, 110, 199
Patrick, St., 93, 98, 127
Patron saints, 126-30
Patronal festival, 61, 130
Peach Festival, 173
Pearly Kings, 66
Penance, 114, 119
Pentecost, 19, 62, 97, 199
Pentecostal Churches, 23
Perahera (Procession), 15, 101, 105,
    113, 200
Persia, 29, 33, 89
Persians, 51, 101, 105, 113
Personal festivals, 104, 188
Phylacteries (see Tefillin)
Pilgrim festivals, 62, 101, 108,
    110, 112-3, 135
Pilgrimage, 2, 27, 110-3, 127, 144
Pilgrims, 110-1, 113, 144
Pitcher Fair, 110
Plague Sunday, Eyam, 200
Plays, 44, 95, 106, 124, 151
Plough Sunday/Monday, 43, 198
Plymouth Brethren, 23
Poetry, 148-9, 151
Polytheism, 6-9, 12, 26
Pomona, 69
Posadha, 119
Poson Perahera, 15, 105, 200
Prayer, 4, 18-9, 25-27, 31, 36,56,
    63, 71-2, 74-5, 91, 100, 108,
    111, 114, 116, 118, 122, 175

Presbyterians, 22–3
Priests, 11, 46, 49, 56, 73, 114, 117, 177, 182
Primal religions, 2, 6
Prizegivings, 159
Processions, 3, 132–9
  Carnival and celebration, 133, 136–9, 153, 162, 192
  Ceremonial, 93, 132, 134, 165–7
  Festival, 88, 104, 135, 189
  Funeral/mourning, 118, 132, 187
  of Witness, 95
  Religious observance, 56–9, 61, 63, 88, 93, 143, 192
  Rogation, 56–9, 138, 143, 145, 147
  Seasonal, 38–40, 48–9, 53, 56–9, 88
  Temple, 13, 101, 105–6, 113, 135
Prophet's Day (Muhammad's Birthday) 27, 193, 202
Prostration, 4, 27, 100
Protestants, 22–3, 169
Pure Brightness, Festival of, 48, 199
Puri, 101, 113
Purification, 3, 73, 144
Purification of BVM, 73, 99
Purim, 19, 107, 198

Quakers, 23, 91
Queen, 63, 123 132, 160–1, 162–6, 167, 183
Qur'an, 26–7, 72, 86, 100, 102, 118, 176–7, 193

Rain dances, 45, 145
Raksha Bandhan, 13, 172, 200
Ramanavmi, 13, 190, 198
Rama, 12, 87, 106, 190, 198
Ramadan, 27, 102, 115, 118, 175, 202
Ramakrishna, Sri, 13, 191, 198
Ramayana, 12, 190
Ram's horn, 85, 117, 145
Rastafarianism, 25
Ratha Yatra, 13, 101, 113
Ravana, 87, 106, 190
Red Indians, 4, 7, 38, 42, 46, 60, 67, 71, 76, 145, 149
Red Letter Days, 169
Reformation Day, 169, 201
Regatta, 136, 147

Relics, 2, 15, 112, 130
Religions and festivals, 5, 11–34
Remembrance, 120–5
  Festival of, 123
  Sunday, 123, 133, 201
Requiem Mass, 187
Resurrection, 18, 20, 44, 51, 96, 99, 109
Reunions, 39, 48, 172, 174–5
Ridván, 29, 193, 199
Rigveda, 12, 47
Ritual, 3–4, 11, 46, 60, 73, 91, 100
Rivers, 142, 144
Robigalia, 56
Rogation, 56–7, 96, 143, 147, 199
Roman Catholic Church, 22, 23, 50, 56, 75, 91–3, 96, 99, 114–5, 125, 181–2, 187
Roman festivals, 2, 52, 56–8, 69, 78, 124, 138, 142
Romans, 58, 69, 116, 124
Rome, 9, 22, 110
Rosh Chodesh, 19, 37
Rosh Hashanah, 19, 85, 196, 201
Royal Company of Archers, 165
Royal Hospital, Chelsea, 140, 159
Royal International Agricultural Show, 155, 200
Royal Maundy, 94
Royal National Eisteddfod, 148–9, 200
Royal occasions, 132, 136, 162–3, 171
Royal Tournament, 161
Rush-bearing, 61, 200
Russian Orthodox Church, 22–3, (34), 81

Sabbath, 3, 19, 24, 37, 72, 75, 90, 91, 116, 122, 177, 179,
  – of Blessing, 37
  – of Sabbaths, 117
Sackcloth and ashes, 114, 119
Sacred rivers, 142, 144
Sacred Thread, 178
Sacrifice, 6, 12, 45, 58, 62, 72, 106, 108, 111, 119, 121, 135, 156, 174
  Human –, 58, 146, 156
St. Andrew's Day, 126, 201
St. David's Day, 127, 198
St. George's Chapel, Windsor, 166

St. George's Day, 126, 133, 199
St. Giles' Cathedral, Edinburgh, 166
St. Lucia's Day, 79, 202
St. Nicholas, 79, 202
St. Patrick's Day, 93, 127, 198
Saints, 75, 125, 126–30
Saints' Days, 93, 125–7, 130, 184
Sakyamuni, 14, 189, 199
Salat, 27, 100, 175
Salvation Army, 23
Samhain, 76
Sangha, 15
Santa Claus, 79
Sarasvati Puja, 13, 149, 198
Sat Guru, 30
Saturnalia, 2, 78
Saum, 27, 118
Scotland, 38, 126, 148, 150–1,
    161, 165–6, 171
Scrolls, 74, 102–3, 107, 179
Sea festivals, 146–7
Sekiten, 149, 191, 199
Separatists, 22–3
Setsubun, 41, 48
Seveners, 28
Seventh Day Adventists, 24
Shahada, 27, 28
Shahenshai, 33, 89, 197, 200
Shakespeare Festival, 151
Shaman, 6, 46
Shavuoth, 19, 62, 102–3, 110, 199
Shema, 18, 20
Shen-Tao, 11
Shetland, 135
Shi'a:Shi'ites, 28, 118
Shichi-go-san, 173, 201
Shimenawa, 11
Shinto, 6, 11, 39, 45, 73, 138
Shiva, 12, 47, 98
Shiva Ratri, 13, 47, 198
Shofar, 85, 117, 145
Shows and exhibitions, 155
Shri Yantra, 13
Shrines, 2, 11, 15, 27, 29, 39, 45,
    101, 112, 135, 138, 189
Shrove Tuesday, 51, 137, 198
Shrovetide, 50
Sikh:Sikhism, 3, 30–1, 36, 49, 87–8,
    102, 104, 112, 149, 176–7, 180,
    184–5, 187, 192
Simchath Torah, 19, 63, 102–3, 201
Simnel cake, 174

Sita, 12, 87, 106
Sky gods, 8, 12, 72
Sleipnir, 77
Snake dance, 145
Society of Friends, 23
Sol Invictus, 58
Soldiers, 106, 160–1
Solemnity of Mary, 99
Soul cakes, 124
Souls, 7, 12, 32, 47, 124, 186
Spalding Flower Parade, 139, 199
Spenta Mainyu, 33
Spirits, 6–7, 41–3, 46, 54, 124
    – of the dead, 7, 120–2, 124
    – of water or sea, 142, 144, 146
Sport, 152–3, 159, 171
Spring, 8, 41, 44, 48–51, 109, 140
    – Bank Holiday, 97, 199
    – Equinox, 41, 89, 198
    – Festivals, 45, 48, 76, 108, 140,
    142, 198
    – Flowers, 48, 109, 139, 141
Sri Lanka, 15, 101, 105–6, 110,
    113
State ceremonial, 132, 163–7
State funerals, 132, 187
State Opening of Parliament, 164
State visits, 163
Statues, 3, 12, 101
Stone laying, 156
Stonehenge, 59
Stoning the Devil, 111
Stratford-on-Avon, 151
Stupa, 2, 15, 112
Sudreh, 178
Sufis, 28
Sukkoth, 19, 63, 103, 110, 145, 201
Summer, 8, 58–61
    – festivals, 42, 60
    – solstice, 58–9, 200
Sun, 3, 8, 13, 58–9, 76
    – dance, 4, (42), (45), 60
    – god/goddess, 8, 11, 58–9, 135
    – worship, 58–9
Sunday; Sunday Schools, 91
Sunna:Sunni, 28
Swan upping 167
Symbols; symbolism, 2–4, 11–12,
    14, 16, 18, 20, 26, 29, 30,
    32–34, 38–9, 42, 44, 51, 61,
    72–4, 82–3, 92–3, 95, 108–9,
    117, 122, 126–7, 178, 181

Synagogue, 19, 36–7, 62–3, 72, 74, 77, 90, 102–3, 107–8, 116, 122, 179

Tabernacles (see Sukkoth)
T'ai-chi T'u, 16
Tallith, 4, 18, 116, 179, 187
Talmud, 18
Tandava, 47
Tango-no-seku, 173, 199
Taoism, 16
Tattoo, 150, 161
Tefillin, 4, 18, 116, 179
Temple, 2, 3, 11, 15, 31–2, 39, 41–2, 45, 59, 72–3, 75, 88, 101, 105–6, 116, 124, 144, 173, 190
 – at Jerusalem, 45, 63, 74, 99, 103, 116, 145
 – festivals, 13, 15, 101, 110, 113, 135–6
 – image, 32, 101, 106, 113, 189
Temple of the Tooth, 101, 113
Teng Chieh, 48, 198
Tenth of Muharram, 27, 118, 202
Terminalia:Terminus, 57
Thanksgiving Day, 71, 175, 201
Theravada Buddhists, 14–5, 75, 105, 189
Three Baskets, 14
Tisha b'Av (see Fast of 9th Av)
Tissington, Derbyshire, 143
Tokyo, 101, 120, 138, 200
Topping-out ceremony, 157
Torah, 18, 62–3, 72, 85, 90, 102–3, 108, 117, 179
Torii, 11
Tower of London, 160, 162–3
Towers of Silence, 122, 187
Trade Fairs, 155
Trafalgar Day, 169, 201
Tree planting, 157 – 8
Tree spirits, 6, 42
Trees, 2, 42, 53, 158
Tribal Religion, 6
Trinidad, 137
Trinity, Holy, 21, 24, 98
Trinity Sunday, 21, 98, 199
Tripitaka, 13
Triple Refuge, 189
Triumph over evil, 45, 74, 87, 106–9
Trooping the Colour, 161
Tu b'Shevat, 19, 158, 198

Tuan Yang Chieh, (17), 147, 200
Tulip fields, 139–140
Turban, 30, 88, 104, 180, 184
Twelfth Night, 83, 137, 198
Twelvers, 28
Tynwald Day, 165, 200

Uji-gami, 39
Ulster, 133, 165
Unitarians, 24
United Nations Day, 169, 201
United Reformed Church, 23
United States of America, 51, 60, 67, 69, 71, 76, 79, 109, 120, 133, 137, 145, 149, 154, 168, 200, 202
Up-Helly-A', 135, 198
Upanishads, 12
Uposatha, 115

Varanasi (Benares), 2, 14, 32, 105, 144
Vardhamana, 191
Vedas, 12–3
Vesakha Puja, 15, 189, 199
Vigil, 95, 130, 190
Vintners Company, 167
Virgin Mary, 75, 99, 144
Vishnu, 12, 47, 98, 113, 172, 190
Vivekananda, Swami, 13, 191, 198

Wahabbis, 28
Wakes, 61, 130, 143
Wales, 127, 148, 200
Warriors, Festival of, 106
Wassailing the Apple Trees, 42, 198
Watchnight Service, 38
Water, 3, 63, 142–7
 – Spirits, 6, 142
Wedding, 141, 185
 Anniversaries 188
Week of Prayer for Christian Unity, 23, 198
Weeks, Festival of (see Shavuoth)
Well Dressing, 96, 138, 143, 199
Wells, 142–4
Wesak, 15, 189, 199
Wesley, John, 23, 98
West Indians, 25, 136–7
Westminster Abbey, 123, 132
Wheel, 3, 14, 58–9
Whitebait Festival, 147

Whitsun, 21, 97, 199
Windsor, 161, 166
Wine, 3, 90, 92, 108, 173
Winter, 2, 8, 44–5, 77, 79
Winter clothes to Ancestors, 17, 121, 201
Wishing wells, 142
Witch doctor, 6, 46
Witches, 46, 69
Work and business, 154–5, 156–7
Worship, 6, 12–3, 22, 24, 26, 32, 36, 45, 75, 88, 90–101, 104, 109, 112–3, 141, 169, 170, 189

Yahweh, 9, 18
Yang-yin, 16
Yantra, 12–3
Yasna, 178
Yathrib, 27, 86
Yaum ul-Jum'a, 100

Yeomen of the Guard, 83, 164–5, 183
Yeomen Warders of the Tower, 160
Yom Ha'Atsma'ut, 168, 199
Yom Kippur, 19, 85, 115, 117, 201
York, 80, 97
Yuan Tan, 40, 198
Yue Lan Festival, 17, 121, 200
Yule, 2, 77

Zakat, 27
Zam-Zam, 27, 111
Zarathustra, 9, 33, 191, 199–201
Zarthostno Diso, 33, 191, 199–200
Zen Buddhism, 15
Zoroaster (see Zarathustra)
Zoroastrianism, 9, 33, 72, 89, 114, 122, 178, 191, 197
Zulus, 7, 46